Freedom as Marronage

Freedom as Marronage

NEIL ROBERTS

The University of Chicago Press
Chicago and London

Neil Roberts is associate professor of Africana studies and a faculty affiliate in political science at Williams College.

The University of Chicago Press, Chicago 60637
The University of Chicago Press, Ltd., London
© 2015 by The University of Chicago
All rights reserved. Published 2015.
Printed in the United States of America

24 23 22 21 20 19 18 17 16 15   1 2 3 4 5

ISBN-13: 978-0-226-12746-0 (cloth)
ISBN-13: 978-0-226-20104-7 (paper)
ISBN-13: 978-0-226-20118-4 (e-book)
DOI: 10.7208/chicago/9780226201184.001.0001

Jacket illustration: LeRoy Clarke, *A Prophetic Flaming Forest*, oil on canvas, 2003.

Library of Congress Cataloging-in-Publication Data

Roberts, Neil, 1976– author.
  Freedom as marronage / Neil Roberts.
      pages ; cm
  Includes bibliographical references and index.
  ISBN 978-0-226-12746-0 (cloth : alk. paper) — ISBN 978-0-226-20104-7
(pbk : alk. paper) — ISBN 978-0-226-20118-4 (e-book) 1. Maroons. 2.
Fugitive slaves—Caribbean Area. 3. Liberty. I. Title.
  F2191.B55R62 2015
  323.1196'0729—dc23

                                                        2014020609

♾ This paper meets the requirements of ANSI/NISO Z39.48-1992
(Permanence of Paper).

For Karima and Kofi

Time would pass, old empires would fall and new ones take their place, the relations of countries and the relations of classes had to change, before I discovered that it is not quality of goods and utility which matter, but movement; not where you are or what you have, but where you have come from, where you are going and the rate at which you are getting there.

—C. L. R. JAMES, *Beyond a Boundary*

CONTENTS

ACKNOWLEDGMENTS

I was born at the precipice of death, lungs flooded with fluid. A Jesuit priest read me my last rites. My life was expected to last only a matter of hours. My heart was failing me, but my family did not. My family maintained hope. I fought, even though the memory of that struggle escapes me. Years later, I came upon Audre Lorde's words in *Sister Outsider* imploring those who "were never meant to survive" to persevere, never give up, and excel despite the circumstances. This adage continues to resonate with me.

Unlike the specter of death, composing a book is a creation of the new. Writing takes patience, vigilance, perseverance, and often a great deal of assistance. I have amassed numerous debts over the years and wish to offer my profound respect and thanks. Several colleagues offered meticulous comments and inspiration: Danielle Allen, Kathy Anderson, Antonio Vázquez-Arroyo, Lawrie Balfour, Armando Bengochea, Sara Berry, Greg Beckett, Jane Bennett, Devyn Benson, Denise Buell, Jennifer Culbert, Andrew Dilts, Thomas Donahue, Andrew Douglas, John Drabinski, Enrique Dussel, Lydia English, Sibylle Fischer, Heath Fogg-Davis, Robert Gooding-Williams, Jane Gordon, Lewis Gordon, Everet Green, Michael Hanchard, Floyd Hayes, Clevis Headley, Paget Henry, Fredric Jameson, Robin Kelley, Ferentz LaFargue, Jacob Levy, Rupert Lewis, Keisha Lindsay, James Manigault-Bryant, Michael Monahan, Patchen Markell, Howard McGary, Charles Mills, Emily Nacol, Robin Nagle, Marilyn Nissim-Sabat, Kashia Pieprzak, Mark Reinhardt, Dorothy Roberts, Mérida Rúa, Julie Saville, James Scott, Tommie Shelby, Shanti Singham, Rogers Smith, Jack Turner, Dorian Warren, Stefan Wheelock, Sylvia Wynter, and Iris Young.

The early foundations of the book began at the University of Chicago. Patchen Markell, Danielle Allen, Julie Saville, and Iris Young taught me there how to mean what I say, and they served as excellent models of professionalism. Patchen's exhaustive philosophical knowledge and clever humor, Danielle's gift for decoding politics in literature, Julie's historicism on slavery, and Iris's knack for making the abstract relevant to our contemporary world were an unforgettable constellation of attributes for the study of political theory that I consistently learned from. Iris would become an ancestor far too early, but her spirit and thought live on. The Caribbean Studies Workshop, the Workshop on the Reproduction of Race and Racial Ideologies, and dialogues with Jacob Levy on Francophone thought offered a complementary and lively intellectual community.

Sylvia Wynter's suggestion to consult a little-known work by Aimé Césaire turned out to be beneficial beyond its intended scope. My subsequent time as a postdoctoral fellow at Johns Hopkins University helped me to develop my evolving rationalizations of the project in that not uncommon moment of post-PhD fatigue. Intense discussions with Michael Hanchard and Floyd Hayes then and now still have resonance, as do the ongoing exchanges with Jane Gordon, Lewis Gordon, and Paget Henry. At the institutional level, it has been wonderful to complete the book at my current workplace, Williams College. The faculty, administrative assistants, and students of the Africana Studies Program and Political Science Department, along with colleagues in French, Comparative Literature, and Religion, enriched my rethinking of the project's scale and my ruminations on interdisciplinary philosophy. Kashia Pieprzak and Mark Reinhardt deserve special mention for reading the entire manuscript—several chapters more than once! I am forever grateful. Devyn Benson also added useful commentary on chapters added after expanding the book's original architecture.

Audiences in conferences, symposia, and workshops at the following venues provided invaluable feedback on draft chapters and intimately related ideas: American Philosophical Association, American Political Science Association, Association for Political Theory, Caribbean Philosophical Association, the Claremont Colleges, Columbia University, Dartmouth College, Johns Hopkins University, Temple University, Society for the Study of Africana Philosophy, University of Chicago, University of Pittsburgh, University of Virginia, University of Washington, University of the West Indies at St. Augustine, and Williams College. Support from the Andrew W. Mellon Mays Fellowship program, the Oakley Center for Humanities and Social Sciences Resident Fellowship, and the Woodrow Wilson National Fellowship Foundation Career Enhancement Fellowship provided essential financial and office resources that allowed me to incorporate the input of these public talks into prose.

I would be remiss if I did not underscore the amazing staff of the University of Chicago Press, particularly Elizabeth Branch Dyson. Elizabeth is the gold standard of editors. She is easy to work with, and her acumen, vision, and enthusiastic belief in this book from proposal to finish are greatly appreciated. Russ Damian and Nora Devlin also supplied stellar editorial assistance. The thorough and constructive criticism of the anonymous manuscript reviewers certainly strengthened the book's argument. Any errors that remain are mine.

My parents, Barbara and Franklin Roberts, sister Lisa, and relatives between Jamaica and Washington, DC, have been a constant source of encouragement that words alone cannot capture. Thank you! And thank you to close friends who function as family and have heard my periodic musings on marronage more times than they can likely count: Kevin Anderson, Winnie Eng, Josh Guild, Alex Harris, Ferentz LaFargue, Keisha Lindsay, Victor Muñiz-Fraticelli, Michelle Murray, Emily Nacol, and Dorian Warren. "Uncle" Ferentz, a kindred soul, provided vital feedback in the book's final stages, as did Emily. "Auntie" Emily is my best friend from graduate school and an academic Power Ranger whose humanism my family and I continue to cherish.

This book is dedicated to Karima Barrow and Kofi Roberts, their first and middle names respectively meaning "generous." Karima is the consummate definition of a godsend, a wife whose endless love and generosity sustain me. Our son, Kofi, is a daily reminder that we stand on the shoulders of not only elders and peers, but also the next generation. On nights returning home from writing to smile over Karima and Kofi sleeping, I knew they wished I was present during those missed evenings together. Hopefully this work assures them that the late office hours were worth it.

Neil Roberts
Williamstown, Massachusetts
May 2014

PART ONE

On Slavery, Agency, and Freedom

Why do we find it so difficult to follow the conceptual logic of episodes and materials we uncover even when scholars studying similar sorts of developments elsewhere in the world have already paved the way? Why are there interpretations we are reluctant to embrace even when the empirical evidence invites us to do so? And why are there subjects we can so easily avoid or disown, even when it is clear that they are of genuine historical significance?

—Steven Hahn, *The Political Worlds of Slavery and Freedom*

We said in our introduction that man was a *yes*. We shall never stop repeating it. Yes to life. Yes to love. Yes to generosity. But man is also a *no*. No to man's contempt. No to the indignity of man. To the exploitation of man. To the massacre of what is most human in man: freedom. . . . To induce man to be *actional*, by maintaining in his circularity the respect of the fundamental values that make the world human, that is the task of utmost urgency for he who, after careful reflection, prepares to act.

—Frantz Fanon, *Black Skin, White Masks*

Introduction

Who were the first persons to get the unusual idea that being free was not only a value to be cherished but the most important thing that someone could possess? The answer, in a word: slaves. Freedom began its career as a social value in the desperate yearning of the slave to negate what, for him or her, and for nonslaves, was a peculiarly inhuman condition.
—Orlando Patterson, *Freedom* (vol. 1)[1]

To raise the question, what is freedom? seems to be a hopeless enterprise. It is as though age-old contradictions and antinomies were lying in wait to force the mind into dilemmas of logical impossibility so that, depending which horn of the dilemma you are holding on to, it becomes as impossible to conceive of freedom or its opposite as it is to realize the notion of a square circle.
—Hannah Arendt, *Between Past and Future*[2]

PROSPERO: Come here, Caliban. Have you got anything to say in your own defense? Take advantage of my good humor. I'm in a forgiving mood today.
CALIBAN: I'm not interested in defending myself. My only regret is that I've failed.
PROSPERO: What were you hoping for?
CALIBAN: To get back my island and regain my freedom.
—Aimé Césaire, *A Tempest*[3]

This book answers two central and related questions: What are some distinct concepts of freedom emerging out of the experience of slavery? What important insights does analyzing the relationship between slavery and freedom provide to political theorists that they do not know, have ignored, or have not sufficiently investigated? My project examines a specific, highly overlooked form of flight from slavery—*marronage*—that was fundamental to the experience of Haitian slavery, is integral to understanding the Haitian Revolution, and has widespread application to European, New World, and black diasporic societies. I call the theory derived from such flight *freedom as marronage.*

Slavery and freedom are intertwined and interdependent terms. My inquiry aims to deepen our understanding of freedom not only by situating slavery as freedom's opposite condition, but also by investigating the significance of the equally important liminal and transitional social space *between* slavery and freedom. Experience teaches us lessons about flight and the dialectics of human and all-too-subhuman conditions. Political theorists, therefore, must pay more attention to the experience of the process by which people emerge *from* slavery *to* freedom.

I defend the claim that freedom as marronage presents a useful heuristic device to scholars interested in understanding both normative ideals of freedom and the origin of those ideals.[4] A corollary to this proposition is that freedom should not be understood exclusively as a social practice applicable only to specific historical conjunctures. Marronage is a normative concept forged in a historical milieu, yet it has trans-historical utility.

Modern political theory provides the intellectual resources for rethinking the dialectic of slavery and freedom from ancient to contemporary times. This study investigates a motley array of ideas in Hannah Arendt, Philip Pettit, W. E. B. Du Bois, Angela Y. Davis, Frederick Douglass, Samuel Taylor Coleridge, the Haitian Revolution, and Édouard Glissant in order to develop a theory of freedom that offers a compelling interpretive lens for examining the quandaries of slavery, freedom, and political language still confronting us today. Its structure is thematic; its temporality, nonlinear. Marronage is the underlying principle uniting it all.

The Concept of Marronage

Marronage (marronnage, maroonage, maronage) conventionally refers to a group of persons isolating themselves from a surrounding society in order to create a fully autonomous community, and for centuries it has been integral to interpreting the idea of freedom in Haiti as well as other Caribbean islands and Latin American countries including the Dominican Republic, Jamaica, Suriname, Venezuela, Brazil, Cuba, Colombia, and Mexico. These communities of freedom—known variously as "maroon societies," *quilomboa, palenques, mocambos, cumbes, mambises, rancherias, ladeiras, magotes,* and *manieles*—geographically situate themselves from areas slightly outside the borders of a plantation to the highest mountains of a region located as far away from plantation life as possible. The term *maroon* derives etymologically from the vocabulary of indigenous Arawaks and Tainos in the Caribbean. The Spanish word *cimarrón* developed on the island of Hispaniola in reference initially to Spanish colonialists' feral cattle, which fled to the hills, then to enslaved Amerindians seeking refuge in those areas, and ultimately (by the early 1530s) to enslaved Africans seeking escape from chattel slavery beyond plantation boundaries. The introduction of *cimarrón* into written language led to the coinage of the French and Dutch term *marron* and the English *maroon*, each word garnering regular usage in political vocabulary by the Age of Revolution.[5]

The French *marron* now also refers to both a large chestnut and the color brown, the latter meaning intimately linked to the racialized origins of the word in the modern slavery period. Maroons reside in liminal suspension between slaves on a plantation and colonizers dictating standards of normativity. Moreover, they exemplify a unique manifestation of the more general category of "hill people" that James C. Scott describes in *The Art of Not Being Governed*. These heretical, non-state actors construct a clandestine series of hidden transcripts in opposition to the zones of governance and appropriation intrinsic to existing state regimes of slavery. Maroons do so by cultivating freedom on their own terms within a demarcated social space that allows for the enactment of subversive speech acts, gestures, and social practices antithetical to the ideals of enslaving agents. For Scott, "zones of refuge" most accurately describe maroons' regions of existence and cultivation away from state power.[6]

Reflecting on the theme of marronage, the Martinican poet and politician Aimé Césaire composed a poem in 1955 for the prominent black internationalist journal *Présence Africaine* entitled "The Verb Marronner, a Reply to René Depestre, Haitian Poet." Different versions of the poem were published subsequently, but the tenor of each remained the same. The poem appeared slightly more than a decade after Césaire's "Poetry and Knowledge" speech on Haitian soil, one year before the *Letter to Maurice Thorez* announced his resignation from the French Communist Party, and in the same year as both the Asian-African Bandung Conference of nonaligned nations and the release of the revised edition of the landmark anticolonial treatise, *Discourse on Colonialism*. In *Discourse*, Césaire issued the following moving statement: "My turn to state an equation: colonization = 'thingification.'"[7]

"The Verb Marroner" specifically served as a response to Louis Aragon and others in the French Communist party who issued a call for the usage of traditional poetic forms in their written works. The radical Haitian poet Depestre was living in exile in Brazil at the time, and, surprisingly, Depestre supported this call by those in the French metropole to use traditional meters. All of this transpired in the context of debates within the Francophone world about national language, especially in the former colonies. Césaire's rejection of traditional meters took the nontraditional form of a passionate poem addressed to comrade Depestre in which Césaire invented his own verb, *marronner*. "Poetic knowledge," Césaire stated, "is born in the great silence of scientific knowledge."[8] Césaire utilized poetic knowledge to employ a politics of neologism that drew directly on the image of the Haitian Revolution and Caribbean marronage.[9]

Marronage means "flight," and the terms *maroon* and *marronage* are each nouns. While flight evokes in one's mind movement from one state or location to another, it still remains a noun in lexicon. Césaire, therefore, invents a verb to denote the action and collective agency against slavery entailed in marronage. English translators often equate *marronner* with "to escape like slaves," but a more accurate translation of *marronner* is either "to maroon" or "to flee," thus denoting the intransitive act of marronage and its particular notion of flight. Césaire, however, does more than simply invent a verb. He invokes marronner to go beyond the historical phenomenon of marronage in the Haitian Revolution and the Caribbean, and he uses the verb marronner to articulate a creative, conceptual marronage. Césaire states:

> It is a Seine night
> and as if in drunkenness I recall
> the insane song of Boukman delivering your country
> with the forceps of the storm
> DEPESTRE
> Courageous tom-tom rider
> is it true that you mistrust the native forest
> and our hoarse voices our hearts that come back up on us bitter
> our rum red eyes our burned out nights
> is it possible
> that the rains of exile
> have slackened the drum skin of your voice?
> shall we escape like slaves Depestre like slaves?
> [*marronnerons-nous Depestre marronnerons-nous?*][10]

After conjuring up the memory of Boukman Dutty, the maroon credited with starting the Haitian Revolution, Césaire continues. Yet before discussing the relationship between poetry and revolution, he reflects on the nature of poetry and brings up the memory of Haiti's leader at independence, Jean-Jacques Dessalines, in the revolution's final decisive Battle of Vertières:

Bah! Depestre the poem is not a mill for
grinding sugar cane absolutely not
and if the rhymes are flies on ponds
without rhymes
for a whole season
away from ponds
under my persuasion
let's laugh drink and escape like slaves
[*rions buvons et marronnons*]
Gentle heart
the necklace of the Order of the Moon around my neck
the tightly wrapped coil of the sun's lasso around my arm
my chest tattooed as if by one of night's wounds
I too remember
as a matter of fact *did* Dessalines prance about at Vertières[11]

The poem contains three overlapping valences: the ethical, the sociological, and the political. The political relates most closely to understanding the idea of freedom that Césaire seeks to convey, although the sociological and ethical valences each play a part with respect to Césaire's choice of images and figures. While the images of leaders are invoked, Césaire's primary concern remains the act of marronage, marronner, enacted by the masses of slaves as a flight from slavery to freedom and the conceptual lessons one can learn from revolutionary slaves themselves. Césaire wishes to impart to Depestre that, by looking at and extrapolating from the phenomenon of marronage in the history of Depestre's native land, one may think about marronage as an ideal of freedom and that those in the Caribbean must not think of their concepts as solely derivative of European discourse or as retreating from struggle. Marronage involves flight as well as a societal transformation resulting from the struggle to institute a distinct concept of freedom.

Césaire's idea of marronage underlies subsequent works, including the plays *A Tempest* and *A Season in the Congo*, and it relates closely to the notion of a political imaginary. A political imaginary refers to an agent's imagined state of existence within the body politic. Its temporality is oriented toward the present as well as the future, and it includes a concern for the social.[12] In *Modernity Disavowed*, Sibylle Fischer writes trenchantly about the political imaginary that developed in the aftermath of the Haitian Revolution:

In response to the colonial slaveholders' structuring of the hemisphere through slave routes and slave markets, a radically heterogeneous, transnational cultural network emerged whose political imaginary mirrored the global scope of the slave trade and whose projects and fantasies of emancipation converged, at least for a few years, around Haiti. This interstitial culture cannot be grasped by the teleological narratives that conventionally dominate postindependence national literary and cultural histories. The traces and remnants of radical politics and their attendant cultural practices are scattered across languages, histories, and continents. Most of the cultural and ideological production that pertained to this hybrid formation—reports of traveling revolutionaries and radical abolitionists, trial records about the practices of insurgency among slaves and free colored populations, remnants of popular forms of cultural production, letters exchanged between colonial reformers and radicals, manuscripts that circulated between colonial territories and metropoles—did not become part of the canons of high culture and respectable political theory. . . . Haiti and the Haitian Revolution were central to this landscape although often only as the unspeakable, as trauma, utopia, and elusive dream. Imaginary scenarios became the real battleground.[13]

Although the various documents and testimonials cataloguing the political imaginary surrounding the Haitian Revolution "did not become part of the canons of high culture and respectable political theory" during the nineteenth century following independence, the revolution's impact was felt globally nevertheless. The political imaginary of those outside the Caribbean became a barometer for gauging its international impact in much the same way as the European political imaginary in the wake of Bartolomé de Las Casas's sixteenth-century writings became an indicator for assessing the impact of European colonization in the Americas on metropolitan policies and concepts. The legacy of the Haitian Revolution's imagined body politic and corresponding ideals was also interrogated by later Afro-Caribbean thinkers of the twentieth and twenty-first centuries such as Césaire, C. L. R. James, Édouard Glissant, Maryse Condé, Derek Walcott, Anthony Bogues, David Scott, Edwidge Danticat, and Michel-Rolph Trouillot. These thinkers developed an idea of a creolized, Afro-Caribbean political imaginary, fusing together the poeticist and historicist dimensions of modern and contemporary political theory in the now rich Caribbean intellectual tradition.[14]

Dimensions of Flight

Contemporary political theory lacks a sufficient vocabulary to describe the activity of flight and the dialectical mechanisms operating during the flight process. In existing theories of freedom, there is a dearth of scholarship on what happens during the act of flight itself. Much of the extant literature frames unfreedom and freedom as inherently inert conditions. This body of writing posits slavery as a state that agents are locked into without any mobility, and it describes freedom as a motionless attribute of agents who are simply in a condition antithetical to the unfree. Acts of struggle and assertion have at best descriptive value, and they are of no normative significance. Recent works inspired by Gilles Deleuze, Félix Guattari, and Sheldon Wolin on fugitive thinking are opening up conversations contesting narratives of inertia.[15] While their discussions of lines of flight and fugitive democracy are transforming interpretations of justice, democratic theory, and capitalism, the effects of this turn largely bypass how we talk about freedom and the experiences of agents in flight.

The multiple definitions of freedom in the *Oxford English Dictionary* include "exemption or release from slavery or imprisonment," "liberation from the bondage of sin," "exemption from arbitrary, despotic, or autocratic control," "independence," "the state of being able to act without hindrance or restraint," "the power of self-determination attributed to the will," "readiness or willingness to act," and "capability of motion."[16] Nowhere in the *OED*, current philosophical literature, or discourse on the social sciences is "flight" at the foreground of defining freedom.

John Hope Franklin's catalytic 1947 work, *From Slavery to Freedom*, set the foundations for black studies two decades later and for studies of freedom in myriad disciplines outside the field that disregarded freedom's relation to slavery. Likely unintended, the legacy of that text is Janus-faced. While it brilliantly challenged Kantian notions of freedom in autonomy that were devoid of inquiry into slavery, it reified a polarized, static conception of slavery and freedom with no attention to the liminal spaces between these states and the relational nature of freedom.[17] Marronage fills the discursive conceptual void.

Marronage is a multidimensional, constant act of flight that involves what I ascertain to be four interrelated pillars: distance, movement, property, and purpose. Distance denotes a spatial quality separating an individual or individuals in a current location or condition from a future location or condition. Movement refers to the ability of agents to have control over motion and the intended directions of their actions. Flight, therefore, is directional movement in the domain of physical environment, embodied cognition, and/or the metaphysical. By property, I mean the designation of a physical, legal, and material object that is under the possession and ownership of an individual, institution, or state. Property can be private, collective, or common, thus spanning a range of property relations from atomistic conceptions to the communitarian. Purpose denotes the rationale, reasons for, and goal of an act begun by an individual or a social collective. Movement is the central principle of marronage to which the other three are inextricably connected.

These pillars explain the spectrum of human activities from individuated micropolitics to mass collective revolution. Activities between micro- and macropolitics, such as the middle-range "coagulate politics" described by Michael Hanchard, are also captured by this fourfold constellation.[18] During marronage, agents struggle psychologically, socially, metaphysically, and politically to exit slavery, maintain freedom, and assert a lived social space while existing in a liminal position. Agency here is temporally fluid in contrast to prevailing modern Western theories, particularly Aristotelian and Hegelian systems, which obscure the degrees of agency and their pertinence to freedom due to their inattentiveness to flight and mistaken rigid division between potentiality and actuality. In marronage, there is agency within potentiality. Actuality is merely the manifestation of a heightened form of activity in the action of flight.

Why Marronage?

The studies on marronage hitherto are primarily anthropological and historical.[19] As a consequence, they tend to treat marronage with an inflexible historicist logic that relegates the poeticist political imaginary of marronage to a confined time period and isolationist conception of individual and community formation. This characterization of marronage scholarship aligns with Steven Hahn's assertion in *The Political Worlds of Slavery and Freedom* that "[p]erspectives on marronage, like perspectives on slave rebellions more generally, have for the most part been informed by rather limited and one-dimensional images and understandings of what a maroon is."[20]

Presently, marronage refers to either individual fugitive acts of truancy (*petit marronage*) or the creation of communities of freedom outside of the parameters of a plantation society (*grand marronage*) within which a majority of agents live. Under this bifurcated conception, marronage cannot address the dimensions of flight experienced and envisioned through large-scale revolts, revolutions, and the personalities of a polity's political leadership. I radically reconfigure marronage trans-historically to account for these previous understandings of flight while expanding the idea of marronage.

My aim in coining the phrases *sovereign marronage* and *sociogenic marronage* is to supply a resource for describing the activity of flight carried out by lawgivers, or sovereign political leaders, and agents of mass revolution.

Sovereign marronage is the mass flight from slavery in which the socio-political goal of independence is achieved through the agency and vision of the lawgiver, not the people. Sociogenic marronage classifies the supreme ideal of freedom. It denotes a revolutionary process of naming and attaining individual and collective agency, non-sovereignty, liberation, constitutionalism, and the cultivation of a community that aligns civil society with political society. Flight can be both real and imagined. That pronouncement bolsters a central maxim of the theory of marronage: Freedom is not a place; it is a state of being.

To comprehend how a modified concept of marronage helps to serve as a general political theory of freedom beyond its conventional Caribbean historical usage, one must first understand why the turn to diaspora is fractionally useful but not a panacea. Diaspora studies is a field forged in the twentieth century as a result of inquiries into the migrations of peoples both from a homeland outward to other lands and from dispersed lands back into homelands, established or imagined. Diaspora is thus able to describe flight either unidirectionally or, for lack of a better analogy, flight and return over time in a boomerang trajectory.[21] Although it can describe elements of intrastate flight, including the great migration of African-Americans from the South to the North and Jamaican and South East Asian maroons fleeing lowland states and plantations for life in highland, non-state spaces, in addition to flight across state borders, diaspora is unable to explain evanescent flight, modes of fugitivity, and intrastate flight focused on the attainment of freedom through the macro-level reorientation of civil society and state institutions—most notably revolutions.

The fundamental nature of a concept's relationship to phenomena reveals another important facet of a broadened intellectual compass for marronage. Understanding the relationship between a concept and phenomena is essential to grasping the ways in which an idea is not only thought about but also manifested in the world of lived experience. In *Politics, Language and Time*, J. G. A. Pocock notes the challenges that political language poses to understanding this relationship and the implications of political language for the study of revolutionary events.[22] The implications of political language also pose challenges for methods utilized in the study of politics.[23] Since the work of Ludwig Wittgenstein, political theorists and social scientists have paid closer attention to concepts by analyzing their meanings before initially embarking upon empirical investigations.[24] Wittgenstein describes the role of language-games and grammar in contributing to new forms of life. That language involves games indicates potential roadblocks preventing the generation of fresh terrain for navigating language's complexities.

A political theorist faces the special problem of communication in light of these language-games when she hopes to change the conceptual framework of an audience about a term.[25] The audience already has an understanding of a word's meaning, yet that meaning differs from the meaning the theorist proposes. The theorist hopes to change the way the audience views the word, and this change in perspective has as an implication the creation of a new political vocabulary. In this study, the special problem occurs when attempting to articulate the concept of marronage in an original manner while retaining the terminology of marronage. My inquiry, then, involves a "grammatical" investigation. A grammatical investigation is "directed not towards phenomena, but, as one might say, towards the *'possibilities'* of phenomena."[26] Put another way, investigations into the possibilities of phenomena are conceptual investigations.

Evidence in addition to Césaire's poem demonstrates the conceptual relevance of marronage to the Haitian Revolution and to normative theories of freedom more broadly. Laurent Dubois contends that marronage in Haiti is as old as the existence there of slavery itself and that the "practice of running away laid the groundwork for an uprising that united slaves across plantations and in so doing enabled them to smash the system from within" in their struggle for freedom.[27] Kamau Brathwaite describes Haiti as "the greatest and most successful Maroon polity of them all," and the example of Haitian marronage both prior to and during the Haitian Revolution is uniquely related to the Afro-Caribbean political and intellectual tradition detailed by Paget Henry.[28] In the year between the start of the French Revolution and the beginning of the Haitian Revolution, British critic Edmund Burke, in *Reflections on the Revolution in France,* described (albeit misguidedly) the French revolutionary notion of freedom and compared it with the idea of freedom that maroons desired. According to Burke, French revolutionaries were a "gang of Maroon slaves, suddenly broke loose from the house of bondage."[29] Perhaps the most visible contemporary memorial to marronage is the statue of the *Unknown Maroon* (*Le Marron Inconnu de Saint-Domingue*) that was constructed directly in front of the Haitian Presidential Palace in Port-au-Prince. The statue withstood the catastrophic January 2010 earthquake that wrecked the palace's infrastructure and killed hundreds of thousands of Haitians. Its aesthetics and symbolism remain a primary marker of freedom and lasting tribute to the maroon (*Le Nègre Marron*) in Haiti.[30]

The *Unknown Maroon* conveys Édouard Glissant's notion of "a prophetic vision of the past," a vision not locked in the grammar of historicism but rather conjuring a mental picture utilizing past ideals for imagined transhistorical politics.[31] A student of Césaire, Glissant is one of the few Caribbean theorists whose *oeuvre* repeatedly calls for interrogating the creative dimensions of marronage beyond its historical associations.[32] Marronage is a total refusal of the enslaved condition. Interpreting maroons' systematic opposition means developing alternative imagined models of freedom through the process of intellectual marronage (*le marronnage intellectual*), an epistemological blueprint functioning as a corollary to the enactment of actual flight.[33] As Glissant remarks in *Caribbean Discourse*, "The rigid nature of the plantation encouraged forms of resistance, two of which have a shaping force on our cultures: the camouflaged escape of the carnival, which I feel constitutes a desperate way out of the confining world of the plantation, and the armed flight of *marronnage*, which is the most widespread act of defiance in that area of civilization that concerns us."[34]

This study privileges the trope of Haitian marronage, yet it refutes provincializing marronage as relevant merely to Caribbean regional discourse. Moreover, while careful attention is paid to historical detail where germane, the overall argument is a normative one. The chapters survey a group of thinkers and a revolution that rarely are examined together for the express purpose of showing scholars the normative value that marronage affords.

Alternative Theories of Freedom: Negative and Positive

Two alternative streams of thinking about freedom have been prominent in Western political theory from early to late modernity. These theories may be called *negative* and *positive*. What these streams have in common is the rejection of freedom as a process of flight bridging the negative and positive polarities. Negative theories of freedom refer to static ideals that construe freedom as an absence of a condition encroaching upon an agent. The notions of freedom as non-interference and freedom as non-domination are representative of this current. Thomas Hobbes ushered in the liberal tradition of conceptualizing freedom as non-interference when he wrote in *Leviathan*, "LIBERTY, or FREEDOME, signifieth (properly) the absence of Opposition; (by Opposition, I mean externall Impediments of motion;)."[35]

Isaiah Berlin revised the liberal tradition three centuries after Hobbes by introducing the language of negative liberty to describe the state of non-interference. In the seminal essay, "Two Concepts of Liberty," Berlin argues for the adoption of freedom as non-interference after asking the basic question that negative liberty aims to answer: "'What is the area within which the subject—a person or group of persons—is or should be left to do or be what he is able to do or be, without interference by other persons?'"[36] Freedom is not about rational self-realization, autonomy, instrumental reason, or retreating to an inner citadel of self-direction.[37] For Berlin, freedom demands procuring "an area within which I am not frustrated." Agents strive to live in societies with demarcated "frontiers of freedom which nobody should be permitted to cross." As Berlin notes, "By being free in this sense I mean not being interfered with by others. The wider the area of non-interference the wider my freedom." "Non-interference" is negative insofar as it denotes the absence of physical coercion or the credible threat of coercion. "To coerce a man is to deprive him of freedom."[38] The liberal formulations of Hobbes and Berlin are both a freedom *from* instead of a positive freedom *to*.

Philip Pettit, Quentin Skinner, and theorists associated with the turn to neo-Roman republicanism provide another example of negative theorizing. Pettit's version of freedom within the Roman tradition eschews the Berlinian dichotomy of negative versus positive liberty, choosing instead the notion of non-domination. "Non-domination" denotes the condition of an agent who is not subject to the arbitrary interference of another agent. Pettit suggests that a state's commitment to track the common avowable interests of citizens results in the non-arbitrary reduction of private *dominium* and public *imperium*. Although he accepts the Roman tradition's grounding of freedom as the antithesis of slavery, Pettit disavows the agency of slaves. I use the word *disavowal* to indicate the simultaneous acknowledgement and denial of an agent or event. A disavowal differs from silence, and it leads to traumatic effects. Negative and positive theorists each succumb to the pitfalls of disavowal with respect to the dialectics of mastery, slavery, and the flight of agents.

Positive theories of freedom, in contrast to negative models, emphasize self-mastery, participation, and the active, collective practice of pluralistic humanism. Hannah Arendt and Jean-Jacques Rousseau exemplify this stream. The positive stream cultivates the capacity for agents to will legislation and found lasting institutions. Generality and plurality share aspirations for the active life. Rather than focus on preventing other agents from imposing their will on a subject, positive theories invent political vocabularies for the purpose of either willing or constituting collective action. Arendt's idea of freedom as non-sovereign human action and Rousseau's notion of freedom in the general will radically diverge on the issue of sovereignty. Arendt and Rousseau nonetheless mutually champion the creative positivity of agents.

While Pettit disavows only slave agency, Arendt engages in the disavowal of slavery as a sociopolitical institution. Rousseau transcends the negativity of Pettit and the disavowal of Arendt by conceiving of slavery and freedom in dialectical terms that question those who deem agents slaves by nature.

Rousseau does not evade the problems of sovereignty, and a major reason for this blind spot has to do with his lived experience. As I document in the analyses of Douglass and the Haitian Revolution, theorists of slavery such as Rousseau arrive at different conclusions than theorists who are slaves.[39] Experience holds a more central place in positive conceptions. However, the function of the negative dialectic of liberation is not given sufficient attention.

Marronage is a flight from the negative, subhuman realm of necessity, bondage, and unfreedom toward the sphere of positive activity and human freedom. Flight is multidimensional, constant, and never static. Negative and positive theorists overwhelmingly conceive of freedom as a stable condition. Negative formulations articulate stability as security against interference and domination. Positive ideals endorse a vision of freedom that agents can imagine arriving at, and they classify agents either as participators in the active life or as unfree. There is no consideration of the transitional space between unfreedom and freedom. Agency exists prior to and during a slave's dialectical encounter with the stages of liberation and freedom. Agency is temporally fluid because of the political imaginary underlying it in the minds of the slave and the free. Modern Western theories of freedom obscure the degrees of agency and their relation to freedom due to their inattentiveness to the act of flight.

The concept of marronage is not anti-Western, but post-Western. *Post-* designates neither a comprehensive jettisoning of the past nor the bracketing of a particular intellectual tradition in favor of another. It is an acknowledgement of subject formation in shifting regions of the in-between, what Homi Bhabha identifies as the "emergence of the interstices."[40] Western thought alone cannot explain flight emerging from the interstitial, yet languages emerging outside its tradition are able to represent this phenomenon among actors internal to it. By looking at the idea of marronage and then rethinking conceptualizations of freedom in Western theory through the marronage heuristic, we are able to use marronage as a tool applicable respectively to Western and non-Western thinkers and movements. Work critically integrating lived experience, slavery, and slave agency highlights the stakes of uniting the negative and positive streams of thought on freedom. The writings of Patterson belong to this unifying category of research.

Patterson's Dialectic

Orlando Patterson is a scholar who has been at the forefront of dialectical studies bridging historical and normative analyses. One observes this in

Patterson's initial work on Caribbean slavery, the trilogy of novels *The Children of Sisyphus*, *An Absence of Ruins*, and *Die the Long Day*, the comparative studies of ancient and modern slave societies, and the philosophical meditation on ethnicity, *Ethnic Chauvinism*. This is evident as well in Patterson's later writings on American geopolitics. Prominent are social scientific texts such as *Rituals of Blood* and *The Ordeal of Integration*, numerous *New York Times* op-ed columns, and public intellectual essays including "Freedom and 9/11."[41] Patterson's theorizing, however, extends beyond the scope of the Caribbean and North America.

In the award-wining *Freedom in the Making of Western Culture* (vol. 1 of *Freedom*), Patterson claims that freedom emerges out of the experience of slavery and that freedom, "like love and beauty, is one of those values better experienced than defined."[42] Nonetheless, in the wake of this assertion, contemporary theorists of freedom not only fail to point out the primary benefits and limitations of Patterson's system; in their definitions of freedom, they also avoid engagement with the relationships among freedom, slavery, and the recombinant form of slavery, serfdom, that are integral to comprehending the concept of freedom itself.

The phenomenological and historical claims of Patterson are equally pertinent to marronage and normative conceptual inquiries into freedom's origins. If conceptions of freedom indeed emerge out of the experience of slavery, why do so few contemporary political theorists engage with slavery and the varying notions of slavery that give rise to different conceptions of freedom? The problem of slavery is not a dilemma about inquiring into the reasons for the loss of freedom. On the contrary, it is a quandary dealing with explaining the conditions under which individuals and social collectives may achieve freedom through a process of exiting a foundational unfree state of slavery. Patterson's dialectic over the last forty years has provided original ways to think through our present impasse.

Patterson's early essay, "Slavery and Slave Revolts," explores social dialectics in colonial Jamaica's First Maroon War between the English and the Leeward and Windward maroons.[43] Like pirates, maroons are essential to the Jamaican slavery period. Also like pirates, maroons gain the status of myth that unfortunately obscures discourse on their ruminations on freedom. Patterson moves beyond the mythical veil, and he arrives at three normative conclusions out of this specific historical episode: the first pertains to marronage, the second to defining slavery, and the third concerns moral psychology. He argues that "all sustained slave revolts must acquire a Maroon dimension."[44] By "Maroon dimension," Patterson means strategies of flight, guerrilla warfare, ambush, blowing of the abeng horn, and other hidden transcripts used to protect the capacity of slaves and runaways for individual and collective agency. Circumstances inevitably provide the enslaved with real or imagined maroon techniques if revolt and revolution are the objective. Slaves have to come to terms with their unfreedom by recognizing what the premises behind slavery are. Patterson provisionally defines slavery as a denial of all freedom and humanity.[45] Slavery, he claims, is not a condition pertinent to the psychological. The slave's psychology has nothing to do with his idea of what freedom entails.[46]

The arguments made in "Slavery and Slave Revolts" serve as the basis for Patterson's subsequent celebrated conception of slavery as a state of *social death*. In *Slavery and Social Death: A Comparative Study*, Patterson develops a theory of slavery grounded in the constituent elements of powerlessness, dishonor, and natal alienation.[47] The powerlessness of the slave is indicative of slavery as a relation of domination between slave and master. To dishonor another is to strip an agent of the ability to feel social self-worth. The slave insider/outsider is thus alienated from birth. Natal alienation corresponds to the secular excommunication experienced by the slave. Being born estranged from any claims to rights, property, and ownership already moves slaves outside the boundaries of social norms. Slavery does not consist in property relations alone, and slavery's constituent elements show why. For Hannah Arendt, natality means a new beginning, rebirth, and a sign of freedom. Natality in Patterson's dialectic signals the slave's birth into social ill repute. Taken together, powerlessness, dishonor, and natal alienation create a slave existing in a condition of social death, a state of being alive while socially irrelevant.[48]

Slavery is social because its institutional network situates slaves as part of a polity's structural institutions. States include slaves in the political system as liminal beings who are paradoxically marginal yet socially integrated. A successful, large-scale slave society must balance its incorporation of liminal populations with a sizable free population that promises the possibility of manumission even if the professed scope of manumission is uttered in bad faith. Freedom involves the negation of slavery, but it does not require recognition of a laboring slave as the basis for the dialectical struggle.[49] The dialectics of recognition misrepresent slaves' overall intentions. Patterson's ultimate slave exists as a human parasite. Slaves feed off the master until the time when they can exist on their own. Patterson conceives of slavery as a relation of domination, although he has reservations about equating slavery with domination in political language.[50]

Freedom in the Making of Western Culture investigates the other side of the dialectical problem of slavery's freedom with which *Slavery and Social Death* concluded—namely, the problem of freedom's slavery. Patterson focuses on the experiential genesis of freedom out of slavery during ancient Greece and Rome, the rise of Christianity, and the Western, medieval reconstruction of freedom under feudalism. According to Patterson, freedom is the supreme value of the Western world, and it was socially dead slaves who got the unusual idea that freedom was to be cherished and considered the preeminent social value to attain.[51] Non-Western societies privileged values such as rights, community, filial piety, glory, nirvana, justice, and equality, yet they did not make freedom supreme. Many of these societies did not have words in their lexicon to denote freedom. Why is this so? Patterson's answer uses the musical metaphor of the *chordal triad* buttressing centuries of Western thought.[52]

The chordal triad represents the tripartite value of freedom invented by slaves: personal freedom, sovereignal freedom, and civic freedom. Personal freedom is the capacity to do as one wishes insofar as one can; sovereignal freedom is the desire for power to act as one pleases; and civic freedom is the aspiration of adult members in a community to participate in life and governance. Female slaves invent personal freedom, and sovereignally free persons have the ability either to empower agents beneath them or to restrict the freedom of others. Only during the era of Pericles did the chordal triad first become fully aligned.[53] Henceforth, a society's level of slavery fluctuated depending on whether the chordal triad was in harmony.

Struggles among Roman patricians, plebeians, and slaves produced a version of the chordal triad universalized around a notion of *libertas*. Different notes of the chord were dominant from the Republic to the Empire. The slave's point of view was made prominent in the figure of Epictetus, one of the few major Roman theorists born a slave. By the Middle Ages, freedom had attained a spiritual dimension but was still linked to the political. With medieval Christendom came the triumph of the sovereignal conception of freedom. That triumph coincided with theocratic societal decadence, the doctrine of heresy, the transformation of mass slavery into the political language of serfdom, and the introduction of the root word *Slav* to refer to serfs across Europe. Heretics privileged their personal freedom over sovereign orthodoxy. Being burned at the stake was a consequence.[54]

Of the three triadic notes, Patterson suggests the sovereignal chord has been an overwhelming Western tendency from antiquity to the present. The desire for sovereignty predates the nation-state, and it tragically explains some of the best and worst moments in the Western world. Connecting the conclusions of the past and present to his general theory, Patterson writes, "It is no accident that the first and greatest mass democracies of the ancient and modern worlds—Athens and the United States—share this evil in common: they were both conceived in, and fashioned by, the degradation of slaves and their descendants and the exclusion of women. The chronic, identical evils of Athenian xenophobia and misogyny, and antebellum American racism, nativism, and sexism, served a common purpose and nourished a common good: the profound commitment of both cultures to the inspired principle of participatory politics."[55] Patterson paves the way for a retreat out of historicism, detailing how a theory of freedom uniting the negative and positive streams can be applied across time to social dialectics of mastery and slavery. The ideal of marronage does the same, but with two important differences.

First, Patterson's dialectic consistently excludes psychology as a relevant factor in understanding a slave's conception of freedom. This explains in part a paradox noted by Vincent Brown: although Patterson's early work delves ostensibly into slave resistance, his overall body of writing, past and present, ironically continues to come under recurrent critique by slave-resistance scholars who find limited use for the idea of social death due to Patterson's lack of attention to the agency of slaves themselves—agency closely associated with slaves' responses to the psychodynamics and corporeality of slavery.[56] Patterson asserts that there "is no evidence from the long and dismal annals of slavery to suggest that any group of slaves ever internalized the conception of degradation held by their masters."[57] My study rejects this premise. Furthermore, Patterson's trenchant contention is puzzling, given his provisional intuitions reached previously in his overlooked novel *The Children of Sisyphus*.

The Children of Sisyphus focuses on the Rastafari movement in Kingston, Jamaica, during the early 1960s. Patterson bases the title on Albert Camus's explorations into the myth of Sisyphus, the psychodynamics of perennially pushing a rock up a precipitous hill, and the question of the absurd in human existence. The opening line is seemingly indicative: "'Oh, what a life, what a worthless, lousy, dirty life,' one of them cursed beneath his breath."[58] Patterson, though, does not create a nihilistic tale mirroring Camus's. He delves into the beliefs and aspirations of Rastafari, a twentieth-century maroon movement whose members at the time were labeled cultists and that considered its followers to be agents enslaved in the Babylonian political state of Jamaica. Rastafari sought inspiration from Garveyism, oneness with the *Geist* of Emperor Haile Selassie I, repatriation, and freedom in Zion qua Africa.

Although many Rastafari reside in rural spaces, the novel takes place in The Dungle, an urban enclave based upon the impoverished Kingston ghetto, Back-O-Wall. Rastafari in The Dungle imagine that another world is possible, and they are far from being socially dead. Instead, they struggle to achieve freedom as they negotiate late modern forms of mastery, slavery, and the condition of the mental slave, the "worst kind of slaves."[59] The protagonist, Dinah, is a prostitute who has the "ambition" to alter her life course.[60] Dinah's complex interactions with Cyrus, Brother Solomon, Shepherd John, and the dwellers of The Dungle point to challenges of millenarian prophetism. Yet Dinah's actions reinforce the ability of agents to enact flight and become free against the existential logic of the absurd. Patterson's social scientific studies unfortunately retreat from core intuitions illuminated in his fiction.

In my book, I offer an account divergent from the Pattersonian concept of social death by detailing why the interpretation of slave psychology serves an integral function in comprehending a slave's imagined ideal of freedom. The chapter on Douglass marks the beginning of my analysis of psychology's significance regarding a slave agent's persistent pursuit of political subjectivity and intersubjectivity. In the ensuing chapters on the Haitian Revolution, I borrow Frantz Fanon's conception of the *zone of nonbeing* to illustrate further the importance of slave psychology. The *damnés* (the damned, the condemned, slaves) exist in this zone, which is a sterile and arid region where an authentic upheaval can be born. Flight from the zone of nonbeing involves struggle and assertion, and it creates the possibility for actualizing revolutions against slavery through the natality embedded in its processes of movement.

Second, for all its investigations into marronage and slave societies globally, Patterson's system remains Eurocentric. He locates the birth of freedom as an inherently Western European ideal, and much of his justification revolves around brief references to political language.[61] However, as Hanna Pitkin details, not only did societies such as that of ancient Greece, which lacked words for "representation," still have notions of representation that those living today would recognize.[62] Societies including ancient Western polities themselves also had different words to describe the state of freedom. Explaining the emergence of the words *freedom* and *liberty*, each with divergent roots, poses problems for Patterson's lexical claims.[63] Instead of avoiding engagement with the social groups examined by Patterson, we must develop a creolized conception of slavery and freedom that blends ancient and modern, Western and non-Western thought. Comparative analysis helps us locate the multiple sources of freedom's genesis in enslavement at the same time that we make clear the unique conceptualizations that those sources offer.

Theories of freedom from modernity's underside disclose alternative transmodern solutions for agents seeking to subvert the omnipresent dialectics of slavery and mastery. Freedom as marronage isolates a modern disavowal of slavery and slave agency that complicates the dilemma Patterson only partially solved. Political theory can become enlightened so long as it shuns the entrapments of disciplinary provincialism.

Political Theory from the Underside of Modernity

Building upon recent developments in postcolonial theory, Africana thought, Latin American philosophy, subaltern studies, indigenous political thought, critical race theory, multiculturalism discourse, feminist political theory, and comparative political theory, Afro-Caribbean political theorists are furthering efforts to show the multiple faces of oppression and their relationship to the state of contemporary political theory by looking back at past events in order to theorize the conceptual meanings and implications of those occurrences.[64] It is in these more recent reflective investigations, along with the chronicles of individuals and events before, during, and after the Haitian Revolution, that one may best interpret the current relevance of this cataclysmic upheaval, which for too long has been deemed by Western scholars an "unthinkable" occurrence in need of disavowal.[65] My project, which bridges Caribbean, Continental, and North American political theory, contributes to shifting the geography and scope of political theory itself.

To fully appreciate the stakes of forging new directions in political theory, we must come to terms with changes in modern political geography. Revolutionary slaves possessed their own political imaginary, an imaginary with its own notions of reason and freedom that developed during the process of struggle against a form of slavery. Like the slave Caliban portrayed in William Shakespeare's 1623 play *The Tempest*, Haitian slaves battled Prospero, the European conqueror, literally and figuratively for the right to exist as free. These slaves refused what Stephen Greenblatt describes as the curse of slavery by transforming the system of unfreedom from the bottom up.[66] Nonetheless, alterations in the conceptualization of global geography did present several obstacles to the enactment of revolutionary slave agency.

Walter Mignolo aptly notes how Christopher Columbus's October 12, 1492, arrival on the Caribbean shores of the Bahamas ushered in the "modern/colonial" world, reconfiguring global designs through "discovery," conquest, the creation of the idea of America, newly invented mapmaking, and the matrices of colonial governance.[67] Columbus set sail with a Ptolemaic conception of the universe. Shifts in political geography after

Columbus's major voyages across the Atlantic affected the dominant Eurocentric political language, which rendered indigenous communities *terra nullius* and forcibly transformed Africans into invisible subhumans. Abraham Ortelius's *Orbis Universalis Terrarum* (Universal World) map (c.1575), for example, built upon the Western Christian T-in-O map in order to create a geographical world divided into the four regions of Africa, Asia, America, and Europe, with Europe serving as the global center.

Global political discourse, international law, and what Carl Schmitt refers to as the *nomos* of the earth were forever destabilized and reconstructed, thereby leading to a series of paradoxical negotiations between agents' consciousness of their identity and their difference from others.[68] The emergence of maps such as Ortelius's supports the claim of Sylvia Wynter that post-1492 thought unsettled medieval scholasticism's order of knowledge and marked a "New World View." In turn, the consequences of the 1550–1551 public Valladolid debate on the conquest of the Americas between the converted Dominican priest, Bartolomé de Las Casas, and the Renaissance humanist, Juan Ginés de Sepúlveda, strengthened adherents of the latter's transumed, neo-Aristotelian rationalizations of enslaving bodies classified as inhuman and subordinate by nature to the objectives of the political state.[69] The dialectics of coloniality in the modern/colonial world rested upon asymmetrical master-slave relations between Caliban and Prospero.

Unlike imperial Prospero, who represents the bearer of language and guardian of civilization, the character Caliban is a cannibal stuck in a state of nature, a being without language, and a not-so-noble savage without the capacity to reason. The Haitian slave is an archetypal Caliban figure.[70] As Paget Henry states in *Caliban's Reason*,

> To imperial Prospero, native Caliban (the Carib) was identical with nature—a cannibal, a child, a monster without language, and hence a potential slave to be subdued and domesticated along with nature and history. Much like the raw materials of nature, the labor of Caliban was there to be exploited for the purposes of imperial Prospero. In return for his labor, Prospero would give Caliban language and endow his "purposes with words that made them known." But even with this revelation of purpose, Caliban will only experience a small measure of humanization . . . In the Caribbean, this process of racialization turned Africans into blacks, Indians into browns, and European into whites . . . In short, this new racialized identity was also the death of Caliban's reason.[71]

Rejecting Prospero's ideal of freedom imposed from above, Haitian slaves instead embark upon the radical act of marronage from the standpoint of what Latin American philosopher Enrique Dussel calls the *underside of modernity*.[72] Those situated on modernity's underside craft a detailed system for escaping the state of enslavement. Caliban's conception of freedom, however, comes into being after the lived experience of deplorable exploitation.

Las Casas depicted the Spanish destruction of colonial Haiti, detailing graphically the manner in which indigenous women and men "found themselves condemned to a lifetime of captivity and slavery."[73] C. L. R. James remarks further, "The Spaniards, the most advanced Europeans of their day, annexed the island, called it Hispaniola, and took the backward natives under their protection. They introduced Christianity, forced labour in mines, murder, rape, bloodhounds, strange diseases, and artificial famine (by the destruction of cultivation to starve the rebellious)."[74] European slave traders rounded the Cape of Good Hope and made their way up through the West Coast of Africa in search of bodies deemed inherently unfree. The Torrid Zone previously considered by slavers to be the heart of darkness became the primary commodity locale for colonialists' New World mode of production. Slaves transported from Africa subsequently replaced Hispaniola's decimated indigenous populations. They were New World Calibans racialized as black and shackled until death. Haitian slaves imagined an alternative future without chains and devoid of the enslaving doctrines of colonial authorities. That future would necessitate marronage. This novel act fundamentally reshaped the conceptual landscape of modern political thinking not only for Haiti and the Caribbean, but also for peoples and movements across space, time, and locales.

Prospectus

Freedom as Marronage makes six contributions to the study of freedom. First, it offers a critique of theories that disavow the relationships among slavery, slave agency, and freedom. Chapter 1, more than the rest of the book, is theme-centered, with authors invoked insofar as they describe a problem we can and must eliminate. It defines disavowal and slave agency, highlights the importance of probing slavery ancient and modern, and outlines the consequences for freedom when disavowing slave agency. To accomplish this task, the chapter examines the republicanism espoused by Hannah Arendt and Philip Pettit and illuminates their thought's relevance to flight.

In the later explication of marronage, I reconstruct Arendt's distinction between liberation and the foundation of freedom. Whereas liberation is the moment of release from bondage, the foundation of freedom denotes natality and lasting principles of constitutionalism buttressing a new political order. The work of W. E. B. Du Bois points to the impasse of disavowal, first by depicting the utility of studying the actions and experiences of the enslaved, and second by introducing how the vector of race affects fugitivity, unfreedom, and flight.

Second, the project engages the work of Frederick Douglass—an example of a theorist who supports the claim that freedom must be understood in relation to slavery but does so in ways that still remain insufficient in describing freedom. Douglass's prime significance is in his detailing, with painstaking precision, the value of experience. For Douglass, it is our mutating struggles and assertions in the face of enslavement that offer context to the meanings of the free life and its betrayal. Chapter 2 provides an exegesis of Douglass's middle autobiography, the text in which Douglass supports this position through developing the concept of comparative freedom. The analysis of this book is mediated by inquiry into the work of African-American thinker Angela Y. Davis, the British Romanticist poet-philosopher Samuel Taylor Coleridge, and the hemispheric influence of the elder Douglass, particularly the period of the early, postcolonial Haitian state. This makes more apparent the stakes of understanding fugitivity and acts of marronage in revolutionary Saint-Domingue during the previous decades.

Third, the book focuses attention in chapters 3 and 4 on the Haitian Revolution—the only known successful slave revolution—in order to explain a more robust notion of freedom that I contend best portrays the dialectic of slavery and freedom. In the process, I highlight the value of marronage for our modern political vocabulary by redefining its conventional usage so as to delineate freedom's meaning in the Haitian Revolution and to present freedom as marronage as a heuristic device useful to political theorists working in multiple geopolitical contexts. The work of another Césaire student, Frantz Fanon, supports this objective.

Chapter 3 examines two central Francophone documents of the seventeenth and eighteenth centuries in order to uncover a juridical paradox unresolved by the revolution's beginning. It outlines thereafter three types of marronage that serve as a response to questions left unanswered in previous chapters. The crux of the chapter is inquiry into the benefits and limitations of sovereign marronage and its manifestation in the figure of Toussaint L'Ouverture during the Haitian Revolution. It challenges enduring rhetoric in the popular imagination that collapses into one Toussaint's freedom and all the principles forged during the revolution. Toussaint's vision of a future is not the only notion of freedom operative in the uprising. Chapter 4 continues the analysis of the Haitian Revolution, but with a focus on sociogenic marronage, non-sovereign activity, and decipherment of principles developed by slave masses, known and obscure, through flight. A close examination of naming, architectonics, Haitian constitutionalism, the state of society, and a postrevolutionary short story bolster support for the opening corollary that freedom is not a social practice applicable solely to bounded historical periods.

Fourth, inquiry into Édouard Glissant's thought marks a shift in the text to the relevance of my argument for late modernity. A philosophical examination of a novel and an essay collection by Glissant frame both Glissant's idea of freedom and the implications of his conception of marronage for contemporary debates over France's commemoration of abolition, the Arab Spring uprisings of 2011–2013, and the relation between mainland France and French overseas *départements*, including Martinique. This is followed by a brief discussion of immigration politics and the figure of the refugee-immigrant as a late modern maroon.

The relation of the book's argument to liberalism and neoliberalism constitutes the fifth contribution. But first, a few caveats: you are not going to find a comprehensive critique of liberal and neoliberal thought. This work does not introduce an alternative system of governance to liberal statecraft, as do treatises, intellectuals, and movements advocating genres of Marxism, Pan-Africanism, anarchism, absolutism, and conservatism. It does delve into varieties of republicanism and also draws from principles and figures associated with the latter traditions. There is an immanent critique of genres of modern liberalism descended from Hobbes, Berlin, and Kant that, whether negative or positive, reify beliefs in inertness and center freedom on the individual outside interstitial acts of flight connecting us with one another. Neoliberalism, at least in typologies after Friedrich Hayek and the Austrian school of moral philosophy and political economy, is an extension of these modern liberal prescriptions—particularly the negative Western stream—applied to self and economy. For Hayek, excessive state intervention in human lives is the route to serfdom. In general, since the end of World War II, adherents of neoliberalism view freedom as rooted in the market, personal choice, reduction of state intervention into the lives of individuals, and the ability of individuals through effort and hard work to partake of the resources of the market economy without state interference and domination. The insufficiencies of freedom as non-interference and non-domination are as applicable a rejoinder to neoliberalism as they are to the liberal and republican voices explored at the start of the book.

Sixth and finally, the project explores the meaning of *unfreedom*. The significance of unfreedom is a theme that connects every chapter. In much the same way that centering attention on the notion of injustice to understand justice significantly shifted debates in contemporary political theory,[75] this book aims to contribute to the transformation of contemporary thinking on freedom by elucidating the importance of conceptualizing freedom's opposite condition and the experience of flight from that state. Unfreedom is a condition the *damnés* reside in. It also contains the resources for the their revolutionary flight from slavery. I explore at length this often-ignored axiom.

The afterword opens up a conversation on the significance of Rastafari, a movement whose contours demonstrate overlapping forms of marronage and late modern complexities of flight in a world of difference. Rastafari speech acts and dialogue on dread and love set the terms for freedom and an evolving disposition of its members toward the state. The ongoing benefits and challenges of Rastafari present us with a rubric to appreciate the meaning of freedom and why marronage still matters.

Fanon and James dared theorists of freedom to cast aside old enslaving norms, work out new concepts, and set afoot a new imaginative humanism in regions Prospero never knew. Freedom as marronage is one answer to this challenge.

ONE

The Disavowal of Slave Agency

In other words, the social question could not very well be solved by revolution in America for the simple reason that at the moment no such solution was required—if we leave out of account, as we must here, the predicament of Negro slavery and the altogether different problem it posed.
—Hannah Arendt, "Revolution and Freedom: A Lecture"[1]

This opposition between slavery or servitude on the one hand and freedom on the other is probably the single most characteristic feature of the long rhetoric of liberty to which the experience of the Roman republic gave rise.
—Philip Pettit, *Republicanism*[2]

There are many people today and some of them radicals and revolutionaries who sneer at the fact that this [Greek] democracy was based on slavery. So it was, though we have found that those who are prone to attack Greek Democracy on behalf of slavery are not so much interested in defending the slaves as they are in attacking democracy.
—C. L. R. James, *Every Cook Can Govern*[3]

Introduction

A glaring problem exists that receives little attention in the voluminous appraisals of freedom: the lack of attention paid to slavery and slave agency. Hanna Pitkin asks whether freedom and liberty are conceptual twins, observing how these terms might denote distinct notions with their own original roots and implications. Implicit in this inquiry are the ways in which thinkers posit probing questions without exploring crucial aspects required for comprehensive explanation.[4]

Although philosophers and political theorists persist in thinking about the association between freedom and liberty, they often perpetuate the unfortunate act of disavowing a much more fundamental relationship between freedom and slavery. If the relationship between freedom and liberty is one of twins or siblings, then the connection between freedom and slavery is one of a child to a parent. Slavery serves as the foundational notion that gives rise to freedom.

Slavery should not be understood as a mere metaphor. Slavery denotes a state of unfreedom and zone of nonbeing conceptually and phenomenologically antithetical to freedom, and any theory of freedom failing to take this association seriously remains inadequate. The use of slavery as metaphor is ubiquitous in Western thought, ancient and modern. The literatures of Greek and Roman antiquity, discourses on sin of Pauline and Augustinian Christianity, documents of medieval jurists, treatises of Enlightenment *philosophes*, battle cries of revolutionary America, the French national anthem, and the rhetoric of contemporary libertarians are suffused with it.[5] The metaphor of slavery is a trope in the Western imagination that overextends itself, the metaphorical eclipsing the experiences of the real. The analytical juxtaposition of slavery ancient and modern, though, is not a formula for conflating the historical circumstances of eras, for whereas ethnicity, gender, and class are primary identifiers of enslaved peoples of the ancient West, race is foremost among other intersections for modern slaves. Nonetheless, peering deeper into ancient and modern slave societies, thinkers, and revolutions discloses experiences of flight that excavate common submerged discursive knowledges.

In the modern period scholars espousing genres of republicanism and reading the ancient into the modern devise influential ideas of freedom beyond the parameters of liberalism and neoliberalism. To a differing extent, however, cadres of republicans disavow slavery and the actions of the enslaved, obscuring the importance of a slave's capacity for revolutionary action. Through their disavowals, they obscure the constituent elements of freedom.

Disavowal does not mean silence, as a silence denotes a complete failure to mention the relevant subject.[6] In everyday language, the verb *to avow* is to acknowledge. Regarding the opposite of *avow*, the *Oxford English Dictionary* defines the verb *disavow* as meaning "to refuse to avow, own, or acknowledge, to disclaim knowledge of, responsibility for, or approbation: to repudiate; to deny." Disavowal, then, in its everyday usage, denotes the "action of disavowing or refusing to acknowledge; repudiation, denial."[7] Sigmund

Freud usually describes disavowal (*Verleugnung*) with respect to castration anxiety and fetishism. To a lesser degree, Freud associates disavowal with death. Children, for example, acknowledge the lack of a penis in females while at the same time repudiating the belief that they in fact imagined a female possessing the male sexual organ. The resulting neurotic castration fear leads to the creation of a fetish that is disavowed internally in the children's minds.

Freudian psychoanalysis expands the understanding of disavowal by relating it to specific traumatic experiences and pointing out that acts of disavowal exist alongside recognition and acknowledgment of the traumatic event.[8] While trauma plays a large part in disavowal, Freud does not differentiate between its internal and external consequences. The example of disavowal regarding the castration fear illustrates internal trauma; events such as the Haitian Revolution and revolutionary antislavery illustrate external trauma; and acts of race and racism illustrate forms of both. Repetitions and reversals produce external transgenerational trauma at the individual and collective levels.

Disavowal centrally requires what I take to be a simultaneous *double movement*: an acknowledgment *and* a denial. By simultaneously acknowledging and denying an event, one does not silence its existence. Rather, one strategically locates an event and then rejects its relevance, knowing full well that it occurred. The double movement produces negative traumatic effects more damaging than silence. Locating and establishing the implications of the disavowal of slave agency is the goal of what follows.

The chapter begins with an analysis of two republican notions of freedom: the first, freedom in the founding of non-sovereign human action; and the second, the concept of freedom as non-domination. I outline the claims of each while highlighting the locus of their respective disavowals of slavery and slave agency. The second republican ideal does not hide the importance of slavery to freedom in the Roman tradition it seeks to revive. It makes a point of addressing slavery explicitly in a manner that the first notion fails to articulate. Strict, doctrinaire adherents of these two systems nevertheless disavow the experiences, thoughts, and agency of slaves, and this act unites them. After explaining the adverse effects of disavowal, I turn in the next section to the meaning of slave agency and underscore Toni Morrison's adage that "modern life begins with slavery."[9] By identifying the actions of slaves and spheres of fugitivity, we discern the importance of lived experience, the intersections between race and slavery that inform modern sensibilities, and overlapping ancient and modern discourses on flight derived from experience.

Founding Non-Sovereign Action

Justice, power, order, and rights are essential features of our existence in the world. On their own, they are not first principles of what it means to be human. The relation of humans to politics complicates this appraisal. Hannah Arendt observes that the *"raison d'être* of politics is freedom, and without it, political life would be meaningless."[10] In "What Is Freedom?" and *The Promise of Politics*, she reiterates this statement.[11] Arendt conceives of freedom as the central category shaping the human condition, and constant attempts to formulate a compelling notion of freedom pervade her oeuvre. Arendt's ruminations on freedom navigate an inherited "hostility between philosophy and politics" that "has been the curse of Western statecraft as well as of the Western tradition of philosophy ever since men of action and the men of thought parted company—that is, ever since Socrates' death."[12] Understanding the hostile abyss between politics and philosophy brings to the fore the contested gulfs between *praxis* and *poiesis*, acting and making, beginning and ending, thought and contemplation, and natality and death.

Arendt shares several of Immanuel Kant's positions on judgment and spontaneity. Even more fundamental is Arendt's agreement with Kant on conceptualizing freedom as independent of slavery.[13] For Arendt, "Kant saved freedom from this twofold assault upon it by distinguishing between 'pure' or theoretical reason and a 'practical reason' whose center is free will."[14] Kant's critical philosophy locates freedom *a priori* in the noumenal realm of intelligible things-in-themselves, a sphere separate from the phenomenal world of the senses. In the Kantian framework, one does not come to realize or feel freedom through casting judgment on the experience of slavery, since a universal idea of freedom is thought to exist throughout time and space regardless of our everyday lived activities.

In Arendt's estimation, despite his originality, Kant falls prey to the limitations of a Western philosophical tradition unable to integrate concepts and phenomena into comprehension of how humans living in an interactive "web of relationships" may best live free. Actions and experiences matter more to Arendt than *a priori* intuitions. Philosophy mistakenly banishes freedom from the domain of politics, turning its optic narrowly inward toward the will.[15]

We must come to terms with the meaning of freedom externally by recognizing the actuality of human plurality, "the fact that men, not Man, live on the earth and inhabit the world."[16] A return to the ancient Greek *polis* is the basis for Arendt's neo-Athenian republicanism and proposed solutions to the dilemmas facing us.[17] By *neo-Athenian*, I mean a conception of republicanism that bridges concerns about the life and economy of the ancient city-state with modern forms of governance and statecraft. Neo-Athenian thought introduces elements of ancient Athens applicable to republicanism and freedom in the modern world.

The agonal spirit of the *polis* is the passionate human drive for self-assertion against others. Becoming a part of the *polis* means participating in public modes of governance. This has a range of scales. Size matters less than the capacity for agents to cultivate a free existence. For Arendt it "was the *polis*, the space of men's free deeds and living words, which could endow life with splendour."[18] To speak of freedom in modernity, unencumbered by the limitations of Western philosophy, requires delving into the phenomenon of revolution.

In *On Revolution* (1963), Arendt reflects on two of the eighteenth century's formative events: the American Revolution and the French Revolution. While the American Revolution represents the realm of freedom and the political, the French Revolution is Arendt's definitive example of the apolitical site of necessity and unfreedom. Arendt claims the French Revolution's negative totalizing effects overshadow the lost treasure of the American revolutionary tradition. A symptom of this loss is "the very fact that these two elements, the concern with stability and the spirit of the new, have become opposites in political thought—the one being identified as conservatism and the other claimed as the monopoly of progressive liberalism."[19] Reclaiming the lost tradition established by American revolutionaries and the Founding Fathers, particularly Thomas Jefferson, is paramount to achieving freedom in dark times.

When looking to the physiognomy of the twentieth century, Arendt identifies the rise of the atomic bomb and notes the staggering omnipresence of wars and revolutions. Unlike the phenomenology of war, revolution emerges only with the advent of the modern age. Revolution occupies a key role in thinking about freedom since the "aim of revolution was, and always has been, freedom." Nonetheless, in the twentieth century, "nothing indeed has seemed to be more safely buried than the concept of freedom."[20] Arendt's exhumation starts with an etymological observation.

The term *revolution* first related to the natural sciences, and it was nonpolitical. Revolution had an astronomical association with the revolving motion of the stars. It carried the backward-looking connotation of restoration, the exact opposite of the word's current usages. In the seventeenth century, revolution took on a political designation, remaining wed to the notion of restoration as a return to a preestablished point. The subsequent onset of the

American Revolution also operated to a significant degree under the rubric of revolution as restoration.[21]

With the storming of the Bastille, French revolutionaries forever changed the political language of revolution, shifting its meaning from a backward-looking to a *forward-looking* concept. Revolution in its modern form now denoted a beginning, the birth of a *novus ordo saeclorum*. The people irresistibly sought nothing less than the entire abolition of absolutist feudalism and the asymmetrical relationships among peasants, lords, legislators, and monarchs that feudalism established.[22] The idea of irresistibility took a sad, violent turn in Arendt's view, as the unalterable movement in search of radical change collapsed into the violent Jacobin Terror of historical necessity. Arendt remarks, "It was the French and not the American Revolution that set the world on fire, and it was consequently from the course of the French Revolution, and not from the course of events in America or from the acts of the Founding Fathers, that our present use of the word 'revolution' received its connotations and overtones everywhere, the United States not excluded."[23]

Modern revolutions confront the problem of beginning directly. Beginning is *natality*, dually referring to "the fact that human beings appear in the world by virtue of birth" and "the capacity of beginning anew, that is, of acting."[24] Arendt develops an unorthodox conception of the experience of beginning, which has in its theorization a desire to dismantle hierarchical systems of rule while holding onto the ideals of naissance and action. Experience here is significant. In her German translation of *On Revolution*, Arendt underscores this through the repeated invocation of the word *Erfahrung* for "experience"—understood in a processual manner as the experience of "movement" and a "journey"—instead of *Erlebnis*, an immediate experience.[25] The problem of beginning something new in the domain of politics resides in the existence of nonpolitical and antipolitical factors that disrupt the formation of a new order of things. The foundation of freedom, nonsovereignty, and the social question are phenomena that either obviate or exacerbate the problem's challenges.

Anchoring Arendt's republicanism is differentiation between *liberation* and the *foundation of freedom* (*constitutio libertatis*). The lack of acknowledging the distinction is another facet of loss in late modernity that we are to recover. Liberation describes the negative moment of necessity "whose fruits are absence of restraint and possession of 'the power of locomotion.'"[26] It is a condition that precedes the institution of freedom. To attain liberation means be released from one's chains. Violence characterizes the moment of liberation, an unavoidable phenomenon in many instances of flight.

Violence, nevertheless, must not dictate the course of revolutionary projects, for in Arendt's estimation violence's subsumption of speech and situatedness outside the political sphere produces a clear outcome: the implosion of freedom.[27] Whereas power is the human ability to act in concert, violence is the instrumental, illegitimate, antipolitical quality that destroys power.[28] Under this rationale, a "rebellion," as a violent uprising, describes the final result of the liberation process rather than the nomenclature of "revolution." The French Revolution is a misnomer in these terms, because it ends in the liberatory violence of the enraged, failing to arrive at the next constituting phase.

Freedom moves beyond the stage of necessity through its central act: foundation. Arendt imagines foundation as spontaneously constituting a lasting rubric for a republic unsusceptible to the necessities of violence, political closure, and time.[29] Freedom demands the constitution of a republic, and it is not to be mistaken for either free enterprise or civil rights. In this sense, notwithstanding an inverse appraisal of will and constituent power, Arendt echoes Carl Schmitt's dictum that constitutionalism and foundation are more than the sum total of constitutional laws.[30] To enact constitutionalism, agents must be participators in governance. Otherwise, their actions become meaningless.[31] Unlike liberation's focus on tearing down, freedom involves positivity and the creativity that natality instills.[32] Resolving concurrent tensions between liberation and the foundation of freedom is a dilemma that Arendt believes is unsolvable. Hers is also a premature judgment.

The idea of non-sovereignty, the second integral aspect of Arendt's system, is diametrically opposed to notions of generality embraced by French revolutionaries under the influence of philosophers including Rousseau. The basic miscalculation of the French insurrection lies in equating freedom and sovereignty. Sovereignty, "the ideal of uncompromising self-sufficiency and mastership, is contradictory to the very condition of plurality."[33] The compassionate desire of autonomous agents for self-mastery, willed conformism, and unity into an indivisible multitude perpetuates, rather than solves, the crisis of the republic. A republican community cannot found freedom upon spectators harboring a destructive notion of sovereignty, since "a community actually founded on this sovereign will would be built not on sand but quicksand."[34] Freedom requires a non-sovereign imaginary in the body politic, and the American Revolution is Arendt's archetype of founding non-sovereign human action because of its consistent rejection of sovereignty throughout the republic.[35]

On Revolution builds on a primary claim of *The Human Condition* regarding non-sovereign action as the fundamental human activity molding politics. Action, in conjunction with speech, avoids the problems brought on by the biological subsistence of labor (*animal laborans*) and work's meaningless, productive fabrications (*homo faber*). The private, the public, and the social realms reflect the three spheres of human activity (*vita activa*). While labor occurs in private, and work cuts across the private and the public, action is a pluralistic manifestation whose coalescence with speech is the premier form of activity. "To act, in its most general sense, means to take an initiative, to begin"; and "with the creation of man, the principle of beginning came into the world itself, which, of course, is only another way of saying that the principle of freedom was created when man was created but not before."[36] Action alone exists entirely in the public, political realm.

The social is Arendt's bête noire, the rubric of activity that has as its enclosure violence, economic relations, and unanimity. Of greatest consequence for disavowal is the third fulcrum of Arendt's system rooted in this sphere: the social question.

The Ultimate Blob

Where we find Arendt's disavowal is in the discussion of the social question and US racial slavery. Arendt invokes the word *social* in different works; its instances appear to be related in all texts, yet mutable over time. She usually employs a neologism by rendering the adjective *social* into the noun, *the social*. However, chapter 2 of *On Revolution* bears the title, "The Social Question," demonstrating the lexical return to the adjective. Using *social* in either adjectival or noun form occupies a special place in Arendt's lists of negatives, for she conceives the social sphere and the social question as entities of conformity that swallow up and destroy politics. All things social are an abominable quality, considered in Pitkin's opinion to be an evil Blob that Arendt hopes to excise. Pitkin likens Arendt's notion of the social to fantasies of science fiction, wherein a monstrous space invader breaks through Earth's atmosphere, hovers over the human masses, descends on them, and turns humans into robotic, uniform drones devoid of the ability to create individual thoughts and actions. In *On Revolution*, the social question refers to a debilitating manifestation of the social Blob: poverty.[37]

Arendt argues that the existence of poverty in France led French revolutionaries to embrace the cause of liberating those in the polity from their state of destitution. And indeed, the unhappy revolutionaries (*les malheureux*) succeeded in achieving liberation of the poor without founding freedom. "The Revolution, when it turned from the foundation of freedom to the liberation of man from suffering, broke down the barriers of endurance and liberated, as it were, the devastating forces of misfortune and misery instead." French revolutionaries transformed the Rights of Man into the Rights of the Sans-Culottes in an attempt to make a social problem a political issue.[38]

The background to disavowal starts surfacing when Arendt attempts to reconcile the idealism of the American Revolution and the existence of poverty within the republic. Arendt tries to clarify her position by stating that what the new American republic lacked was want and misery, not poverty.[39] This assertion we know to be historically inaccurate, as does Arendt, and the double movement of disavowal, both acknowledgment and denial, of US black slavery ensues. To be certain, Arendt is no stranger to discourse on the experience of race and bondage. Her earlier writings on the Jewish Question in the West, notably "Enlightenment and the Jewish Question," "The Jew as Pariah," "Antisemitism," and columns written in France as a stateless person in limbo between Nazi Germany and the United States serve as affirmation.[40] Furthermore, Arendt does not silence American racial slavery, conceding "that abject and degrading misery was present everywhere in the form of slavery and Negro labour."[41] In fact, she considers, albeit briefly, the meaning of black slavery and the relationship of the several hundred thousand enslaved blacks to the social question in America:

> If it were not for the presence of Negro slavery on the American scene, one would be tempted to explain this striking aspect exclusively by American prosperity, by Jefferson's "lovely equality," or by the fact that America was indeed, in William Penn's words, "a good poor Man's country." As it were, we are tempted to ask ourselves if the goodness of the poor white man's country did not depend to a considerable degree upon black labour and black misery — there lived roughly 400,000 Negroes along with approximately 1,850,000 white men in America in the middle of the eighteenth century, and even in the absence of reliable statistical data we may be sure that the percentage of complete destitution and misery was considerably lower in the countries of the Old World. From this, we can only conclude that the institution of slavery carries an obscurity even blacker than the obscurity of poverty; the slave, not the poor man, was "wholly overlooked." For if Jefferson, and others to a lesser degree, were aware of the primordial crime upon which the fabric of American society rested, if they "trembled when [they] thought that God is 'just'" (Jefferson), they did so because they were convinced of the incompatibility of the institution of slavery with the foundation of freedom, not because they were moved by pity or by a feeling of solidarity with their fellow men. And this indifference, difficult for us to understand, was not peculiar to Americans

and hence must be blamed on slavery rather than on any perversion of the heart or upon the dominance of self-interest. . . . Slavery was no more part of the social question for Europeans than it was for Americans, so that the social question, whether genuinely absent or only hidden in darkness, was non-existent for all practical purposes, and with it, the most powerful and perhaps the most devastating passion motivating revolutionaries, the passion of compassion.[42]

Political questions demand attention. Social questions, tragic as they might be, remain beyond the political sphere no matter how much passion they generate. Arendt situates slavery in a nebulous space between the political and the social. Issues straddling the political-social divide threaten to shatter the Arendtian schema, causing her to engage in disavowal. After acknowledging the overlooked slave and asserting that black slavery carries an institutional "obscurity even blacker than the obscurity of poverty," Arendt quickly disavows the relevance of racial slavery and actions of black slaves to the social question, first to maintain the integrity of her American revolutionary vision, a vision absent of the violence, blood, injury, and terror experienced by the slaves, what Saidiya Hartman calls the sufferance and burdens of flight under subjection;[43] and second to preserve the critique of the violence and poverty in the French Revolution. After this disavowal, slavery becomes a ghost, disappearing from the remaining pages of *On Revolution*.

"Revolution and Freedom: A Lecture," delivered just over a year earlier in October 1961, provides greater insight into the quandary slavery poses not merely for Arendtian freedom but for a circumscribed republicanism. Arendt gave the talk at Connecticut College's fiftieth Anniversary Convocation ceremonies, and in 1962 a publisher based in Tel-Aviv included the text in a compilation of essays mainly in German.[44] More than a prolegomenon to *On Revolution*, the lecture puts forth crucial claims about world politics and slavery that are absent or equivocally stated in the larger work. Arendt frames the talk in an era of "cold peace," a phrased preferred in place of "cold war," as the latter conjures the modern world's fearful preoccupation with nuclear weapons.[45] Although the American and French Revolutions still serve their archetypal functions, the lecture's provocations surround declarations on the twentieth-century revolutions in Hungary and Cuba.

Despite its short-lived success, the 1956 Hungarian Revolution and its council system gain significance as the best post-American revolutionary model for constituting freedom, the social question ostensibly having no role. The then new and uncompleted 1959 Cuban Revolution, similar to the French Revolution, garners contempt due to its inability to act and to found.

This comes neither from its advent, since Arendt welcomed the revolution with enthusiasm, nor from the Cuban response to the failed US Bay of Pigs invasion that occurred only months before the talk. The disdain stems from the actual trajectory of the revolution under Fidel Castro's leadership, the guerrilla tactics, and popular support the Cuban people give to sovereignty through their revolutionary project.

The people passionately desire to walk the urban streets and countryside of Cuba "without yet knowing what it might mean to act in freedom," their compassionate preoccupation with eradicating poverty another devastating attack by the social Blob.[46] The revolution's aim of freedom through platforms designed to curb racial inequality, master-slave relations, and the legacy of racial orders forged during transatlantic slavery and left in place after the truncated Cuban War of Independence are not the objects of this narration.[47] Black slavery has an intimate link to the race question, which Du Bois calls the problem of the twentieth century and Arendt says remains unsolved in mid-twentieth-century America. The issue of the color line and the contradiction of freedom for some and not for all raise queries about the model of freedom itself and markers of achievement.[48]

In "Revolution and Freedom," Arendt explicitly displaces the conundrum of black slavery both in Cuba and, critically, America. Arendt acknowledges that the American Revolution does not solve the social question. In complementary writings on civil disobedience, she discloses disenchantment with the 1857 Supreme Court ruling in *Dred Scott v. Sandford*, which made juridical an American racial state that, in tacit form, already existed following 1776. The framers of the Constitution rely on tacit consent in forging a post-revolutionary America in which the slave population "had never been included in the original *consensus universalis* of the American republic."[49] The Fourteenth Amendment, Fifteenth Amendment, and the spirit of the laws, of consent, supported in the policies of leaders including the antebellum Abraham Lincoln, cannot alleviate the intentional unwillingness of federal and state governments to rectify the "original crime" of black slaves' "*tacit* exclusion from the *tacit* consensus."[50]

Black slavery is the *ultimate Blob*, the preeminent crisis of the new American republic. The United States enters the comity of nations as a *Herrenvolk* democracy, a white supremacist state that, according to Charles Mills, has juridical divisions between masters and slaves, whites and nonwhites.[51] Personhood becomes a subject of law, whiteness an assemblage of power relations vis-à-vis blackness, and mutable human characteristics are treated frequently, through a metaphysics of race, as fixed categories of status. Black slaves are racialized and dehumanized, race seeping throughout the polity from the apparatuses of government to the somatic. The existence of slavery, the facticity of subpersons in bondage, and the way the factor of race structures being, experience, and flight have confounding internal and external traumatic effects that must be denied after recognition. Otherwise, the political-social distinction collapses, as does another measure to sustain the American Revolution's positive significance:

> Hence, when I said the American Revolution succeeded where all others failed, I did not mean to say that it succeeded in solving the social question, that is, it found political ways and means to cure a country from the curse of poverty. This is not to deny the enormous and enormously revolutionizing influence of the New World's prosperity upon the events and the hopes in the Old World. On the contrary, it is perfectly true that here, for the first time, men began to see and to believe that misery and want do not have to be part and parcel of the human condition on earth. John Adams said: "I always consider the settlement of America as the opening of a grand scheme and design in Providence for the illumination of the ignorant and the emancipation of the slavish part of mankind all over the earth." But he wrote these words ten years before the outbreak of the revolution, in a state of perfect unawareness of such a possibility. In other words, the social question could not very well be solved by revolution in America for the simple reason that at that moment no such solution was required—if we leave out of account, as we must here, the predicament of Negro slavery and the altogether different problem it posed. Therefore, undisturbed by any outside factors, the revolution could accomplish its original aim: the establishment of institutions which guarantee liberty for all, and the foundation of a new public realm, called a republic, as opposed to a monarchy, where everybody, in the words of Jefferson, could become a "participator in government."[52]

Telling an exceptionalist story without thorny quotidian realities does not invalidate exceptionalism, though it might. It does decontextualize the struggles of the experience of freedom trans-historically between past and future. *Erfahrung*, after all, is the experience of a journey and varieties of movement in flight. The consideration of slaves as political agents with social problems, whether New World black slaves, Athenian pedagogues, or the Zandj of premodern Iraq, is useful to properly capture action and constitution.

The novelist Ralph Ellison's public dispute with Arendt over school desegregation in the Battle of Little Rock reveals the futility of separating the political and the social. For Ellison, there are no political versus social spheres, but rather an interrelated "social-political" world to inhabit.[53] Another consequence arises that Ellison misses: freedom pertains to more than physical spheres of private, political, and social activity. The psychological and the metaphysical are also domains informing what it means to be free. The trauma of slavery is not only its effects on statecraft and institutionalism. The slave's trauma is also existential, its effects capable of distorting awareness of an agent's inherent capabilities. The promise and perils of resuscitating a second significant notion of freedom from the Roman republican tradition begin to elucidate why.

Non-Domination

The resurgence of Roman republican thought is now well-known among political theorists and circles of academe. In Maurizio Viroli's assessment, republicanism "not only is a noble tradition of the past but also is meant as a new, or rediscovered, utopia of political liberty."[54] Many in the neo-Roman republican movement conceive their principles of freedom as a vigorous, viable alternative to forms of liberalism, neoliberalism, and communitarianism.[55] At the forefront of the revival is Philip Pettit's *Republicanism: A Theory of Freedom and Government*, first published in 1997 and revised in 1999 with a postscript.[56]

Republicanism is a manifesto urging the adoption of a neo-Roman notion of freedom as "non-domination." According to Pettit, the Western liberal tradition develops an influential concept of freedom as "non-interference," beginning with Thomas Hobbes and Jeremy Bentham and culminating in Isaiah Berlin's inaugural lecture, "Two Concepts of Liberty."[57] Berlin further transforms the language of freedom in the modern liberal tradition by introducing a distinction between negative liberty and positive liberty, where, as we recall, negative liberty corresponds to the ideal of non-interference and positive liberty to the ability for self-mastery. The distinction between negative liberty and positive liberty is reminiscent of Benjamin Constant's division of the liberty of the moderns from the liberty of the ancients.[58]

Pettit suggests that Berlin's distinction and the liberal non-interference ideal have done us ill. He aims to recover an anterior Roman notion of freedom and the "supreme political value" of this tradition's lost conception.[59] This tradition traces its roots from classical Rome to Machiavelli and Renaissance Italy, the English Commonwealth thinkers, Montesquieu and Rousseau, proponents of the American Revolution, and elements of French revolutionary thought connecting freedom, structural egalitarianism, and people's social and common goods.[60]

Domination in the Roman tradition consists in the capacity of an agent to interfere on an arbitrary basis in certain choices that another agent is in a position to make. "An act is perpetrated on an arbitrary basis, we can say, if it is subject to the *arbitrium*, the decision or judgment, of the agent." Pettit refers to this elsewhere as *alien control*: the condition of an alien agent exercising arbitrary positional control over the deliberations and decision making of another.[61] Roman republicanism does not denounce interference entirely, as does the liberal tradition; only *arbitrary* interference. An agent's ability to make choices informed by context and parameters that do not obstruct well-being and life options is critical. This agent-centered approach is principally person-based, with the component of choice having an integral secondary function.[62]

Integral to the *law-and-liberty theme* of republican freedom is the ability for the state to engage in non-arbitrary interference of citizens under a just, properly constituted rule of law.[63] Such non-capricious interference, which champions an empire of laws, can take the form of a state tax on its citizenry. Accordingly, freedom as non-domination is compatible with legislated state interference, so long as the state tracks the "common, recognizable interests" of its citizens.[64] Tracking this helps to curb the debilitating effects of two types of power: individuals' private power of arbitrary interference (*dominium*) and the public power of the state (*imperium*).[65] Combating *dominium* and *imperium* assists in releasing an agent from the condition of domination.

The central feature of Roman republicanism, the *liberty-versus-slavery theme*, highlights the grounding of republicanism in the phenomenon of enslavement. Slavery, the antonym of *libertas*, is the tradition's quintessential unfreedom. "The condition of liberty is explicated as the status of someone who, unlike the slave, is not subject to the arbitrary power of another: that is, someone who is not dominated by anyone else."[66] Domination derives from *dominus*, meaning "master" or "owner," and *dominus* originally referred to a Roman slave master. To be dominated thereby means being subject to the arbitrary will of a *dominus*. An individual exists under the master's power of domination even in the case of a benevolent, non-interfering master.[67] Capricious domination of the slave wielded in the twin forms of *dominium* and *imperium* can occur in many permutations, including the domination of a Roman master over a slave, a wife-beating husband in a heterosexual marriage, a pedophilic in-law over a defenseless child during a baby-sitting session, a prison warden over inmates, and a commanding monarch over her or his subjects.

Libertas carries a "predominantly negative," "passive," and "defensive" connotation, never active participation in interest-group politics and democratic government, despite differences in rival conceptions among the Roman republic's nobility and plebeians. Gaining protection and security from personal and institutional caprice far precedes those positive aspirations. It is the negativity of *libertas* in Roman thinking that undergirds freedom as *non*-domination.[68] Neo-Roman republicanism reorients thought on how we can move from domination to non-domination and hence acquire freedom without relinquishing our private security and trust in the political state to uphold a non-dominating rule of law.

Yet concern for the nuances of political language brings with it a heightened attentiveness to the historical legacies that language carries and the political repercussions of its normative usage. Pettit appropriates crucial terminology derived from ancient Rome without properly spelling out the full political significance given to their traditional Latin tags.[69] This points toward two levels of disavowal that Pettit enacts, both related to the gradual disappearance from *Republicanism* of the vocabulary of slavery. Pettit introduces a distinction between slavery and domination, shifting the meaning of unfreedom away from the Roman tradition. The linguistic vanishing of slavery is not the locus of disavowal. It is a symptom of the act. In the first level of disavowal, Pettit establishes another distinction between the *unfree* and the *non-free* that undermines the value given to the law-and-liberty theme. Of greatest consequence, in the second level of disavowal, Pettit simultaneously acknowledges and denies the being and activities of slaves. These two levels combined produce traumatic effects.

Pettit's *Republicanism* begins by establishing a set of synonyms that we can characterize by the following equation: domination = slavery = unfreedom. In his preface, for example, Pettit states that the "antonym" of freedom in classical Rome "was slavery." He comments in the introduction, "No domination without unfreedom." By chapter 2, Pettit remarks that "slavery and unfreedom [are] consistent with non-interference: that it [domination] can be realized in the presence of a master or authority who is beneficent, and even benevolent."[70] After the last statement, the word *slavery* vanishes from the text's vocabulary, becoming a floating signifier.

The disappearance of *slavery* in favor of *domination* is intentional. Pettit henceforth changes the equation domination = slavery = unfreedom *to* domination = unfreedom, dropping the language of slavery altogether. With the linguistic evaporation of slavery, Pettit concurrently aligns himself with the Roman tradition's revival and creates distance from its notion of unfreedom in full, choosing instead a less stringent conception of domination. Unfreedom in his revised typology no longer corresponds to domination's original meaning, understood as a slave existing under the master's arbitrary powers of private *dominium* and public *imperium*. *Dominium* and *imperium* have not left the world for Pettit, nor has the institution of slavery. The barometer Pettit uses to classify an agent's flight has been recalibrated, as has freedom's antonym.

The topic of state non-arbitrary interference brings us to the first-order disavowal. This entails an additional conceptual maneuver to change the meaning of domination and, by extension, of non-domination by establishing a distinction between the *unfree* and *non-free*.[71] Recollect that Pettit's system endorses state non-arbitrary interference so long as the state tracks citizens' common, recognizable interests, as in the example of a government tax levy. One would deduce that a state's non-dominating tax levy would be compatible with an individual living the free life. That deduction is incorrect.

An individual agent subject to a state tax does not exist in a state of domination and thus is not unfree. Even so, the person is still subject to a state's "suitably constraining, constitutional arrangement."[72] The individual remains in a non-free state between freedom and unfreedom resulting from the constraints imposed by the rule of law: "As we may say that someone is unfree so far as their freedom is compromised by domination, so we may say that they are not free in this or that respect—they are non-free, though not strictly unfree—insofar as their freedom is subject to certain conditioning factors."[73]

Pettit later upholds the unfree/non-free dichotomy in "Keeping Republican Freedom Simple," a sign of its enduring status.[74] If freedom as non-domination means neither the absence of slavery nor existence as citizens residing under a properly constituted rule of law, what is it? Are we to escape domination and live as non-free agents ostensibly failing to achieve comprehensive freedom? This seems right and wrong.[75] Situating persons constrained by a noncapricious rule of law in a liminal space of non-freedom complicates domination's meaning at the same time as it gestures to the unexamined experience of a slave's liminality, of borders, of fugitivity, of actions betwixt and between the interstices.

The contradictions of political language expose a second-order disavowal: the disavowal of the slaves of slavery. This form refers to the acknowledgment and denial of slave agency. By *slave agency*, I mean two points in concert: (1) the capacity of slaves themselves individually and collectively to *imagine* their conception of freedom; and (2) the ability of slaves individually and collectively to *enact* their imagined ideal of freedom into practice. Slave agency accentuates the experience of slaves, privileging the slave viewpoint in describing existence within enslavement and strategizing what would be required to achieve lasting conditions of subjectivity, intersubjectivity, and political freedom. By definition, slave agency denies metaphysical articulations of slaves as naturally fixed, inert, coerced beings without the ability to change conditions.

C. L. R. James underscores the lack of attention paid to slave agency in the pamphlet *Every Cook Can Govern*.[76] In reflecting on the modern relevance of ancient Greek democracy in the wake of the Hungarian Revolution, James notes how self-proclaimed radicals and revolutionaries in 1956 attacked ancient Greek democracy under the guise of criticizing its reliance upon slavery as a bedrock institution of social and political life. However, these persons invoke slavery not to defend the slaves, but out of a desire to denigrate the system of Greek democracy. James observes the phenomenon of theorists invoking the political language of slavery, only later to disavow slave agency in pursuit of criticizing a specific movement, intellectual current, or thinker. We are all cooks who can govern, so to speak, insofar as all humans have the capacity to maintain degrees of self-activity, intersubjective actions in governance, critiques of coercive external agencies, and imaginings of alternative models of existence beyond solely negative or positive models of freedom. If theorists of the disavowal school would acknowledge slave agency, James argues, they would enrich their projects and discern the value of slaves as thinking beings.

Republicanism is *A Theory of Freedom and Government* whose emphasis on the governance valence eclipses the actions of agents whose struggles in flight define the free life. Trauma results from the contamination of a republican tradition and disavowed memory. There is the trauma of disciplines circumscribing discussions of particular experiences. The internal trauma of slaves, their response to bondage, and the effects of their actions on institutions are tabled not just by Pettit but by a substantial portion of those in the neo-Roman movement. Pettit's account of domination and freedom is in stark opposition to agent-centered narratives of subordinate groups premised on deciphering codes of gossip, songs, whispers, laughs, euphemisms, grumblings, theater, and varieties of what James Scott calls "infrapolitics," fugitive tactics of being and organization employed by the unfree.[77] A deliberate focus on the perspectives of the battered wife, sexually abused child, Roman slave, plantation slave, and prison inmate could illuminate the facticity of the *damnés*. Inquiry into slave agency offers us a way forward.

Beyond Disavowal: Slave Agency

Imagining the foundation of non-sovereign human action without domination requires a radical transformation in framing the art of being free. To envisage a condition beyond slavery and slave agency's disavowal entails a return to the phenomenology of lived experience and discussion of mass insurrection internal to polities.

While revolutions provide profound insights, so too do other upheavals. In the case of America, an upheaval prominently absent from Arendt's *On Revolution* and "Revolution and Freedom" is the US Civil War. Its absence is logical, since revolutions in the Arendtian system are sites of natality and moments to enact freedom. Civil wars do not possess a revolution's "pathos of novelty."[78] Whether this is true or not, the centrality of black slave agency in the Civil War and black slaves' efforts to constitute and reconstruct freedom in the American republic offer several lessons, signaling the virtues of learning from the humanity of slaves and the world the slaves made, as urged by Eugene Genevose, Herbert Aptheker, Angela Davis, Moses Finley, and Stephanie McCurry. Revisionist documentation of the actions of black slaves during the Civil War to reckon with and dismantle the slaveholding Confederacy through contestation of Confederate welfare, tax, and enlistment policies is instructive.[79]

Organizations created in the wake of the war were also demonstrative. The Freedmen's Bureau was founded in 1865 at the moment W. E. B. Du Bois called in *The Souls of Black Folk* (1903) the "dawn of freedom."[80] The purpose of the bureau—whose full name was the Bureau of Refugees, Freedmen, and Abandoned Lands—was to increase the political agency of former slaves by the expansion of choices and options as well as the mitigation of complexities and possibilities associated with race, racialization, the problem of the color line, and, in Du Bois's terminology, the experiences of double-consciousness and second sight.[81] Awareness of one's unmitigated strivings on race and nation could be a gift or a curse, especially when the eyes and opinions of onlookers shape our vision of the world. It was belief in an innate potential to build ourselves and our world anew that was for Du Bois a lasting resource.

In Du Bois's estimation, the Freedmen's Bureau symbolized "one of the most singular and interesting of the attempts made by a great nation to grapple with vast problems of race and social condition." It was the measure of progress, a condition that, like the log hut schoolhouse in the hills of Tennessee where Du Bois briefly taught years before, while enrolled at Fisk, has obstacles in its materialization and survival. The bureau's termination by 1872 also signified then what "all men know; despite compromise, war, and struggles, the Negro is not free."[82] This did not mean the end of blacks' actions. There were activities at the time, unaddressed in *Souls*, demanding closer examination.

The post–Civil War reconstruction of America necessitated national introspection at the abyss between the promise of freedom and the realities of an illusory freedom among the ex-slave population. Alexis de Tocqueville saw the apprenticeship of freedom as being harder than marveling at the art of becoming free. But Tocqueville's focus on aspects of apprenticeship presupposed that the maintenance of the free life was more arduous than the original process of attaining that freedom, which is still unrealized for many.[83] *The Souls of Black Folk* admonished readers not to evade inquiry into the meaning of progress and the strivings of folk even in times of sorrow, the dark times to which Arendt often referred. The assertions of Du Bois developed into working claims on the Negro Question made in "The Conservation of Races," "The Study of the Negro Problems," "The Development of a People," and the Harvard University commencement address, "Jefferson Davis as a Representative of Civilization," in which Du Bois first limned the meaning of the Civil War, the Confederacy, and the paradox of its leader, a "peculiar champion of a people fighting to be free in order that another people should not be free."[84] Du Bois expanded upon core aspects of *Souls* in subsequent works such as *John Brown*, "The Damnation of Women," articles in *The Crisis* magazine, *The Gift of Black Folk*, and, above all, his towering inquiry into slave agency, *Black Reconstruction in America*.[85]

Black Reconstruction (1935) demonstrates the impasse of the disavowal school and utility of studying freedom in the context a broader plane of human action.[86] It surveys the role blacks had in refashioning democracy and American republicanism from the start of the Civil War through the period of Reconstruction and the rollback of Reconstruction policies leading to the establishment of Jim Crow segregation. Judith Shklar's conviction that slavery haunts the American imagination and that America was a democratic republic from its founding, but only in principle, has its first major twentieth-century defense within this work.[87] Du Bois also advances with ample documentation a stunning position rendering previous forms of disavowal impossible to uphold: it is the actions of black slaves that decisively shift the justification for the Civil War. Whereas rationalizations to enter into war begin with calls to preserve or sever ties with the Union, slaves alter the argument for war, asserting it as a confrontation between the Union and the Confederacy, with the Union's revised intention being the end of slavery and the Confederacy's aim being to preserve it.

The leading accounts of the Civil War and Reconstruction prior to Du Bois—notably those of William Dunning, John Burgess, Claude Bowers, and their disciples—marginalize or neglect altogether the contributions of African-Americans to this period. Their creation of a so-called propaganda of history misconstrues the past, failing to distinguish between authors' functions as objective reporters of human actions and subjective interpreters of them. Writing at the heart of the Great Depression and advised by educator and feminist philosopher Anna Julia Cooper to respond to the propaganda, Du Bois takes on the task of filling in this gap.[88]

Du Bois describes the *white world* and the *black world*, the psychological and public wage of being white, the trauma of black unfreedom, and the doctrine of racial separation reifying differentiation between the white and black worlds. The Southern States of South Carolina, Alabama, Florida, Georgia, Louisiana, and Mississippi receive particular attention, though the description of black education and the founding of public schools cuts across the Northern and Southern territories. Du Bois's opening note, "To the Reader," indicates the "especial reference to the efforts and experiences of the Negroes themselves" and his objective: "to tell this story as though Negroes were ordinary human beings."[89]

Besides its place in historiography, *Black Reconstruction* is of philosophical value for slave agency and flight. This is evident in Du Bois's portrayal of what he labels "the Safety Valve of Slavery": the fugitive slave.[90] Du Bois contends that the very existence of runaways fleeing from Southern plantations and deserting their masters infringes on the economies of slaveholding states. In addition to the economic stakes, planters' larger worry is the fear of future runaways and the chance that fugitive leaders may influence the masses in bondage, causing them to revolt. Slave agency is part imagination, part enactment, each reinforcing the other. Harriet Tubman and the Underground Railroad facilitate fugitives' physical flight from the South to the North, genres of abolitionist ideologies flow from North to South, desertion occurs inside states of the Confederacy, and discursive communication arises among slaves. All these fortify a context that slaveholders hope to limit, if not suppress. Fugitives, real and potential, are catalysts for reinforcement of the brutal codes and mores of mastery. For these reasons, according to Du Bois, there is heightened monitoring of the sites and bodies of slavery.

Black Reconstruction captures the capacity of the enslaved for collective action by way of a two-word phenomenon: general strike.[91] The strategy of a general strike has roots in the nineteenth century and it goes against principles of autonomous, self-directed desires for nonwork. A general strike is a mass strategy requiring a substantial portion of a workforce to agree in concert that they are no longer going to work until specified demands are agreed upon. It is, as Walter Benjamin put it, a "pure means" that can have as an outcome the abolition of state power.[92] A general strike is irreducible to non-domination under a master or participation in non-sovereign action.

It is both/and rather than either/or. In this case, the general strike is aimed at slavery.

Du Bois makes the provocative argument that the refusal of black slaves to work, along with the fleeing of slaves to Union Army enlistment camps, changed the course of the Civil War and made the implosion of the Confederacy possible. Fugitives are the slaveholder's safety valve as well as the leaders of general strikes. Some help to orchestrate recruitment to Union troops, others motivate collectivities to say no to the conditions of unfreedom. Undoubtedly, cadres of fugitives either fend for themselves and their families or become the propaganda of Northern abolitionists. According to Du Bois, a noteworthy number of fugitives do not follow those paths.

In terms of scale, Steven Hahn notes that by the end of the war, roughly a hundred and fifty thousand slaves fight on behalf of the Union military and nearly half a million flee to lines of the Union.[93] By the time of Abraham Lincoln's declaration in the Emancipation Proclamation that, in the midst of the Civil War, slaves are to be "henceforth and forever free," the general strike is a mechanism for holding the postbellum government responsible and helping to ensure materialization of the promissory pledge to ex-slaves.[94]

The influence of Northern abolitionist philosophies on the individual and collective activities of slaves is undeniable, as we shall see in the evolution of the thought of Frederick Douglass, whom Du Bois regularly references. Nonetheless, the slaves' concerted stoppage of work proves to be a decisive turn: "It was not the Abolitionist alone who freed the slaves. The Abolitionists never had a real majority of the people of the United States back of them. Freedom for the slave was the logical result of a crazy attempt to wage war in the midst of four million black slaves, and trying the while sublimely to ignore the interests of those slaves in the outcome of the fighting. Yet, these slaves had enormous power in their hands. Simply by stopping work, they could threaten the Confederacy with starvation."[95] When assessing sentiment during the Civil War on the postbellum future, Du Bois notes two opposing visions. One bases itself on industrial private profit, the continuation of slavery, and upholding *Herrenvolk* democracy; the other, on freedom and the abolition of slaveholding republicanism.[96] The Freedmen's Bureau, while fleeting, results from the general strike and the postwar second vision.

In the war's aftermath, Du Bois bemoans "the great American Assumption" permeating the republic: the belief that we are our own sources of wealth creation, that individual thrift shall lead inevitably to economic prosperity, that trade-offs between personal effort and laziness determine our successes and failures.[97] The idea of equality of opportunity—an individual's access to resources within a polity thought to be equally accessible to all inhabitants— trumps equality of outcome policy measures— specified programs for individuals and groups believed to require targeted support to achieve stated ideals of an egalitarian order. Versions of this are still familiar: the Horatio Alger story, rags-to-riches tales, the language of the American Dream, the rhetoric of personal responsibility. The assumption, while strong in the white world Du Bois observes, is also present in the black world and its leadership. Du Bois rejects its premises and uses the historical experiences of blacks to nullify its future impact throughout all worlds.

The problem of the "American Assumption" resides in its disregard for structural factors. In spite of the amendments to the Constitution (Thirteenth, Fourteenth, and Fifteenth) passed in the years following the end of the war, there remain in Reconstruction disturbing holdovers from antebellum slave society centered on racial orders and the division between the white world and the black world.[98] Du Bois begins his study with the context of war, shifts to the uprising, evaluates the postwar period, and then returns back to slavery in order to find meaning in this gulf and the ensuing breakdown of Reconstruction. The assumption also universalizes certain characteristics of the human, excluding how lived experiences affect our options, choices, and our entire being.

This brings us to a final signpost of *Black Reconstruction*: race and its relationship to the experience of flight. It is productive to study ancient and modern slavery together, a point addressed at the outset. The modern idea of race, nevertheless, does present specific considerations. Race marks the black body.[99] Flight has different forms, and the physical modes organized around space and place are ones that allow for the external ascription. The sight and site of moving black bodies in flight and the aesthetics of flight have repercussions for observers who wish to deny such movement. In forms of flight based on condition instead of spatial geography, race affects the ontology and phenomenology of unfreedom and freedom. The actors of Reconstruction and their legacy show this.

Du Bois rates Reconstruction a "splendid failure," an abandoned project unable to maintain the desired hope of American postbellum abolition-democracy following the "price of the disaster of slavery and civil war."[100] While there are disputed costs and benefits associated with the price of disaster and what James Baldwin later refers to as the price of the ticket,[101] Du Bois nonetheless concludes that the agency afforded and attempted by the enslaved and ex-slaves offers lessons to learn from: "And yet, despite this, and despite the long step backward toward slavery that black folk have been pushed, they have made withal a brave and fine fight; a fight against ridicule and monstrous caricature, against every refinement of cruelty and gross insult, against starvation, disease and murder in every form."[102]

Black Reconstruction does not provide an alternative theory of freedom to the models of republicanisms examined previously. Where it succeeds is in revealing the humanity of slaves, the experience of actors in the interstices of flight, the slave's capacity for natality and imagination, and the benefits of "looking out from slavery."[103] It demonstrates as well the critical consequences for flight not only of revolutions, but also of civil wars. This all has bearing on freedom beyond disavowal. We would do well to remind ourselves constantly of this.

The Political Language of Freedom

Three major implications result from our provisional investigation into freedom's meaning. The first pertains to political language. Only recently is emphasis on political language resurfacing in work on freedom covering a range of methodological approaches. A major reason for this is the current movement to overcome the separation of political thought into historical and normative camps. This chapter illustrates that these methodological distinctions do exist, but they should not prevent the exchange of ideas and approaches. Political language arises in specific historical contexts. Being attentive to that allows us to navigate its normative usage across space and time, so long as we do not relegate those contexts to a subsidiary role.

Second, disavowal serves as a useful conceptual tool beyond the political language of silence. Silence is an important notion only if there is in fact the complete lack of utterance or written record. Once an event or idea has been uttered, written down, or catalogued in some form, silence as a concept loses its weight when a theorist seeks to point out conceptual and phenomenological oversights. Disavowal offers a compelling idea for theorists of freedom and for those interested in concepts and events that have been simultaneously acknowledged and denied.

Finally, slave agency provides an essential perspective from which to think about those living in a condition of unfreedom. Charting in greater detail the experience of the enslaved does not only disclose the relational qualities of an agent's struggle to become free; it also reveals how micro-acts of flight have macro-consequences for freedom.

PART TWO

Slave Theorists of Freedom

Slavery was woven into the warp and woof of American life, especially in the South but also in the North. Words alone were not sufficient to make it go away. If slavery was pronounced dead, it was simultaneously reincarnated in new institutions, new practices, new ideologies. Existing institutions of punishment served as receptacles for these structures and ideologies of slavery that were translated into the terms of freedom. In other words, slavery was translated into the terms of freedom. This notion of slavery being translated into the terms of freedom clearly complicates our original question about the meaning of freedom. What has it meant to negotiate passages of freedom over the last two hundred years?

—Angela Y. Davis, *The Meaning of Freedom*

The slaves had revolted because they wanted to be free.

—C. L. R. James, *The Black Jacobins*

TWO

Comparative Freedom
and the Flight from Slavery

Well, my dear reader, this battle with Mr. Covey,—undignified as it was, and as I fear my narration of it is—was the turning point in my *"life as a slave."* It rekindled in my breast the smouldering embers of liberty. . . . After resisting him, I felt as I had never felt before. It was a resurrection from the dark and pestiferous tomb of slavery, to the heaven of comparative freedom.
—Frederick Douglass, *My Bondage and My Freedom*[1]

By a principle essential to Christianity, a PERSON is eternally differenced from a THING; so that the idea of a HUMAN BEING, necessarily excludes the idea of PROPERTY IN THAT BEING.
—Samuel Taylor Coleridge, epigraph to *My Bondage and My Freedom*[2]

In combating his ignorance, in resisting the will of his master, Frederick Douglass apprehends that all men should be free, and thus deepens his knowledge of slavery, of what it means to be a slave, what it means to be the negative counterpart of freedom.
—Angela Y. Davis, *Lectures on Liberation*[3]

Introduction

The scholar-activist, philosopher, and black feminist Angela Y. Davis was on the cover of *Life* magazine's September 11, 1970 issue when she was listed on the Federal Bureau of Investigation's Ten Most Wanted List. Above an ominous picture of Davis with a now iconic, large Afro aesthetic, the caption to the cover page read "The Making of a Fugitive." Davis was a fugitive in the eyes of the American government, a twentieth-century maroon, a terrorist challenging the prevailing inegalitarian society's secular theodicy, a being on the run eerily referred to by various popular media outlets in terms reminiscent of advertisements that appeared after passage of the 1850 Fugitive Slave Law offering rewards for chattel slaves in the South who took flight from a plantation in search of freedom in the North. When the warrant for her arrest was issued, Davis was both teaching in academia and organizing grassroots protests on behalf of three African-American political prisoners known as the Soledad Brothers.

Davis was already under heavy surveillance by J. Edgar Hoover's covert FBI Counterintelligence Program (COINTELPRO) as a result of her prior associations with the Communist Party USA (CPUSA) and the Black Panther Party for Self-Defense (BPP). Davis also faced constant death threats by anonymous political adversaries. In August 1970, a member of her bodyguard staff was killed along with other persons connected to an act intended to raise awareness regarding the Soledad Brothers' case and prison reform. Although she was not in northern California when the incident occurred, Davis was accused of conspiracy, murder, and kidnapping. Fearful of being considered guilty before due process could take place, Davis evaded authorities for two months. Police subsequently apprehended her, and Davis spent sixteen months in prison during which she was put on trial for a crime that she did not commit.

In prison, Davis received more than a half million letters and appeals on her behalf from a wide spectrum of allies, including the widow of Rev. Martin Luther King Jr., Coretta Scott King, Rev. Ralph Abernathy, Bettina Aptheker, Shirley Graham Du Bois, the Soviet Union, the Women's Secretariat of the African National Congress, Georg Lukács, James Baldwin, fellow prisoners, and Davis's mentor, Herbert Marcuse. Marcuse declared Davis to be the object of political prosecution. Lukács compared the Davis ordeal to the Dreyfus Affair that shook Europe from the end of the nineteenth century to the beginning of the next. For Baldwin, everyone had to care about Davis's outcome, for the fate of Davis foreshadowed our own potential unfreedom. The trial, *People of the State of California v. Angela Y. Davis*, generated massive worldwide attention, causing many to reevaluate the predicament of political prisoners and the meaning of freedom in a time of Cold War and repression. After evaluating the evidence and hearing extensive testimonies, a jury acquitted Davis of all the charges.[4]

A year before her imprisonment, Davis taught a class at UCLA on recurring philosophical representations of slavery and freedom in black literature. Not long before the inaugural session, California Governor Ronald Reagan, in consultation with the state Board of Regents, fired Davis from her position as Acting Assistant Professor in the Philosophy Department because of her membership in the CPUSA. Upon appeal, the Los Angeles Superior Court overturned the dismissal order. More than fifteen hundred students and colleagues attended the first meeting of the course, partially to show support for Davis's constitutional right to have private political views separated from the sphere of classroom pedagogy. The majority of those enrolled registered to hear Davis's framing of the semester's aims and objectives through the thought of the fugitive-turned-ex-slave Frederick Douglass.

W. E. B. Du Bois famously deemed Douglass "the greatest of American Negro leaders," and Booker T. Washington equated Douglass's life with "the history of American slavery epitomized in a single human experience."[5] Douglass's role as a major political leader intrigued Davis, but it was his brilliance as a thinker that captivated her.[6] Whereas Jean-Jacques Rousseau's work engages in a mode of thought grounded in thinking through how a shackled slave can once again become free, Douglass shifts attention in the modern period toward the figure of the fugitive, the experience of fugitivity, and authors who are either current or former slaves. The experience of slavery informs the imagined concept of freedom.[7]

"Philosophy," Davis writes, "is supposed to perform the task of generalizing aspects of experience, and not just for the sake of formulating generalizations." We can, and must, "learn from the experience of the slave."[8] In Judith Shklar's estimation, "Rebellious Europeans might cry out that they were enslaved, but they have never seen the real thing. Americans lived with it in pain, guilt, fear, and hatred. It [slavery] was a profound experience."[9] Davis adopts the experiential writing genre that fugitive and former slaves such as Douglass made prominent—so much so that her autobiography and prison writings have been dubbed "neoslave narratives."[10] Experience alone does not explain the uniqueness of these fugitive ideas. It is the combination of experience and the interpretation of experiences that matter.

During Davis's incarceration, the National United Committee to Free Angela Davis published the first two lectures from the fall 1969 UCLA course under the title *Lectures on Liberation*. Rarely commented on today, these lectures would be published later in a curtailed version bearing the heading "Unfinished Lecture on Liberation—II."[11] The truncated essay, however, excludes the full second lecture's commentary on Douglass's idea of freedom. Although Davis's investigations provide keen insights into Douglass's existential thought, as Lewis R. Gordon has shown,[12] the talks more importantly illuminate the successes and failures faced by previous scholars attempting to describe Douglass's concept of freedom and his interpretation of the origins of freedom in slavery. The lectures probe the following modern paradox, to which Douglass supplies an answer:

> The idea of freedom has justifiably been a dominating theme in the history of Western ideas. Man has been repeatedly defined in terms of his inalienable freedom. One of the most acute paradoxes present in the history of Western society is that while on a philosophical plane freedom has been delineated in the most lofty and sublime fashion, concrete reality has always been permeated with the most brutal forms of unfreedom, of enslavement. . . . Is man free or is he not? Ought he be free or ought not he be free? The history of Black Literature provides, in my opinion, a much more illuminating account of the nature of freedom, its extent and limits, than all the philosophical discourses on this theme in the history of Western society.[13]

Davis and Douglass have an aversion to Western negative and positive traditions that construct freedom in fixed, static terms. To decipher the contradiction at the underside of the modern West, we must understand "the crucial transformation of the concept of freedom as a static, given principle into the concept of liberation, the dynamic, active struggle for freedom."[14]

Enslavement is the absolute condition of unfreedom. Douglass fuses experience and theory not simply to narrate the mere incidents of his life and times. He presents a structural analysis of slavery and strategies for overcoming the enslaved condition. For Douglass, movement is a cornerstone of the human condition and essential to reform and progress. Humankind, like the world, moves over the long term, whether political states in the present rise and fall, or the representatives of enslaving state policies uphold norms of unfreedom. Movement is inevitable.[15]

Douglass's reactions to Nat Turner's rebellion, the Christianity of slaveholders, the alienating qualities of religion, and the metaphysics of master-slave relations shape his worldview. For Davis, therefore, freedom, liberation, and resistance are the interdependent terms in the phenomenology of unfreedom.[16] Davis's lectures on Douglass remain unfinished since, in her view, Douglass conceived of the flight from slavery as a continual process of release from bondage. This position, however, rests on a pair of insufficiencies. First, contrary to Douglass, it conceives of struggle as a principle pertinent only to liberation, as if struggle ends with liberation from bondage. Second, it presents the case for Davis's ongoing theorizing on the negative dialectics of *liberation* rather than the dynamic movement that Douglass's relational conception of freedom entails. Davis shares Douglass's interest in imagining both liberation and elements of constitutionalism used by agents in founding a new order, as her work on the prison-industrial complex and recent arguments in *The Meaning of Freedom* attest.[17] The incomplete nature of the Davis 1969 lectures is not due to inadequacies in Douglass's thought. We must therefore explore how Douglass envisions liberation *and* freedom in concert to explicate fully the intricacies of his system.

The stakes of analyzing the theory of freedom proposed by Douglass are threefold. First, Douglass moves beyond modern thinkers writing in the aftermath of Rousseau through his acceptance of the premise that slavery is the foundational human condition. Second, he discerns more clearly than Hannah Arendt and Angela Davis the importance of differentiating liberation from freedom by suggesting that we conceive of freedom as a condition involving liberation from bondage. Third, as a mediating figure between the forms of republicanism explored in the last chapter and the Haitian Revolution, Douglass develops a tradition of political theory centering attention on the psychological and physical acts of struggle and assertion that are integral to slave agency. Although the Haitian revolutionaries provide solutions to the dilemmas of slavery in ways Douglass does not, Douglass's conceptual innovations about freedom and the agency of slaves allow us to identify the distinct, interrelated facets of fugitivity and marronage.

Studies of eighteenth- and nineteenth-century autobiographical slave narrative authors such as Quobna Ottobah Cugoano, Olaudah Equiano, Mary Prince, William Wells Brown, Henry "Box" Brown, Henry Bibb, Harriet Jacobs, and Douglass were, for several decades, written primarily by literary critics.[18] Davis's perspective did not reflect the scholarly norm at the time. Beginning in the 1990s, philosophers and political theorists started to probe these texts. Howard McGary and Bill Lawson concluded that these narratives "provide important insights that will enable us to rethink our views about certain concepts." For Paul Gilroy, they revealed the antinomies of modernity, slavery's role in the Enlightenment, and the elements of hybridity underlying black Atlantic cultures. These more recent revelations have impelled Michael Dawson and those outlining the rival tendencies in African-American political thought to ascertain the "competing visions of freedom" within and outside of black communities.[19] In addition to outlining what Robert Gooding-Williams noted is Douglass's distinctive model of black political solidarity, Douglass's narratives in particular illuminate his vision of freedom and the intricacies of master-slave relations in ways that similar autobiographical accounts do not. This is why philosophers and political theorists have now begun to address intuitions that Davis sensed long before.[20]

Beyond editing and contributing copious articles to the newspapers *The North Star* (1847–51), *Frederick Douglass' Paper* (1851–59), and *Douglass'*

Monthly (1859–63), Douglass composed three autobiographical slave narratives: *Narrative of the Life of Frederick Douglass, An American Slave, Written by Himself* (1845), *My Bondage and My Freedom* (1855), and *Life and Times of Frederick Douglass* (1881, revised 1892). Whereas Davis focuses solely on the last autobiography, what follows examines in detail *My Bondage and My Freedom*. *Bondage* has been labeled "the best philosophical analysis of human nature in slavery ever" with good reason.[21] Douglass's *Narrative* is a moving, short tract, much like Immanuel Kant's *Groundwork of a Metaphysics of Morals*. Yet, like the *Groundwork*, which lacks the sustained rigor of the larger *Metaphysics of Morals*, the *Narrative* suffers from its reduced scope. *Life and Times* covers more years in Douglass's life. Nonetheless, the middle autobiography contains crucial theoretical devices that the other two do not have.[22] The devices at work show a Douglass who has broken with the moral suasion philosophy of the Garrisonian abolitionists, a Douglass who has been on the run, a fugitive who traveled to Great Britain and then returned to the United States de jure a freed man in a society that de facto continued to treat him as subhuman. It is this period to which the middle autobiography speaks and with respect to which Douglass most insightfully analyzes the dialectic of slavery and freedom.

The first section of this chapter investigates Douglass's relationship to British Romanticism.[23] Specifically, I analyze the connection between Douglass and the Romanticist writer Samuel Taylor Coleridge. Coleridge's ideas on property explicitly and implicitly serve a spectral function throughout Douglass's rumination on slavery's meaning. Background information relevant to Douglass's *Bondage* is offered in the process. An explication follows of the idea of freedom that Douglass calls "comparative freedom." The third section raises objections to Douglass's thought, pointing out how Douglass was in a certain sense blind to his own marronage. Brief inquiry into Douglass's political work as the US Ambassador to Haiti in the years after *Bondage* clarifies Davis's own conceptual dilemmas and enables a transition to the chapters on marronage in the Haitian Revolution. To the romanticizing of slavery we now turn.

Textual Context

Frederick Douglass was born in February of 1818, Talbot County, on the eastern shore of Maryland. Douglass surmised that he was a year older than his actual age, but he admitted no definitive knowledge of his birth. "Like other slaves, I cannot tell how old I am." *Time* was a confounding variable, less so than awareness of *place*.[24] In his life, Douglass had four slave masters with farms, plantations, and domiciles located in geographic spaces from bays east of the Chesapeake to Baltimore: "Old Master" Captain Aaron Anthony, chief clerk on Colonel Edward Lloyd's home plantation rumored to be Douglass's father; Thomas Auld; Hugh Auld, Thomas's brother; and William Freeland. The depictions of Mr. Sevier and Austin Gore portray the logic and actions of a third class, the overseers, who structure the public plantation sphere.[25] Douglass fled slavery in Maryland by impersonating a sailor, boarding a section of a North-bound train reserved for blacks, exiting the train in Delaware, transferring to a steamboat headed to Philadelphia, ultimately making his way to New York City, then New Bedford, Massachusetts, and later Rochester, New York. Douglass withholds several details of the escape in *Bondage* to protect his personal security. The experiences as a slave and a fugitive are fulcrums in Douglass's intellectual formation, phenomenological explorations, critique of white supremacy as a political system, solutions to the Negro Problem, and disposition toward black politics.

Douglass begins one of the two long-standing traditions in African-American political theory in the *Narrative*'s assimilationism along with his early political activities.[26] Assimilationists strive for a color-blind society in which the economic, political, and moral facets of racial difference are irrelevant to human well-being because they view such a society as possible or desirable. Douglass's expression of assimilationism while he was still a fugitive slave made him an ally of William Lloyd Garrison and Anglo-American Garrisonians, whose core prophetic principle of moral suasion denounced racially charged language, abhorred any calls to violent, revolutionary slave resistance, and privileged rhetorical morality over physical struggle.[27] As Frank Kirkland observes, "moral suasion is *prima facie* the use of rhetoric to persuade others about the moral wrongness of slavery and the moral rightness of abolition." [28]

Assimilationism contrasts starkly with the emigrationist tradition initiated by the modern black nationalist Martin Robson Delany, which rejects any talk of a color-blind society in favor of a separate space for blacks, either in territories abroad in Africa and the African Diaspora or in a distinct territory within the United States. Although Douglass and Delany inaugurate rival traditions that still produce heated debates, their views on assimilationism, emigrationism, and the eradication of slavery start converging at critical points as they mature. In Douglass's case, Romanticism contributes heavily to his changing outlook.

With the exception of a planned trip to Haiti, where he intended to inquire into potential refuge for American blacks, Douglass never retreats from his anti-emigrationist stance.[29] His evolving experiences after releasing the *Narrative*, however, cause him to reinterpret the concepts of slavery and freedom from an internationalist perspective. The internationalist viewpoint leads the author to rethink the ways in which his association with the Garrisonians limits the structural tale he hopes to tell the world. Douglass discerns little about abolitionists up until his Baltimore teenage years. Once he learns how to read with the temporary assistance of Hugh Auld's wife, Mistress Sophia Auld, and his own private sessions thereafter working through the written speeches in Caleb Bingham's *The Columbian Orator*, Douglass gains an increased awareness of the meanings of written as well as spoken words.[30]

The teenage Douglass wants to know why abolitionist political language poses a threat to masters. "Of *who* and *what* these were, I was totally ignorant . . . I therefore set about finding out, if possible, *who* and *what* the abolitionists were, and *why* they were so obnoxious to slaveholders."[31] Douglass, the young adult fugitive slave, interacts with abolitionists intimately but comes to the realization that he must define himself independently of them. Narrating a slave experience under the strictures of rigid moral suasion philosophy, which does not allow for the full explication of slave agency, can lead only to an incomplete rendering of a slave's imagined ideal of freedom.

Reflecting on how Garrisonians introduced him during speaking tours in the North in front of large white audiences seeking to hear evidence of an escaped slave's travails, Douglass remarks,

> I was generally introduced as a *"chattel"*—a *"thing"*—a piece of southern *"property"*—the chairman assuring the audience that *it* could speak. Fugitive slaves, at that time, were not so plentiful as now; and as a fugitive slave lecturer, I had the advantage of being a *"brand new fact"*—the first one out. . . . During the first three or four months, my speeches were almost exclusively made up of narrations of my own personal experience as a slave. "Let us have the facts," said the people. So also said Friend George Foster, who always wished to pin me down to my simple narrative. "Give us the facts," said Collins, "we will take care of the philosophy." Just here arose some embarrassment. . . . "Tell your story, Frederick," would whisper my then revered friend, William Lloyd Garrison, as I stepped upon the platform. I could not always obey, for I was now reading and thinking.[32]

Douglass remained assimilationist to the degree that he stayed committed until his death to the elimination of slavery in America. Douglass did not forever remain content with simply narrating the facts as he experienced them. "It did not entirely satisfy me to *narrate* wrongs; I felt like *denouncing* them."[33] Douglass wanted not only to narrate, but also to think. Romanticism attracted Douglass in its emphasis on cultivating the use of one's imagination for the purpose of action-oriented theory. To think rigorously about slavery and freedom required expanding an individual and a social collective's ability to imagine themselves in a state other than their present condition.

The structure of *My Bondage and My Freedom* additionally illustrates Douglass's desire to think through his experiences independently, apart from the influence of the Garrisonians.[34] The book title twice invokes the possessive pronoun "*My*" and the first-person inclusion of Douglass's full name marks his authorship ("by Frederick Douglass"). The front cover of the *Narrative*, in contrast, invokes a third-person authorship ("Written by Himself"). The Douglass of the *Narrative* is a phantasmagoria to Garrisonians, as substantiated by representations of Douglass in the same year as the publication of the *Narrative*, such as the image accompanying the popular musical sheet of "The Fugitive's Song."[35]

The frontispiece of *Bondage* prominently includes an epigraph by Coleridge. Also on the cover page is a daguerreotype photograph of Douglass in a three-piece suit, sitting upright in a consciously assertive, dignified fashion. Whereas the *Narrative* included a preface and introductory letters from Garrison and Wendell Phillips respectively, *Bondage* showcases an introduction written by the African-American physician James McCune Smith, who was the author of a treatise on the Haitian Revolution.[36] Moreover, Douglass issues an inordinately lengthy dedication to the honorable Gerrit Smith, a fervent anti-Garrisonian, for ranking slavery alongside piracy and murder.

Upon further investigation, the text outline reveals a larger agenda beyond the deliberate announcement of the break with Garrison. The book is broken up into two parts, "Life of a Slave" (part 1, chapters 1–21) and "Life as a Freeman" (part 2, chapters 22–25). The division best captures Douglass's endeavor to explain "My Bondage" and "My Freedom." Captivating paintings precede the start of each part, especially the image before part 1 depicting a fugitive slave running away from a ferocious dog and a shotgun-wielding slave catcher. The appendix, which comprises excerpts from eight previously delivered Douglass speeches, including "The Nature of Slavery," "The Inhumanity of Slavery," and "What to the Slave Is the Fourth of July?" forms a key coda to the autobiography, an addendum whose words provide a precise definition of slavery and related concepts that Douglass assumes the audience will bear in mind when reading *Bondage*.

The impulse to situate *Bondage* alongside an American Romanticist tradition is enticing, given the context of works and political movements before, during, and soon after the book's release in 1855. Consider Ralph Waldo Emerson's *Nature* (1836), Douglass's reference to John Greenleaf Whittier as the "slave's poet" in chapter 8 of the *Narrative* (1845),[37] Margaret Fuller's *Woman in the Nineteenth Century* (1845), the Seneca Falls Convention on women's rights (1848), the Fugitive Slave Law (1850), Herman Melville's *Moby-Dick; or, The Whale* (1851), Martin Delany's *The Condition, Elevation, Emigration, and Destiny of the Colored People of the United States, Politically Considered* (1852), Harriet Beecher Stowe's *Uncle Tom's Cabin* (1852), William Wells Brown's *Clotel; or, The President's Daughter* (1853), Henry David Thoreau's *Walden* (1854), the Kansas-Nebraska Act (1854), Walt Whitman's *Leaves of Grass* (1855), *Dred Scott v. Sandford* (1857), John Brown's raid (1859), Thoreau's "Resistance to Civil Government" (1859), and the outbreak of the Civil War (1861). American Romanticism emerges prior to the Civil War as a liberal response to the web of human relationships connecting these events. The movement essentially forges, in Nancy Rosenblum's language, "another liberalism."[38]

Alluring as this initial association of *Bondage* to American Romanticism might be, it is misguided. Douglass indeed belongs to the American literary tradition of the time. The inspiration for changes in his political writings at the moment of *Bondage*, though, reveals a more nuanced picture. In *Romanticism and Slave Narratives*, Helen Thomas argues persuasively for studying the often overlooked conjunction between Africana slave narratives and British Romanticist thought.[39] While Thomas does not analyze Douglass, evidence linking Douglass's political theory to British Romanticism exists in three key areas.

First, we must pay close attention to the time Douglass spent in Britain immediately after the publication of the *Narrative*. In chapter 24 of *Bondage*, entitled "Twenty-One Months in Great Britain," Douglass describes the extended period he spent in England, Ireland, Scotland, and Wales at a phase when he was a fugitive slave fearing negative repercussions following the first autobiography's release. "Upon this experience alone," he writes, "I might write a book twice the size of this, '*My Bondage and my Freedom.*' I visited and lectured in nearly all the large towns and cities in the United Kingdom, and enjoyed many favorable opportunities for observation and information."[40] Douglass marvels at how a black fugitive slave could be treated freely in "monarchical" England and remain unfree in "democratic" America. Citing a letter he wrote from Britain soon after his arrival, Douglass states, "In the southern part of the United States, I was a slave, thought of and spoken of as property; in the language of the LAW . . . . In the northern states, a fugitive slave, liable to be hunted at any moment, like a felon, and to be hurled into the terrible jaws of slavery. . . . But now behold the change!

Eleven days and a half gone, and I have crossed three thousand miles of the perilous deep. Instead of a democratic government, I am under a monarchical government . . . When I go to church, I am met by no upturned nose and scornful lip to tell me, *'We don't allow niggers in here!'"* Douglass does criticize aspects of British hypocrisy such as the Free Church of Scotland's acceptance of money from slave traders to build additional churches.[41] But overall he locates a positive, new-found internationalism that radically transforms his conceptual landscape.

Second, Douglass becomes enamored with two lines from the British Romanticist Lord Byron's tract, *Childe Harold's Pilgrimage*, which urges the slave to bypass moral suasion and embrace a qualified, violent rebellion against enslaving agents. He initially invokes the lines in the novella, *The Heroic Slave* (1853)[42]—his only venture into fiction—and then famously at the end of chapter 17 of *Bondage* ("The Last Flogging"), detailing Douglass's fight with the brutal slave-breaker Edward Covey.[43] Du Bois would cite these same lines as an epigraph to the third chapter of *The Souls of Black Folk*, in which he evaluates Douglass's political legacy.[44] Importantly, Douglass adds to *My Bondage and My Freedom* these lines from Byron that do not appear in the same retelling in *Narrative*:[45]

> Hereditary bondmen, know ye not
> Who would be free, themselves must strike the blow?

Third, and most important, is the Coleridge epigraph to *Bondage*. Establishing the connection between Douglass and Coleridge is necessary to understand the centrality of property, passionate reason, political imagination, and agency in Douglass's conception of freedom. A discussion of Coleridge the political thinker must precede an interpretation of Douglass's engagement with Coleridge's Romanticism.[46]

Romanticizing Slavery: Douglass's Coleridge

Coleridge on Slavery, Property, and Agency

Coleridge is among the most romantic of the British Romanticists. His trenchant belief in utilizing the poetic imagination to condemn political slavery—arguably more than his political thinking in other areas—earns him this designation during the most radical phase of his career. Scholars such as Pamela Edwards believe Coleridge's purported fluctuations between Romantic radicalism and Romantic conservatism confound attempts to label his political leanings. Whatever one's position, it is clear that Coleridge did not waver on his stance denouncing slavery.[47]

As early as 1792, Coleridge was awarded Cambridge University's Browne Gold Medal for the poem, "Ode on the Slave Trade," a text written in Greek that questioned slavery in the West Indies. He is known most famously for *The Rime of the Ancient Mariner* (1797/98), a lyrical poem addressing an accidentally slain albatross, mariners at sea, figurative slavery, and slavery's relation to exile and errantry. In addition to discussions of slavery in poems, his public lectures explicitly center attention on the experience of slavery and the role of the imagination in instituting and dismantling slave regimes. Coleridge levels a sustained critique against slavery and the European slave trade, most clearly in his June 1795 *Lecture on the Slave-Trade*, reprinted in a revised version of his March 1796 journal *The Watchman* under the title "On the Slave Trade."[48]

Coleridge delivers the *Lecture* at the Assembly Coffee House on the quay in Bristol, England.[49] He poses the following question at the beginning, "Whence arise our Miseries? Whence arise our Vices?" Coleridge's answer: from "artificial Wants" or what he correspondingly terms *"imaginary* Wants."[50] The *Lecture* draws upon the antislavery writings of Thomas Clarkson and the Abbé Raynal to reject the position espousing the maintenance of slavery in the English and French-speaking Caribbean. The argument does not simply focus on the deleterious effects of slavery. Rather, it goes to the root causes underlying support for reducing other human beings to property. The "faculty of the *Imagination*" has the potential to enslave as much as it can help to free. How we use our imagination determines our social outcome.[51] Coleridge states, "Perhaps from the beginning of the world the evils arising from the formation of imaginary wants have been in no instance so dreadfully exemplified as in the Slave Trade & West India Commerce! We receive from the West Indies Sugars, Rum, Cotton, log-wood, cocoa, coffee, pimento, ginger, indigo, mahogany, and conserves—not one of these are necessary—indeed with the exception of cotton and mahogany we cannot with truth call them even useful, and not one is at present attainable by the poor and laboring part of Society."[52]

Coleridge views "imaginary Wants" as causing the bourgeoisie in European societies to institute inegalitarian political systems premised upon slavery. The unnecessary produce resulting from slave labor reach only the richest citizens of Europe. In this sense, Coleridge echoes Rousseau's theorizing in the *Discourse on Inequality*. Coleridge, like the Rousseau of the *Social Contract*, book 4, chapter 8 on civil religion and like Douglass thereafter, denounces Christians who enslave people in the name of Christianity. "There are two classes of Men I wish that they were always one—Those who profess themselves Christians and those who (Christians and infidels) profess themselves the zealous advocates of Freedom!"[53]

Rapacious colonizers whose conception of property extended solely to the individual, not to a social collective, uprooted Africans in Coleridge's view. That conception allowed for the forceful enslavement of another human group under the belief that individual freedom to own property granted the enslaver the right to place into bondage any entity—human, animal, or inanimate—considered personal private property that could increase the individual's wealth. Coleridge romanticizes property relations in precolonial Africa in a fashion similar to the way Rousseau idealizes indigenous, savage Americans living in a state of nature. Nonetheless, his commentary points toward a Romantic notion of common property grounded in a political imaginary contrary to the liberal individualism used to justify colonial slavery. "The Africans, who are situated beyond the contagion of European vice—are innocent and happy—the peaceful inhabitants of a fertile soil, they cultivate their fields in common and reap crop as the common property of all."[54]

Coleridge extends admiration for a collectivist notion of property in "On the Slave Trade." Turning a people with a positive idea of property into property themselves symbolizes for him the perversion of freedom. Something is wrong when, for example, a wagon licensed to an individual slave master has equal or greater legal status than his human slave. Coleridge denies the pro-slavery argument that the right of property would be injured if New World slavery were to cease. Abolishing slavery in no way precludes maintaining property, whether private, collective, or common. What slavery's abolition does require is the eradication of treating human beings as if they were things. Coleridge explains as follows:

But how would the right of property be invaded by a law which should leave the estate and every thing on it untouched, and only prevent the owner from *forcing* men to work for him? from *forcing* men to leave their friends and country, and live slaves in a climate so unwholesome or beneath a usage so unnatural, that contrary to the universal law of life they annually diminish? Can a man possess a right to commit actual and virtual murder? to shorten and prevent existence? It is a well-known and incontrovertible fact, that in some few plantations in which tyranny has been instructed by an enlightened selfishness to relax and soften her features, there have been no slaves bought for a series of years. By whomever therefore they have been bought yearly, yearly murders have been committed![55]

Coleridge concludes the *Lecture* and "On the Slave Trade" by comparing the plight of the black slave to that of the European peasant. Certain pro-slavery British activists wanted to associate these two groups in order to belittle the actual state of unfreedom in which black slaves existed. Coleridge replies by stating, "For I appeal to common sense whether to affirm that the Slaves are as well off as our Peasantry, be not the same as to assert that our Peasantry are as bad off as Negro Slaves."[56] Coleridge recognizes a poor European's dire situation, but he wishes to highlight how systemic slavery stands as the ultimate bondage. Douglass's remarks in "The Nature of Slavery" as he reflects on his travels to Ireland have a glaring similarity to Coleridge's. "It is often said, by the opponents of the anti-slavery cause, that the condition of the people of Ireland is more deplorable than that of the American slave. . . . Yet I must say that there is no analogy between the two cases. The Irishman is poor, but he is not a slave."[57] The poor and the slave do in actuality have many problems in common, and both Douglass and Coleridge know this. The property dimension nevertheless distinguishes these groups.

Coleridge and his British Romanticist colleague Robert Southey developed a model for a utopian society dubbed *pantisocracy* during the same period that Coleridge wrote most of his tracts against slavery.[58] Pantisocracy imagined the abolition of all property relations in society. Each inhabitant would live on the land that nature provided. Our collective, common interests would be in the imagined, romantic promotion of one another's freedom, absent systems enslaving other human beings.

Coleridge and Southey never put into practice the pantisocracy polity. Despite that, a few points are worth noting. Southey is the thinker credited in the *Oxford English Dictionary* with introducing the term *autobiography* into the English language.[59] This is ironic, as slave narratives, including Douglass's, would be at the forefront of works illustrating autobiography's meaning even though they did not necessarily use the word to describe their interpretive narrations. Next, as Walter Johnson notes, another rarely discussed fact, also rooted in *OED* political language, is that Coleridge offers an early definition of *agency* grounded in self-directed action and the idea of "personal free agency."[60] This idea has been useful to slavery scholars engaged in thinking through the various facets of slave agency, albeit in an adapted form. Lastly, it is the invocation of words from Coleridge's *A Dissertation on the Science of Method; or, The Laws and Regulative Principles of Education* (1818) that brings us back to Douglass—words adorning *Bondage's* cover page: "By a principle essential to christianity, a PERSON is eternally differenced from a THING; so that the idea of a HUMAN BEING, necessarily excludes the idea of PROPERTY IN THAT BEING."[61]

Douglass does not identify the source of the Coleridge epigraph. He also slightly alters the sentence, capitalization, and grammatical emphases placed on terms cited from Coleridge's treatise.[62] As a result, generations of interpreters up to the present day neglect the citation or propagate Douglass's rendition as infallible. In either case, erroneous rationalizations of the purpose of the guidepost words are standard.

Coleridge's *Dissertation* appears initially as part of a multivolume *Encyclopedia Metropolitana* in the year of Douglass's birth, and it goes through several reprints, including a posthumous sixth edition released in 1854, a few months prior to the publication of *Bondage*. It has a tripartite structure, divided into sections on the philosophical principles of method, the illustration of principles, and the application of principles of method to the general concatenation and development of studies. According to Coleridge, the twin principles of union and progression are the basis of method.[63] Douglass extracts from section 2 of the *Dissertation* most, though not all, of the full Coleridge sentence. It is significant that the first clause of the original contains the phrase "the gradual abolition of domestic slavery," thereby situating Coleridge's first-order and Douglass's second-order analyses of the principle of freedom vis-à-vis slavery.

Three themes emerge from Douglass's choice of epigraph. The first is the juxtaposition of spiritual metaphysics and philosophical method in imagining inspirations for transformation of the slave condition. Second, there is a critique of the prevailing Lockean conception of individual property and the Lockean proviso that assumes an individual has entitlement to acquire property and maximize the resources of a habitable land as long as the agent does not disadvantage, harm, or prevent another agent from doing the same. Third, Douglass posits a merger of Coleridge's romantic discourses on method, imagination, and feeling with his specific concern to disaggregate two terms falsely rendered isomorphic in the body and being of the slave: *person* and *thing*.

Douglass's Coleridge, Douglass's Slavery

Romanticism generally garners descriptions as an anti-Enlightenment movement privileging imagination and feeling over reason. In describing the slave system, Douglass says that "reason is imprisoned here, and passions run wild." He remarks elsewhere that "to make a contented slave, you must make a thoughtless one. It is necessary to darken his moral and mental vision, and, as far as possible, to annihilate his power of reason."[64] Slave regimes suspend a particular modality of reason as well among the master class, which creates the conditions for masters to formulate a subjective morality based upon a passion that permits political freedom only for a chosen few. "The morality of *free* society can have no application to *slave* society."[65] Nonetheless, slaves like Douglass do not abandon reason. Instead, they harbor a different conception of reason than their masters. This conception resists the master's desire to strip slaves of the power to reason altogether. Douglass amends Coleridge's ideas on property through reconfiguring the British Romanticist matrix. By incorporating imagination and feeling into a slave notion of reason, Douglass asserts a unique idea of freedom.

The experience of slavery generating Douglass's ideal of freedom builds upon Coleridge's claim that reducing another human being to property stands contrary to political right. A person is entirely different from a thing. Whereas jurists in the late Roman Republic introduced the legal distinction between persons and things so as to render slaves absolute property under the slave master's private power of *dominium*,[66] Douglass adopts the categorical division between person and thing for the purpose of rendering void any claims to justify human enslavement.

A person cannot be excluded from the right to maintain control over property in her own being, as that right contradicts nature. Slaves—whether on the plantation or on the run—inherently have responsibilities and rights to protect their own claims to property in their own person, despite a slave society's refusal to respect them. According to Douglass, the "order of civilization is reversed" within slavery. This epistemic about-face places slaves in a wretched condition at the bottom of the Great Chain of Being.[67] Slavery, hence, fundamentally goes against right and civilized political order.

Douglass's definition of *slavery*, promulgated during the Britain sojourn, incorporates his views on the relationships among property, unfreedom, and the treatment of persons as things. He states in his "Reception Speech" at Finsbury Chapel, England,

> Slavery in the United States is the granting of that power by which one man exercises and enforces a right of property in the body and soul of another. The condition of a slave is simply that of the brute beast. He is a piece of property—a marketable commodity, in the language of the law, to be bought and sold at the will and caprice of the master who claims him to be his property, he is spoken of, thought of, and treated as property. His own good, his conscience, his intellect, his affections, are all set aside by the master. The will and wishes of the master are the law of the slave. He is as much a piece of property as a horse.[68]

The aforementioned normative definition of slavery is a baseline postulation in the autobiography. Douglass combines this designation with the *true
philosophy of slavery* imparted to him when his master, Hugh Auld, irately
reproaches his wife Sophia upon learning that Sophia was teaching Douglass how to read. Auld proclaims that "'if you give a nigger an inch, he will
take an ell;' 'he should know nothing but the will of his master, and learn to
obey it.' . . . 'If you learn him now to read, he'll want to know how to write;
and, this accomplished, he'll be running away with himself.' Such was the
tenor of Master Hugh's oracular exposition of the true philosophy of train-
ing a human chattel."[69] The principle is clear: a master must consign a slave
to the category of things, farther removed from personhood than even the
Athenian *polis* pedagogue, who was, in a functional inversion, a literate slave
who taught the children of masters under the duress of their demands. The
truest slavery philosophy is the elimination of education with the purpose
of abolishing not slavery as an institution, but the slave's awareness of, desire for, and right to the status of personhood.

Douglass's idea of slavery is analogous to Arendt's conception in *The
Origins of Totalitarianism* insofar as he agrees with Arendt that slavery places
slaves "within the pale of humanity" without attributing to slaves any qualities indicative of full humanness.[70] Slavery constructs a category of sentient
entities as things that are spoken of yet not capable of either speech or
action. While having no personality, slaves are thought of by masters to
be useful commodities. Douglass radically diverges from Arendt, however,
both by conceiving of slavery as a sociopolitical institution and by focusing
on the creative capacity of slaves to fight for their freedom despite existing as
property. Theorists such as Douglass who have existed as pieces of property
outline graphically slavery's normative constituent elements.

In Douglass's appraisal, slavery grants the master complete power to treat
the slave as a thing. By empowering the master with the right to force upon
the slave's body and soul the label property, slavery defuses levels of slave
agency through creating an environment replete with amnesia. The slave
must never know what it means to be a person. The process of naming
slaves is one strategy to ensure a slave regime's success at its alienating tactic.
The slave passively receives a name instead of actively choosing one. The
mother of Douglass, Harriet Bailey, named him Frederick Augustus Washington Bailey. Yet Douglass's Bailey name derives from a pool of names
thrust upon imported slaves and their descendants, not the names retained
from the various regions in Africa. Masters endorse slave names, especially
last names, that rubber stamp which master and plantation that slave belongs to. Not until escaping to the North did Douglass have control over

changing his last name to suite his own preferences.[71] The slave, the brute beast, might be called Frederick or Caroline, but the appellation Mr. Y or Ms. X counts equally toward the imposed amnesia a piece of property must have to remain thoughtlessly unfree. Slavery sanctions slave property at the moral level. At the legal level, law allows the slave master to exchange slaves in the commodity market, a human slave being no different than a horse.

Note further how Douglass explains the conception of property in *Bondage*. When recounting the slave-breaker Covey's attempt to obtain ownership of his first slave, he observes that "Mr. Edward Covey was a poor man. He was, in fact, just commencing to lay the foundation of his fortune, as fortune is regarded in a slave state. The first condition of wealth and respectability there, being the ownership of human property, every nerve is strained, by the poor, to obtain it, and very little regard is had to the manner of obtaining it."[72] Covey may have been poor relative to whites overall, but he still sought to experience the bourgeois dream of having property.

Douglass returns repeatedly at pivotal junctures in *Bondage* to the comparison between human slave property and animals. Commenting on the vicissitudes of slave life following the death of his first master, Aaron Anthony, and the subsequent division of slaves among Anthony's heirs, Douglass writes,

> Cut off, thus unexpectedly, Capt. Anthony died intestate; and his property must now be equally divided between his two children, Andrew and Lucretia. The valuation and the division of slaves, among contending heirs, is an important incident in slave life. . . . On the death of old master, I was immediately sent for, to be valued and divided with the other property. . . . What an assemblage! Men and women, young and old, married and single; moral and intellectual beings, in open contempt of their humanity, leveled at a blow with horses, sheep, horned cattle and swine! Horses and men—cattle and women—pigs and children—all holding the same rank in the scale of social existence; and all subjected to the same narrow inspection, to ascertain their value in gold and silver—the only standard of worth applied by slaveholders to slaves! How vividly, at that moment, did the brutalizing power of slavery flash before me! Personality swallowed up in the sordid idea of property! Manhood lost in chattelhood![73]

This conception of property devouring a slave's claim to personhood underlies the gruesome realities that Douglass's characterization of slavery illuminates. As Stephen Best demonstrates, antebellum laws regulate the bodies of slaves and fugitive slaves.[74] These legal parameters rest on the sordid idea of property Douglass describes.

Douglass recollects how he and a fellow slave, Bill Smith, label Covey "the snake" who utilizes "snakish habits." Slaves secretly can speak disapprovingly of slave masters in animalistic, reptilian terms. But there are constraints on the efficacy of language codes with respect to masters. The structure of plantation biopolitics situates slaves, not their masters, in the position of human animals. After all, as Douglass details in "The Nature of Slavery," "A master is one—to speak in the vocabulary of the southern states—who claims and exercises a right of property in the person of a fellow-man. . . . The first work of slavery is to mar and deface those characteristics of its victims which distinguish *men* from *things*, and *persons* from *property*." Douglass's analogy in *Bondage* between oxen and slaves reinforces this point: "I now saw, in my situation, several points of similarity with that of the oxen. They were property, so was I; they were to be broken, so was I. Covey was to break me, I was to break them; break and be broken—such is life."[75]

Since, as Judith Shklar notes, "the first and most radical claims to freedom and political equality were played out in counterpoint to chattel slavery, the most extreme form of servitude," Douglass's interrogation of slavery's meaning must be read with the utmost closeness.[76] His internationalist framework coupled with the interpretative narration experience offers a perspective lacking in chain theorists from Rousseau to Coleridge. Coleridge romanticizes the harsh reality that slavery produces, yet the disjuncture between Coleridge's and Douglass's conceptions reveals phenomenological dissimilarities. Douglass's fugitive chain theorizing transcends Coleridge in its notions of property, person, thing, and slavery rooted in a slave imaginary. Douglass accounts for feeling and imagination in a qualified freedom developed from slave reasoning. His concept of comparative freedom is the central theoretical innovation that divulges this and fills in areas left unanswered in Angela Davis's lectures.

Douglass on Comparative Freedom

Comparative Political Language

Douglass prominently introduces the adjectival political term *comparative* into *My Bondage and My Freedom*. He adds the words *comparative* and *comparatively* before nouns in sentences throughout *Bondage*, mirroring identical passages in *Narrative* as well as novel scenario descriptions that the first autobiography does not mention. Douglass titles a subsection of the opening chapter, "Comparative Happiness of the Slave-Boy and the Son of a Slaveholder," where he reflects upon the ways in which young slaves are relatively protected from the grueling labor that older slaves endure. In evaluating different slave overseers' stern measures, Douglass writes that the slaves on Colonel Lloyd's plantation who worked under Mr. Sevier's watchful gaze were not permitted to take any pleasure in the "comparatively moderate rule of Mr. Hopkins." Douglass's confrontation with Edward Covey resurrects him "from the dark and pestiferous tomb of slavery, to the heaven of comparative freedom." Austere slave life under Covey cannot measure up to the "comparative tenderness" of his life as a slave in Balti-more. Alienated slave property biologically has brothers and sisters, Doug-lass not exempted. Even so, he states that his two sisters and brothers "were, comparatively, strangers to me" because of forced early separation and the breakup of family units under slavery. The fugitive slave's existence in New York after his escape was "comparatively safe," given the possibility of cap-ture and return back to the South. Additionally, on describing changing his last name, Douglass says the measure was a "comparatively unimportant matter" in relation to other issues facing fellow fugitives.[77]

Douglass's invocation of *comparative* and *comparatively* has precise signifi-cance with regard to freedom, since Douglass carefully uses poetic political language with specific intentionality. In "What to the Slave Is the Fourth of July?" delivered July 5th, 1852 at Corinthian Hall in Rochester, New York, Douglass inquires into whether the principles of political freedom embod-ied in the Declaration of Independence apply to American slaves, and if so why in practice are slaves prevented from experiencing what freedom offers individuals and social collectives.[78] Douglass places the address as the fifth appendix item in *Bondage*. That the speech occurs the day after the official American Independence celebrations grounds the context.

American slavery and the "slave's point of view" are the topic and subjec-tive phenomenology of the orator.[79] Douglass speaks of "Fellow-Citizens" while simultaneously distancing himself from the ability to experience the fruits of full citizenship and freedom. The pronouns *you, yours, I,* and *mine* are Douglass's linguistic mechanisms of differentiation. Douglass questions the hypocrisy of republican governance, not the idea of republicanism. Free-dom is comparative, for the unfree slave looks at legally free white citizens and mourns a majority population incapable of acknowledging the funda-mental crime against humanity structuring their society, governmental ap-paratuses, and livelihood. Freedom is irreducible to laws of states. Douglass exhorts:

What have I, or those I represent, to do with your national independence? Are the great principles of political freedom and natural justice, embodied in that Declaration of Independence, extended to us? . . . This Fourth of July is *yours*, not *mine*. *You* may rejoice, *I* must mourn. To drag a man in fetters into the grand illuminated temple of liberty, and call him to join you in joyous anthems, were inhuman mockery and sacrilegious irony. . . . What to the American slave is your Fourth of July? I answer, a day that reveals to him, more than all other days in the year, the gross injustice and cruelty to which he is a constant victim. To him, your celebration is a sham; your boasted liberty, an unholy license; your national greatness, swelling vanity; your sounds of rejoicing are empty and heartless; your denunciations of tyrants, brass-fronted impudence; your shouts of liberty and equality, hollow mockery; your prayers and hymns, your sermons and thanksgivings, with all your religious parade and solemnity, are to him mere bombast, fraud, deception, impiety, and hypocrisy—a thin veil to cover up crimes which would disgrace a nation of savages.[80]

Victims of subjection have the capacity to alter their world. The unfree, Douglass suggests, are perceptive teachers of freedom's meaning.

Upon returning to the United States from Britain, Douglass declares his intention to "restore to 'liberty and the pursuit of happiness' the people with whom I had suffered, both as a slave and as a freeman." Along with inquiry into the Declaration of Independence, Douglass revisits principles of the American Constitution. His activism around slavery faces challenges from competing US constitutional interpreters, most of whom debate the doctrine of original intent and question whether the Constitution is to be understood as an anti- or pro-slavery text.[81] Recognizing the disjuncture between normative philosophical ideals and human social practices, Douglass formulates a relativistic notion of freedom that contains fundamental baseline requirements while being attentive to the comparative experience of freedom in different settings.

The concept of comparative freedom is temporally stretched to account both for real-world debates on constitutionality during the period of slavery *and* for imagined, forward-looking arguments about post–chattel slavery topics from land economics to voting. Comparative freedom is akin to the classifications of certain contemporary scholars of poverty to the extent that international development specialists on the effects of poverty's unfreedom globally and domestically operationalize a comparative capability approach.[82] However, contrary to these poverty analysts' tendency to endorse a form of liberal political theory and to interpreters of Douglass who read him through the framework of liberalism, Douglass embraces a romantic vision that promotes a unique "true republicanism."[83] He does so to demonstrate how to escape a state of enslavement via flight. Douglass wants to point out the gradations of freedom and the ways in which attaining freedom is not simply a moral or physical quality, but is also psychological. Struggle has a role here, albeit not in terms of a struggle for recognition.[84] Comparative freedom necessitates a struggle against the Slave Power, the power of the master class. Struggle, the fact-form distinction, and assertion are the principles of method validating Douglass's rationale.

Struggle

Douglass's oft-quoted words on struggle from the "West India Emancipation" speech echo the position he defends at length in *Bondage*:

> Let me give you a word on the philosophy of reform. The whole history of the progress of human liberty shows that all concessions yet made to her august claims, have been born of earnest struggle. The conflict has been exciting, agitating, all-absorbing, and for the time being, putting all other tumults to silence. It must do this or it does nothing. If there is no struggle, there is no progress. Those who profess to favor freedom and yet deprecate agitation, are men who want crops without plowing up the ground, they want rain without thunder and lightening. They want the ocean without the awful roar of its many waters. This struggle may be a moral one, or it may be a physical one, or it may be both moral and physical, but it must be a struggle. Power concedes nothing without demand. It never did and it never will.[85]

Bondage closes emphasizing the twin pillars of liberty and progress.[86] These pillars, designed to elevate an African-American political imaginary, resurface in speeches buttressing Douglass's trenchant belief in a progressive freedom emerging out of struggle. Without struggle, the slave cannot become free. Douglass articulates slavery to mean the granting of power to an agent to exercise the right of property over the body and soul of another agent. Although in bondage, the slave is agentic. Engaging in struggle serves as a major step endowing the shackled being with heightened slave agency. Douglass's classic fight with the slave-breaker Covey demonstrates this most clearly.[87]

Douglass confronted Covey once and for all at the age of sixteen after coming to the realization that he must oppose Covey's will to treat him as property. Douglass's master, Thomas Auld, hired Douglass out to be broken. The youthful slave could not believe that his master "had now refused to protect me as *his property*." Douglass existed as surrogate property to Covey and the basest type of property to Auld. Douglass pledged to stand up in his own defense. *"I was resolved to fight,"* he pronounced. The decision to resist lay at the heart of the declaration to fight.[88] "My resistance was entirely unexpected and Covey was taken all aback by it, for he trembled in every limb. *'Are you going to resist*, you scoundrel?' said he. To which, I returned a polite, *'Yes sir.'*"[89] Resistance entails self-consciously choosing to counter any forces acting negatively against one. Angela Davis discerns Douglass's staunch determination to resist, though her explanation for this conclusion misses a crucial dimension.[90] Douglass uses the romantic faculty of the imagination throughout his account of the arduous, two-hour fight. Romantic imagination does not signify an aversion to struggle. Rather, the Romanticism of Douglass has as a premise that a slave shall have to struggle. Moreover, it positions the slave to imagine a comparatively positive state of freedom resulting from the confrontation.

Struggle is dialectical, intersubjective, and an inevitable facet of life in a social world replete with inequalities. Rousseau understood this, while Douglass lived its implications. Recognition may be a by-product of some struggles, but this factor alone cannot explain the motivations of slaves who themselves already have a consciousness of self despite a system's asymmetrical structure that legally denies the claims to subjectivity that slaves profess. By the end of the struggle, Douglass successfully prevents Covey from whipping him and drawing any blood.[91] The reader has to question counterintuitively which agent is the one broken.

Douglass elevated the Byronic chant for the hereditary bondman to strike the blow and Coleridge's admonition against slavery. He peered into the depths of the not-so-peculiar institution of slavery, shifting the view toward a comparative idea of freedom rooted in judging political freedom physically, psychologically, individualistically, and collectively. In reassessing the moment when he no longer feared death, Douglass determined why the struggle with Covey marked the turning point in his life. In the process, Douglass developed the concept of comparative freedom:

> Well, my dear reader, this battle with Mr. Covey,—undignified as it was, and as I fear my narration of it is—was the turning point in my *"life as a slave."* It rekindled in my breast the smouldering embers of liberty; it brought up my Baltimore dreams, and revived a sense of my own manhood. I was a changed being after that fight. I was *nothing* before; I WAS A MAN NOW. It recalled to life my crushed self-respect and my self-confidence, and inspired me with a renewed determination to be A FREEMAN. A man, without force, is without the essential dignity of humanity. Human nature is so constituted, that it cannot

honor a helpless man, although it can *pity* him; and even this it cannot do long, if the signs of power do not arise. He can only understand the effect of this combat on my spirit, who has himself incurred something, hazarded something, in repelling the unjust and cruel aggressions of a tyrant. Covey was a tyrant, and a cowardly one, withal. After resisting him, I felt as I had never felt before. It was a resurrection from the dark and pestiferous tomb of slavery, to the heaven of comparative freedom. I was no longer a servile coward, trembling under the frown of a brother worm of the dust, but, my long-cowed spirit was roused to an attitude of manly independence. I had reached the point, at which I was *not afraid to die*. This spirit made me a free-man in *fact*, while I remained a slave in *form*. When a slave cannot be flogged he is more than half free.[92]

Fact versus Form

Douglass radically amends the identical passage detailing the crescendo of the fight with Covey from the first to the second autobiography. In the *Narrative*, Douglass speaks of the glorious resurrection from the tomb of slavery to the heaven of "freedom," not "comparative freedom." Addition-ally, whereas the *Narrative* describes a distinction between "slave in form" and "slave in fact,"[93] *Bondage* includes a demarcation between "slave in form" and "freeman in fact." This latter distinction accentuates the novelty of comparative freedom as an ideal.

Douglass defines *form* as the condition one occupies under articles of law and jurisprudence. A slave regime classifies slaves as property regardless of a slave's personal mental disposition. The slave in form is the legal slave, the slave of an institution, the commodity belonging to the master. Fact, on the other hand, does not refer to juridical articles granting power to the master over his or her slave property. A *fact* for Douglass denotes the psy-chological disposition of the agent. Suspending the lawful ramifications of jurisprudence in the political imaginary of an agent paradoxically amounts to a unique understanding of fact, which crucially brings moral psychology and the philosophy of embodiment into the domain of politics. An agent's conditions in fact and in form can be aligned or nonaligned.

Four possible models illustrate Douglass's system regarding the dialectic of slavery and freedom, alignment and nonalignment. An agent can be (1) a slave in form and slave in fact, (2) a slave in form and free in fact, (3) free in form and a slave in fact, or (4) free in form and free in fact. Table 1 depicts these scenarios.

Table 1: Four models of an agent's fact-form alignment and nonalignment

	Slave in form	Free in form
Slave in fact	Model 1	Model 3
Free in fact	Model 2	Model 4

The least ideal condition is (1) and the most ideal state is (4). Against countless theories that classify slaves solely within model 1, Douglass suggests that slaves can be comparatively free while in bondage. Model 3 of his theory also offers a framework to answer questions posed by several theorists, including Rousseau in *Of the Social Contract* and Bob Marley in "Redemption Song"—the latter echoing Marcus Garvey—who ask how it is possible for one to be free legally and simultaneously unfree in psychological chains of dependence. For Douglass, it is not that the extreme models (1 and 4) are never fully realized. Models 1 and 4 describe conditions prior to and after the dialectical, intersubjective struggles experienced by enslaved agents. The capacity for activity is inherent in all slaves. Moments of struggle are catalytic in that they convert a slave's potential for agency into the actuality of the lived experience of freedom.

What Douglass ascertains is that his own process of flight from slavery to freedom begins as a result of the fight with Covey. Model 2 categorizes Douglass's observations at the fight's end. Douglass remains a slave in form despite winning the struggle against the agent, keeping him in an austere state of constraint. By victoriously preventing Covey from whipping him thereafter, Douglass psychologically experiences an embodied transformation. He has become a freeman in fact through experiencing what it means to be no longer completely under the mental will of the master. Douglass cannot be flogged any longer and is hence more than half free. Under the law, Douglass remains a slave. Nonetheless, he is comparatively free, having attained the status of a freeman in fact. That major psychological victory put him en route to model 4: the path toward jointly aligning freedom in form and freedom in fact. Davis abides by Douglass's injunction in affirming that the "slave is actually conscious of the fact that freedom is not a fact, it is not a given, but rather something to be fought for; it can exist only through a process of struggle" negotiating the form-fact alignment.[94]

Douglass's conceptual breakthrough anticipates a problematic voiced by Abraham Lincoln in Lincoln's famous pre–Civil War "House Divided" speech. During debates with Stephen Douglas in an Illinois Senate race, Lincoln states that "this [United States] government cannot endure, permanently, half slave and half free," for a house divided against itself is unsustainable.[95] Douglass's prescient diagnosis of Lincoln's admonition concerning the *half slave and half free* has to do with moments of nonalignment between fact and form that can lead to the implosion of civil society, political society, and slaves' aspirations for freedom on dual levels. Douglass restates this finding during a postbellum address in Medina, New York: "It is true that we [the emancipated] are no longer slaves, but it is equally true that we are not yet quite free. We have been turned out of the house of bondage, but we have not yet been fully admitted to the glorious temple of American liberty. We are still in a transition state, and the future is shrouded in doubt and danger."[96]

Comparative freedom rejects totalizing models claiming absolute slavery or absolute freedom. Slavery and freedom have extreme states. Struggle emerges within the critical gaps between these absolute conditions. Assertion continues the realignment process begun by struggle.

Assertion

Assertion designates forthright implementation of an imagined conviction into action. Affirming a conviction means more than discussing ideals. Putting ideals into practice contrary to the dominating, usurping, and property-focused intentions of an enslaving agent has grave risks. There is no progress without struggle in the face of risks. Actively asserting a stance places one farther along on the road to freedom. Assertion must be situated in backward-looking, present, and forward-looking contexts. In Douglass's estimation, "The thought of only being a creature of the *present* and the *past*, troubled me, and I longed to have a *future*—a future with hope in it."[97] Douglass temporally gains wisdom from the past and present, using that wisdom to envision a future, comparatively free condition.

W. E. B. Du Bois portrays the core principle of Douglass's freedom to be "ultimate assimilation *through* self-assertion, and on no other terms."[98] Du Bois is only partially right. Douglass conceives the dialectical struggle the slave engages in as a necessary realignment phase. Self-assertion must transpire for the slave individually to gain freedom in fact while remaining slave in form. Douglass extends the individualistic notion of assertion to the collective level. Accordingly, comparative freedom in its most robust manifestation imagines slaves to be free in form and fact both individually and collectively.

Douglass stresses the value of assertion in two interconnected instances as a slave under his last master, William Freeland. Douglass conducts a clandestine Sabbath School in St. Michaels, teaching more than forty fellow slaves how to read at the height of its enrollment.[99] All participants enter with knowledge of their unlawful, perilous activities. At the outset, the meetings take place in the woods behind a barn and shaded trees. Ensuing sessions occur miles away in the home a free black. Douglass refers to the school pupils as "scholars" in a deliberate maneuver to discount the true philosophy of slavery conveyed to him in his youth by former master Hugh Auld. Education is not a practice of freedom, but a part of the material structure of political freedom itself. The Sabbath School has a space, curriculum, instructor, and scholars. Select scholars, chosen on a rotating basis, are class leaders during a day's lesson. Letters, the alphabet, vowel pronunciation, and the formation of sentences organized around subjects, predicates, indirect objects, direct objects, and clauses embolden expression. The skill of reading, grasped through access to words and the tutelage of the teacher, opens gateways to the ontology of individuality and intersubjective modes of assertion. After flight from Maryland, Douglass encounters former scholars whose acts of assertion assist in their escape from the plantation.

In the second experience disclosed in chapter nineteen of *Bondage*, entitled "The Run-away Plot," Douglass affirms, "The intense desire, now felt, *to be free*, quickened by my present favorable circumstances, brought me to the determination to *act*, as well as to think and speak . . . This vow only bound me to make an escape individually, . . . but the year spent with Mr. Freeland had attached me, as with 'hooks of steel,' to my brother slaves. The most affectionate and confiding friendship existed between us; and I felt it my duty to give them an opportunity to share in my virtuous determination."[100]

The voting principle offers a third, forward-looking example of Douglass's assertion principle buttressing comparative freedom. The Garrisonians' moral suasion philosophy that Douglass broke from fundamentally argued against voting in any systems supporting slavery or societies professing ambivalent positions on slavery's abolition. Garrisonians abstained from voting in the North because they believed the US Constitution to be a pro-slavery document. Douglass became a staunch objector to that opinion after he concluded that the Constitution was "an anti-slavery instrument." He came to see voting as an essential attribute of political freedom, a notion without which life, liberty, and the pursuit of happiness would have no meaning. To him, "to abstain from voting, was to refuse to exercise a legitimate and powerful means for abolishing slavery."[101] An agent such as the free abolitionist having the capacity to vote should exercise this capacity, which was denied to the unfree. In his political theory, emancipation proclamations failing to guarantee the ex-slave the right to vote fall short of full freedom. This is why *emancipation* for Douglass, as for other thinkers, does not equal *freedom*.[102] Douglass prophetically foreshadows post–Civil War debates on the comparative freedom of ex-slaves who find themselves excluded from voting, working as underpaid wage laborers, or relegated to the proto-prison convict lease system. Shklar captures Douglass's vision well, noting how, in conjunction with earning, "Douglass is thinking of the vote as a means of self-protection, as a form of political agency."[103]

Douglass's romantic concept of comparative freedom intends to augment the political agency of the slave. Fugitive dilemmas concerning violence, masculinism, and the overemphasis on property pose potential roadblocks preventing the realization of Douglass's innovative theory.

Fugitive Dilemmas

Valences of Violence

Douglass's perplexing position on violence confounds the interpretation of comparative freedom. That he endorses slave resistance in *Bondage* is not in doubt. On this point, Davis's *Lectures on Liberation* furnishes a proper response.[104] Douglass approves of resistance—physical and mental—as a part of a struggle leading toward individual and collective assertion. However, lingering questions overlooked by Davis due to her focus on *Life and Times* still require answering. Does violence relate to Douglass's understanding of struggle, assertion, and freedom from the vantage point of a fight, war, or revolution? In what way does Douglass's amendment to Coleridge's Romanticism actually prevent Douglass from a more radical conception of freedom?

Shortly after the fight with Covey, Douglass laments the unfortunate effect holidays have on the slave. Holidays are delusions that fill the laboring slave with the promise of a break in the future. They function, in Saidiya Hartman's felicitous expression, as scenes of subjection. The terror and injury of violence exceed spectacles of blood. Violence permeates the mundane and quotidian.[105] A slave regime uses holidays to placate any aspirations among the enslaved to collectively organize an insurrection. A holiday suppresses slave insurrection by giving the slave fleeting pleasures short of freedom. Slaves are encouraged to drink alcohol—rum and whiskey to be exact—a conduit for amnesia that prevents recollection of their condition.[106] Douglass rhetorically urges the slave to think like a fugitive, resisting a society's enslaving conventions. The slave must struggle for freedom, but what constitutes struggle's scope for Douglass is unclear.

Violence contains multiple valences. Whereas a violent fight can involve only two people, wars and revolutions involve numerous actors. Just and unjust wars aim to resolve conflicts over ideals, yet changing existing norms is not an objective. A revolution is the complete overturning of a political system, substituting in its place a forward-looking set of foundational principles. Douglass physically fights Covey, and he rhetorically supports the possibility of war. Douglass's fugitive chain theorizing stops short of revolution, and his romanticism explains why.

Recall that Douglass composed his sole fictional work, *The Heroic Slave*, two years before publishing *My Bondage and My Freedom*. *The Heroic Slave* is historical fiction, a novella retelling in its own manner the story of a slave named Madison Washington who led a slave revolt in 1841 on the Baltimore-constructed American slaver, the *Creole*, after the ship had left its Virginia dock, bound for New Orleans.[107] The name Madison Washington is portentous, for its conjures up the legacy of two Founding Founders, inhabitants of Virginia, visionaries of American freedom, orators against enslavement to the British, and proud enslavers of black chattel. Madison Washington is the figure meant to perfect the ontological iniquities of the rhetoricians of freedom.

The novella begins with a Northern traveler named Listwell who overhears, in the state of Virginia, a soliloquy by Washington. Washington speaks of the condition of the slave, the sordid nature of slavery, the contempt of masters, the quotidian dread of slave life, the relative freedom of healthy birds who can fly away any time they wish, unlike human chattel, and Washington announces his desire to be free at all costs.[108] Five years in the future, Washington appears alone, without his wife, at Listwell's home in Ohio. Washington is a fugitive headed to Canada and requests Listwell's assistance to accomplish his escape across national lines. Washington eventually makes it to Canada, returns to the United States hoping to bring back his wife, is captured, and reenslaved in Virginia. Within twelve months, Washington and Listwell encounter each other again in Virginia, and this time Washington seeks an alternative form of flight. Although Listwell helps Washington to construct an escape plan, Washington is the primary agent of the mutiny. When he is able gain status as thing-cargo on board the *Creole*, Madison orchestrates a rebellion in which the owners of the slaves and the captain are killed. The mutineers spare the first mate so that they can have a crew member alive to shepherd the boat to a new destination.

In response to the charge of being a murderer, Washington retorts: "LIB-ERTY, not malice, is the motive for this night's work." "My men," he continues, "have won their liberty, with no other weapons but their own *Broken Fetters*."[109] The slaves defeat their enslavers and reroute the ship to Nassau in the Bahamas, a colonial territory in the British West Indies. Great Britain had voted to abolish slavery in 1833, with abolition taking effect in 1834.

Nassau followed in governance the juridical architecture of the abolition act. In the novella, when black soldiers meet Washington and members of the mutiny at the docks, they inform them, per the laws of abolition, that "they [do] not recognize persons as *property*."[110] The mutineers are no longer chattel, and their escape from a slave society to an emancipated, colonial regime leaves one to ponder the comparative freedom of Washington and the mutineers. Douglass ends the novella with triumphant cheers for the heroic deliverer, Madison Washington.

Why Douglass endorses the Madison Washington insurrection but not direct, violent revolution against slave masters and slavery in the real world has a rationale. Douglass's political imaginary draws a strict line between rhetorical violence and actual violence. In *Bondage*, on the one hand, Douglass denounces moral suasionist apathy regarding voting and violence. On the other hand, he rhetorically explains the intricacies of the Covey fight in addition to various instances involving physical and mental resistance to other enslaving agents within the bounds of the Constitution. Douglass detests the law and jurisprudence classifying him as a slave. To counter such a system necessitates convincing the dominant society of its misinterpretation of the Constitution. An agent's form-fact realignment must happen within the constitutional terms of the society. Hence, Douglass wants to overturn societal norms while at the same time preventing the breach of federal and constitutional provisions that a revolution would require. David Blight comments on Douglass's assimilationist equivocations pertaining to violence:

> As Douglass illustrated, violent language could serve emotional needs in ways just as important as violent action. . . . Douglass firmly believed in the slaves' right to rebel, but revolutionary—"desperate"—violence troubled him. Black bondsmen had been a majority in Santo Domingo [colonial Haiti], but they would never possess such an advantage in America. . . . Thus, the rub came for Douglass in the ends as well as the means. If widespread insurrection succeeded in bringing slavery down in America, what place would black freedpeople have in the society to follow? In the wake of a southern "race war," how would blacks be assimilated into the new order? These were troublesome questions for Douglass. His rhetoric of violence notwithstanding, he clearly preferred the day of jubilee to come by constitutional means. Even after the outbreak of war, certain conditions had to be met before Douglass would join a "John Brown movement."[111]

Bondage provided the blueprint for Douglass's later refusal to join John Brown's attack on the federal arsenal at Harper's Ferry. Douglass espoused a romantic picture and feeling of revolution, of the emotional need to inspire insurrections opposed to a political order that, when applied to the politics of the public realm, concluded that formal revolution was an incorrect course of action. Instrumental violent conflict with a master and entities inside a home, community, and civil society was one issue. An attack on a federal government apparatus based on intrinsic justification of the necessity of violent action was another—and simply beyond the pale.

Not all New World appropriations of British Romanticism avert violent revolutionary struggle, as examples from the Caribbean political and intellectual tradition show.[112] Douglass's engagement with Coleridge's Romanticism, however bounded, logically produced a position embracing rhetorical violence at the expense of revolution. Real-world violence was an intoxicant fostering madness within slaves, causing them to go beyond the rhetorical "temperate revolutionism" that Douglass championed.[113] Douglass's strategy for eradicating the "imaginary Want" of slavery never considered actual mass revolution an option to contest the violence of the slave commodity market.[114]

Douglass lectured on John Brown's legacy after the latter's execution, and he was never able to suppress the specter of charges from adherents and detractors alike who had little patience for the rhetoric of words, did not understand the Harper's Ferry decision, and wanted to know unambiguously Douglass's convictions on invariable strategies to eliminate slavery. As a result, on the topic of entertaining violent revolution as a mechanism against slavery, Brown was right in many regards, and Douglass wrong.[115]

Masculinism

Long before John Brown's raid, Douglass was an advocate of women's suffrage. The same was true when he composed *Bondage*. Less substantiated was the breadth of Douglass's position on the enfranchisement of women. Douglass paired the logic of white supremacy with the subjection of women and consequential unfreedom. When expressing support of the voting principle, Douglass lobbied on behalf of black men and white women, leaving out until his final years consideration of the status of black women's enfranchisement.

Anterior to this point is a second problem with Douglass's conception of freedom that would apply even if black women's suffrage were a mainstay of Douglass's political advocacy. Masculinism permeates the lexicon of *Bondage*, and it functions to justify Douglass's association of freedom with *manhood*. By *masculinism*, I mean discourse affirming the male as the normative agent in a society. Masculinist language uses the lexicon of *man/men* rather than *human* or *woman/women*, treats effeminacy as a weakness, constructs a lack of manhood as an epistemological, physical, and spiritual deficiency, and views progress as an effect of manhood.

The fight with Covey is the *locus classicus* of Douglass's masculinist conception. The struggle "revived a sense of my [Douglass's] own manhood" and the "manly independence" needed as a prerequisite to freedom. "I was *nothing* before" the fight. After the confrontation with the slave-breaker, Douglass asserts, "I WAS A MAN NOW." Here he begins the process of becoming neither a free agent nor a free human being, but a "FREEMAN."[116] Reminiscent of masculinist discourses on duels, Douglass mentions honor and the dissipated fear of death that comes with the ontology of manhood. There are countless instances of Douglass collapsing freedom and manhood in the second autobiography.

Douglass is a prototypical race man, believer in racial advancement, despiser of slavery, romantic on freedom, and unabashed reproducer of prevalent masculinism during his era.[117] Douglass does not question the basic structure of political orders that organize a polity's unfree and free as a consequence of the intersecting dynamics of gender and race.[118] None of this excuses Douglass's systematic faults. At the conceptual level, though, Douglass's masculinism is compatible with profeminism, the framework of comparative freedom, and the long-term, continual elements of sociopolitical restructuring that the idea of comparative freedom promotes.

Masculinism is not a synonym for patriarchy and misogyny. Patriarchy asserts the superiority of men over women, and misogyny asserts the debasement of women in order to advance the status of men. One can assert a man as normative and also support profeminist politics. Masculinist discourse does not necessarily espouse the intrinsic superiority of men, and it can, at times, profess women to be superior. But masculinism does reify the conventional gender roles of an era.[119] The antiquated masculinism of Douglass is a reminder that the *comparative* freedom of agents in political orders during and after the episteme that Douglass occupies can shift, realign, and move for the better.

The Critique of Property

The third factor confounding Douglass's theory concerns his over-reliance on property as the primary variable to which the slave must devote energy in the pursuit of freedom. Douglass the romantic places so much emphasis on slavery's relation to property that he fails to elaborate on other dimensions of slavery relevant to a successful act of flight. Orlando Patterson's magisterial study of slavery across the globe, *Slavery and Social Death*, employs a "comparative" perspective in order to make the case for abandoning theories that reduce slavery to property. Although Patterson shares Douglass's views on power, Douglass uses power as a subsidiary concept insofar as it relates to developing a definition of slavery. "My objection to those definitions," Patterson observes, "is not that I do not consider slaves to be property objects. The problem, rather, is that to define slavery *only* as the treatment of human property fails as a definition, since it does not really specify any distinct category of persons."[120]

Patterson argues that slavery involves property, powerlessness, dishonor, domination, and associated principles. He shares Douglass's reservations regarding Coleridge's unrealized dream of a society without property relations. It is the use and abuse of the terms related to the holding of property that are a predicament. All the same, endowing or restoring the right of property in the being of a slave alone does not represent the foundation of freedom. Establishing property in one's self and for a community after an arduous struggle greatly increases slave agency. It does not supply the comprehensive answer on how a slave can become free in form and fact.

In spite of its flaws, Douglass's notion of comparative freedom reconfigures the conceptual landscape among competing theories of political freedom. To a significant degree, Douglass remains blind to the radicalism of his own flight, which is enshrined in print in the text of *My Bondage and My Freedom*. This is most evident in Douglass's subsequent reflections on misjudging John Brown's actions and his intellectual and diplomatic relations on the island of Haiti. *Bondage* is part autobiography, part literature, and wholeheartedly a freedom manifesto.[121]

Coleridge wrote a series of poetic, autobiographical letters on radical dissenting Protestants' "spiritual autobiographies" soon after delivering the *Lecture on the Slave-Trade*. These letters reveal a Coleridge who was slowly becoming less publicly polemical in his antislavery activism, devoting time instead to poetry's personal, transformative potential.[122] Douglass never retreated from denouncing slavery in public, and he forged a spiritual autobiography in an act more far-reaching than Coleridge's through creating a written text that read like a poem. Douglass's autobiography mirrored the secularized, spiritual idea of freedom that he crafted. Douglass cultivated a comparative poetics of political thinking rendering the soul transformed upon constant realignments. Douglass was an "apostle of freedom" who bore witness to humans born in chains with the fugitive dream that freedom could be consecrated one day.[123] This new, secularized phenomenology of spirit blending imagination, passion, and reason had his distinct trademark, and it also covered the eyes of Douglass to its limitations.

Fugitive Theory between Douglass and Davis

Frederick Douglass challenges those, such as Hannah Arendt and Philip Pettit, whose respective republicanisms disavow the relationships among slavery, slave agency, and freedom. Furthermore, he goes beyond these thinkers by attempting to spell out the boundaries of slavery and freedom as well as the interstitial modes of flight connecting these opposing states. He demonstrates the value of the fugitive for thought and reasoning. Fugitivity is at once episodic and yet a permanent facet of everyday politics. Fugitives can evade and transform the world we live in. Douglass's formidable approach incorporating and transcending the philosophies of the African-American assimilationist tradition and the British Romanticism of Samuel Taylor Coleridge results in equivocations at important moments that threaten to undermine the political space he hopes to open up for the slave mentally, physically, and social-structurally.

Douglass eventually served as the US ambassador to the Republic of Haiti near the end of his life.[124] Haiti was nearly nine decades removed from the cataclysmic Haitian Revolution. The elder Douglass spent most of his ambassadorial time as minister resident and consul general to Haiti, balancing stately duties on behalf of the US government and observing the inner workings of a Haitian society considered heretical in the views of the Western world. To gain political leverage during diplomatic mediations, Douglass interacted on a regular basis with the famed Haitian minister of foreign affairs Joseph Anténor Firmin.

In addition to holding the position of Haiti's secretary of state under the Hyppolite administration, Firmin was already a major figure in the Haitian intellectual tradition because of his groundbreaking text, *The Equality of the Human Races*, which asserted a sustained critique of the racist theories of Count Joseph-Arthur de Gobineau.[125] Moreover, Firmin was a brilliant lawyer and politician formally trained entirely in Haiti. What distinguished Firmin from Douglass was that he put into practice an idea of freedom as marronage emanating out of the Haitian Revolution. Whereas Douglass equivocated on issues conflicting with state constitutional doctrines, Firmin struggled to assert an egalitarian understanding of freedom inspired by Haitian revolutionaries that at times advocated unconstitutional methods for the purpose of supplanting an enslaving doctrinal document with new constitutional and diplomatic doctrines.

Douglass's results in Haiti were mixed. Douglass failed at convincing Firmin to persuade the Haitian president to allow the American government to utilize the upper northwest Môle St. Nicolas territory as a naval base—a contentious proposal tantamount to the contemporary controversies surrounding the American presence at Guantánamo Bay, Cuba, and America's perceived establishment of what Giorgio Agamben calls a nonjuridical, sovereign state of exception.[126] The US press criticized him for being too sympathetic to Haiti and all things Haitian. Douglass refrained from promoting biopolitics, a racial *nomos*, and an idea of sovereignty reducing Haitians and the Republic of Haiti to bare life, much to the chagrin of dominant American political opinion. That being the case, he tried not to fail at brokering proposed US agreements. Douglass did not divide his loyalties, but he did come to reevaluate the romanticist internationalism underlying the arguments in *Bondage*.

This short historical detour has practical implications regarding the scope of Douglass's assimilationism, the extent to which one is willing to struggle, assert, and achieve structural change in form and fact for the individual and social collectives throughout the process of moving from unfreedom to freedom and bridging the historical and normative camps within contemporary political theory. Douglass sees in the Haitian Revolution, Firmin, and the Haitian revolutionary aftermath a radical notion of marronage that is shunned by many of his own acts of flight following his escape to the North. Comparative freedom, in short, contains the ingredients for expansion of the areas that Douglass hesitated to carry out as an ex-slave and postbellum politician.[127] Douglass closes the *Life and Times* by expressing these limitations and paying homage to the enormous insights Haiti revealed to him about freedom.[128] Douglass's late anti-lynching advocacy in his final years marks a long-deferred recognition of the principles of *My Bondage and My Freedom*. Death prevents Douglass from engaging in renewed vistas of activity.

To summarize, in the first two chapters we have learned important guiding principles. First, focusing on the agency of slaves shows why adopting a dialectical approach to the relationship between slavery and freedom is a necessary but insufficient criterion for outlining the full contours of freedom. The perspective of slave agency also accentuates why slavery, and not freedom, is the foundational human condition.

Second, by emphasizing the experience of agents, we understand more clearly the stakes of inquiring into the movement from slavery to freedom. Conceptualizing unfreedom and freedom as fixed states lacking liminal agents moving to and fro between them prevents proper analysis of these agents' imagined and actual acts of struggle and assertion. An enslaved agent's struggle for freedom is a lived, experiential priority, not a static *a priori*. Experience affects our comparative conditions.

Third, political language serves as an asset in comprehending the introduction of a concept into the world of ideas. Douglass's novel interpretation of the words *fact* and *form* underscores how language shapes the way we organize to attain freedom in the body politic. Fourth, exploration of alternative conceptions of freedom in Arendt, Pettit, Du Bois, and Douglass illustrates how these authors and the events they portray are in conversation with one another even at moments of disagreement. Du Bois's insistence on describing the historical activities of slaves made apparent why exploring Douglass's experience as a fugitive would be revelatory and how slaves' concerns about domination, while not the entire story of freedom, nonetheless pertain to their experiences of struggle that render precepts of the disavowal school untenable. The reconstruction of Arendt's liberation-freedom distinction also offered us a vocabulary with which to interpret the differences between Davis's lectures on liberation and Douglass's relational notion of freedom.

Marronage is the concept that subsumes and goes beyond the theories of freedom discussed thus far. What constitutes the elements of marronage is not yet clear. The interrogation that follows of the theory of freedom as marronage and its application during the Haitian revolution broadens our understanding of freedom's typology and valences. The Haitian Revolution matters not because it is flawless but because it has lessons on the causes and consequences of human freedom. As Douglass boldly asserts in the *Lecture on Haiti*, delivered at the dedication of the Haitian pavilion at the Chicago World's Fair,

> In just vindication of Haiti, I can go one step further. I can speak of her, not only words of admiration, but words of gratitude as well. She has grandly served the cause of universal human liberty. We should not forget that the freedom you and I enjoy to-day; that the freedom that eight hundred thousand colored people enjoy in the British West Indies; the freedom that has come to the colored race the world over, is largely due to the brave stand taken by the black sons of Haiti ninety years ago. . . . It is said of ancient nations, that each had its special mission in the world and that each taught the world some important lesson. . . . Among these large bodies, the little community of Haiti, anchored in the Caribbean Sea, has had her mission in the world, and a mission which the world had much need to learn. She has taught the world the danger of slavery and the value of liberty. In this respect she has been the greatest of all our modern teachers.[129]

THREE

Sovereign Marronage and Its Others

The slaves had revolted because they wanted to be free.
—C. L. R. James, *The Black Jacobins*[1]

Of the many and diverse forms of resistance, marronage proved in the end to be the most viable and certainly the most consistent. . . . That marronage had become an explosive revolutionary force in 1791 was due as much to the global context of revolutionary events as to the persistent traditions of resistance which, necessarily, remained narrower in scope.
—Carolyn Fick, *The Making of Haiti*[2]

But no, the same hand which has broken our chains will not enslave us anew. France will not revoke her principles, she will not withdraw from us the greatest of her benefits. She will protect us against all our enemies; she will not permit her sublime morality to be perverted, those principles which do her most honour to be destroyed, her most beautiful achievement to be degraded, and her Decree of 16 Pluviôse which so honors humanity to be revoked. *But if, to re-establish slavery in San Domingo, this was done, then I declare to you it would be to attempt the impossible: we have known how to face dangers to obtain our liberty, we shall know how to brave death to maintain it.*
—Toussaint L'Ouverture, Letter to the Directory[3]

Introduction

In hindsight, it had to happen. If not in the Caribbean, then it would have occurred elsewhere. But the circumstances were ripe. The polity: the "Pearl of the Antilles." The territory: France's wealthiest colony. The regime: slavocracy. The locale: maroon space. The act: bold. The scope: island-wide. The project: freedom. The reverberations: global.

With a single meeting, an entire order was on watch. The event of the late eighteenth century commenced after a clandestine ceremony at Bois Caï-man in the mountainous forests overlooking Le Cap, located on the northern tip of colonial Haiti. Of the major revolutions begun in America (1776), France (1789), and Saint-Domingue (1791) during the Enlightenment, the Haitian Revolution was the only upheaval to denounce both colonialism and racial slavery. The leader and sovereign, Toussaint L'Ouverture, was a military genius whose acumen and letters became known the world over, earning reverence or fear, depending on the audience. Toussaint has been the singular figure often described as synonymous with the Haitian Revolution, and his idea of freedom is memorialized as the only one espoused by its revolutionaries. The long-accepted reference to "Toussaint" by first name on the part of peers, eyewitnesses to the insurrection, slaves, politicians, writers, and intellectuals past and present, as if there was never another Toussaint, is a profound indicator of his eminence.

Toussaint as synonymous with the revolution, however, is a gross oversimplification. Freedom in the Haitian Revolution has multiple valences, and Toussaint's contributions were a critical part of a larger phenomenology. Fugitives, bands of deserters, maroon communities, leaders vying for power, and slaves—those born in Western and Central Africa (*bossales*) and in the New World—have concomitant stakes in the course of this revolution.

The racial order of Saint-Domingue was more complex than that of polities in North America and Europe connected to the triangular slave trade. On Hispaniola, the island comprising modern-day Haiti and Dominican Republic, racial categories with cultural and juridical distinctions included blacks, mixed-race people of color (*gens de couleur*), and whites, with additional differentiation based on class, skin hue, and social hierarchy. Not all blacks were slaves, not all slaves were *bossales*, nor were all whites planters. The *affranchis* (freed) were a case in point, a combination of manumitted blacks and free people of color. By the advent of the Haitian Revolution, however, the vast majority of Saint-Domingue's residents were African-born black slaves who worked on sugar plantations and lived under white planter rule.

Population shifts in Saint-Domingue put the qualitative markers of the racial order in quantitative perspective. In 1687, whites outnumbered slaves on the scale of 4,411 to 3,358. This was a reflection of the early colonial period when white indentured laborers worked on plantations along with the nonwhite slaves. At the turn of the century, the slave population had risen to 9,100. Halfway into the 1700s, slaves outnumbered whites by 150,000 to 14,000. A few decades later, in the late colonial phase, two years before the revolution's start, there were approximately 31,000 whites, 28,000 free people of color, and 465,000 slaves. The slaves of Saint-Domingue had grown to nearly 90% of the population, a startling numerical transformation. In comparison, the entire slave population of the United States in 1790 was only 700,000, a much smaller percentage of the nation's inhabitants.

The number of plantations in Saint-Domingue also grew exponentially over the same time period. Although there were plantations cultivating coffee, indigo, and cotton, the largest cash crop was sugar, and as C. L. R. James once stated, the "history of the West Indies is governed by two factors, the sugar plantation and Negro slavery."[4] Saint-Domingue had sugar plantations before 1690. By the mid-eighteenth century, there were 600. On the cusp of the insurrection, 800 plantations were devoted to sugar, and twenty-four months prior to it, there were roughly 7,000 documented plantations of various trade specializations.[5] The number of slaves and the breadth of sugar development made colonial Haiti a unique slavocracy.[6]

Furthermore, because of the overworking and death of slaves, Saint-Domingue slave society was based on the constant importation of slaves instead of self-reproducing slave communities, which were vital, albeit a numerical minority, to sustaining the social, economic, and political fabric of mastery in the United States. Its magnitude of violence was unmatched in the modern period. These elements structured the contours of revolt. Nonetheless, while the revolution in Saint-Domingue has further notable particularities, not the least of which is its enduring distinction as the only known successful slave revolution, it has continued to offer broader lessons on freedom and the human condition.

The revolution also took place in the Age of Enlightenment. The Enlightenment promoted principles of reason, public opinion, property, equality, solidarity, and freedom, each in the language of universality and habitually articulated through discourses of secularism. To note the existence of an Enlightenment riddled with contradictions is neither new nor our central concern.[7] The proclamation of universals as the only ideals applicable to a circumscribed category of human beings has been a recurring issue.

But there are three areas receiving less attention, the last the most neglected, that pose deeper problems: first, rethinking who the authors of Enlightenment thought were; second, the exceptionalism narrative of Enlightenment discourse that positioned universal values as if they were either previously nonexistent or a triumphant project still awaiting realization; and third, maroon epistemology illuminating a juridical paradox at the heart of the long eighteenth century. The revolution in Saint-Domingue initiates a revisiting of these predicaments.

Revisionist historicism in Haitian revolutionary studies over the last five decades has sought to address the first two areas. Correcting erroneous facts, uncovering new documents, republishing previously inaccessible texts, writing historical fiction, translating into other languages works available in Kreyòl and French, rewriting extant histories of the revolution in more absorbing prose, thickly describing mores and cultural codes of Saint-Domingue inhabitants, focusing on details big and minute concerning what has been called the world of the Haitian Revolution: these things have been done in formidable ways. For thirty of those years, historical and anthropological research took center stage.[8]

Not until the end of the twentieth century did contemporary thinkers explore the impact of the revolution on concepts such as rights, silence, disavowal, emancipation, empire, universal history, and humanism. This, coupled with Haiti's 2004 bicentennial celebration, led to a further spike in revisionist work. If Michel-Rolph Trouillot was right that the "Haitian Revolution thus entered history with the peculiar characteristic of being unthinkable even as it happened,"[9] then it is no longer unthinkable to debate its centrality now. And yet, in spite of these advances, a still largely unfilled chasm yawns between theorizations of freedom in the revolution and marronage.[10]

Explanation of the types of marronage during the Haitian Revolution and the years leading up to it—*petit* and *grand* marronage, both acknowledged in eighteenth-century jurisprudence and late modern normative thinking—and the models of marronage introduced as sovereign and sociogenic, fills in this void. We began with what it means to describe revolution and freedom without focusing on race, and subsequently explored race in fugitive thought that stopped short of revolution. By examining the phenomenology of slavery, race, and revolution in Saint-Domingue, we gain clearer insight into facets of constitutionalism, experience, and the value of freedom in flight. But before we delve into the forms of marronage operative then, we must know more about the law of slavery and a conundrum of universalism.

Juridical Paradox

In March 1685, the Sun King, Louis XIV of France, promulgated from Versailles *The Black Code or Edict of the King, Concerning the Government and the Administration of Justice and the Police of the French Islands of America, and the Discipline and the Commerce of Blacks and Slaves in Said Country.* Commonly referred to as the *Code Noir*, this juridical document was applicable throughout France and the French colonies until the 1848 abolition declaration. Ratified and effective in Saint-Domingue by 1687, the code provided the legal parameters governing slave life at the start of the Haitian Revolution. The code was suspended during the uprising when slavery was abolished temporarily by French decree, but its juridical force resumed once Napoleon Bonaparte reestablished slavery near the revolution's end. In practice, the *Code Noir* governed the rules, actions, and rationalizations of masters and slaves throughout the Saint-Domingue insurrection.

The *Code Noir* contains a preamble and sixty articles. Although amendments to original clauses were made in later years, the substance of the articles remains unchanged. To comprehend the document fully requires understanding the geopolitics of the day, a confluence of ideas from European metropolitan states and their overseas protectorates. As Alexis de Tocqueville notes, *ancien régime* France was a feudal political order premised on monarchical rule, Catholic religious dogmatism, and bureaucratic centralization. The king sanctioned measures of linguistic uniformity in mainland France despite the pluralism of languages spoken in cities and towns.

Provincial liberty in the *pays d'état* conflicted with the monarch's despotic conception of the free life. "Despots themselves don't deny that freedom is a wonderful thing, they only want to limit it to themselves; they argue that everyone else is unworthy of it." "Thus," Tocqueville writes, "one can state that the preference that one shows for absolute government is in direct proportion to the contempt that one has for one's country."[11] The radicalization of peasants, desire for reform, disputes over church doctrine, and challenge to the divine right of kings would lay the groundwork for the storming of the Bastille.

The *ancien régime* was also a colonial political order, and Saint-Domingue was its prized territory abroad. Louis XIV ruled with this epistemology, as did other French colonial leaders afterwards. How best to preserve empire, monarchical authority, and colonial rule with an overwhelming slave population: that was a primary objective of the Francophone law of slavery.

But the *Code Noir* projects principles that are more than the legal strictures regulating the bodies and being of slaves. It is a moral system regulating how masters and slaves treat one another. The code is a juridical paradox, a peculiar mixture of paternalistic humanism and cruel legal subordination, reifying unfreedom by sanctioning small provisions for slaves, promising the enslaved the right to prosecute masters violating terms of the articles, and holding out the possibility of manumission to an unspecified number in bondage.

Masters also have rights in the code, and sanctioned death may await slaves held by masters to be in breach of the law. Colin Dayan observes that the *Code Noir* "contributed a language that at once offered protection and normalized abuse." For Malick Ghachem, the duality of promissory safety nets and the normalization of brutalization is the code's "strategic dilemma."[12] The contradiction between the *Code Noir*'s rhetoric of morality and its callous disregard for human life evident in harsh punitive consequences for legal infractions is a conundrum that will lead to its negation. While masters customarily ignored precepts of the code pertaining to their moral and legal responsibilities, the philosophy undergirding the articles is what matters.

Article 1 established the terms for who was allowed to reside on the island colonies, separating friend from enemy, Christian from heathen: "We charge all our officers to evict from our islands all the Jews who have established their residence there, who we order, as to the declared enemies of the Christian religion, to leave within three months of the publication date of these present [edicts], or face confiscation of body and property."[13] Per articles 2 and 3, Francophone space is Catholic Roman Apostolic Church territory. Unbaptized slaves must convert. Public exercise of other faiths is prohibited. Like the architects of the fifteenth-century Spanish Inquisition and the doctrine of *limpieza de sangre* (cleanliness of blood), causing Jews from Spain and Portugal to flee to the Caribbean, the *Code Noir* defines Jews and *conversos* of Jewish descent as beyond saving. The logics of anti-Semitism and antiblack racism, seemingly differentiated by religious and secular discourses, converge in the political philosophy of white supremacy and the disposition of bad faith.[14]

What slaves can possess and where they can convene are subject to constraints. Article 15 states, "We forbid slaves to carry any weapon, or large sticks, on pain of whipping and confiscation of the weapon, with the sole exception of those who are sent hunting by their master and who carry their note or known mark." Articles 18–21 prevent slaves, themselves commodities, from selling any commodity without the express permission of a master. No slaves are able to sell sugar cane. Assembly is prohibited.

According to article 16, "We also forbid slaves who belong to different masters from gathering, either during the day or at night, under the pretext of a wedding or other excuse, either at one of the master's houses or elsewhere, and especially not in major roads or isolated locations." This same article authorizes truncated due process, and it gives extraordinary police powers to French subjects observing such gatherings: "We charge all our subjects, even those who are not officers, to approach the offenders, to arrest them and take them to prison, even if there is not yet any warrant against them." The code aims to quell options for secret, coordinated escape and revolt.

The *Code Noir* has conciliatory clauses pertaining to work, rest, and food allocations. Article 6 declares that Sunday and holidays are off days for slaves, and a few clauses specify the type and amount of nourishment a master must provide a slave. Article 22 details the weekly ration of cassava, salted beef, or fish, and article 26 explains the legal ramifications of a master's failure to comply. The most significant conciliatory provision is manumission: the act of releasing a slave from legal bondage. Thus, in the social ordering of Saint-Domingue, a slave's status would change to *affranchis*.

The last clauses state the conditions under which manumission is granted. Masters aged twenty, with parental consent, and twenty-five, without another's authorization, are able to manumit. Slaves named an executor to all of a master's property are to be manumitted. Manumitted slaves are "free and absolved of any burdens, services, and rights that their former masters would like to claim," although in the words of article 53, they must "retain a particular respect" for former masters and their families. "Any insult" against their former owners "will be punished more severely than if it had been done to another person."

The final substantive clause, article 59, juxtaposes the "acquired liberty" of the manumitted with the "natural liberty" of French subjects. While rejecting natural slavery as intrinsic, the article nevertheless uses the language of potentiality rather than actuality. The manumitted are wished "the same effects of the good fortune" of French subjects born with natural freedom, but it does not mean the moment of legal release is equivalent to being free. Emancipation rather than freedom more accurately describes the phenomenology of manumission.

Manumission is natality in slave law. Liberation contains the prospect of freedom: as article 56 announces, "We declare that manumissions enacted in our islands will be considered as birth in our islands and manumitted slaves will not need our letters of naturalization in order to enjoy the advantages of our natural subjects in our kingdom, lands, and countries under our obedience, although they be born in foreign lands."

These conciliatory clauses hardly overshadow the punitive measures beneath the code's juridical paradox. Two clauses stand out. The first, article 42, stipulates a normative notion of torture whose litmus test excludes acts of punishment considered torture in several modern juridical systems. "When they believe that their slaves so deserve," masters are able to "chain them and have them beaten with rods or straps." Masters are "forbidden however from torturing them or mutilating any limb at the risk of having the slaves confiscated and having extraordinary charges brought against them." In effect, masters can legally brutalize slaves within a threshold that does not obviate their status as owner of said property.

The second pertains to runaways from plantations. It is in this clause that movement becomes central, and the disciplinary consequences of fugitive flight are the most severe. Article 38 of the *Code Noir* states an explicit "three strikes" rule for failed attempts at escape: "The fugitive slave who has been in escape [*en fuite*] for a month from the day his master denounced him to justice, shall have his ears cut off and shall be branded with a fleur-de-lis on one shoulder; and if he repeats the offense for another month, again counting from the day of report to the authorities, he shall be hamstrung and be branded with a fleur-de-lis on the other shoulder; and the third time, he shall be punished with death." The symbol of Louis XIV, the *fleur-de-lis* branded on a runaway was to be a physical reminder of sovereignty and the limits of moral and legal altruism. Flight infringed on *ancien régime* doctrine and mores. Flight was a doctrine refusing transcendental indoctrination. Recurrent flight in the era of the *Code Noir* was sure death. Political orders premised on the juridical paradox eventually became insolvent.

The *Declaration of the Rights of Man and of the Citizen* was an effort to resolve the paradox. Passage of the *Declaration* in August 1789 by the French National Assembly signaled the end of feudalism. The text was intended to be the preface to a constitution of a nation defining itself anew.

The *Declaration* has seventeen articles following the preamble, which states "the natural, inalienable, and sacred rights of man."[15] Natural rights republicanism is the document's organizing political philosophy. It drives the actions of the French Revolution's Third Estate and the tripartite notions of *liberté*, *égalité*, and *fraternité*. Article 1 begins to make the unequivocal case for this: "Men are born and remain free and equal in rights. Social distinctions can be based only on public utility." The word *social* appears repeatedly throughout as opposed to the individual, privileging the situatedness of agents in relation to a wider world of beings. Social beings are to have unrestricted expression of opinions and thoughts, be they in print or public utterances.

While the third and sixth articles present concepts of law, sovereignty, and general will reminiscent of Jean-Jacques Rousseau's *Discourse on Political Economy* and *Of the Social Contract*, only the opening declaration on naturalism corresponds closely to Rousseau's conception of freedom. Rousseau does not believe, as the *Declaration* asserts, that representatives can stand in for the opinions and participation of the people qua citizens.[16] What the written text replicates are features of generality in the political language of modern republican social contractarianism.

Equally noteworthy is the final article's principle of property: "Property being an inviolable and sacred right, no one can be deprived of it, unless established public necessity obviously demands it, and upon condition of a just prior indemnity." Public force, as article 12 indicates, is the mechanism to guarantee realization of the rights of man and citizens for collective instead of for personal advantage.

Among the clauses mentioned, two phrases and a word are noticeable: *public utility, public force,* and *property.* We have already encountered with Douglass the question of what constitutes the terms *man* and *citizen.* In the *Declaration,* universality and opacity are twin pillars. Universalist claims receive ambiguous policy prescriptions. Freedom is pronounced, but slavery and abolition never mentioned. Yet when read carefully, exceptional clauses to the document's universality become clearer. The *Declaration* allows for French and Francophone territories to have social distinctions if they benefit a category of citizens. Property, whether pen or slave, is not an entitlement for all human agents when public necessity deems it expedient. *Being property* is rendered consistent with the articles, and public force, examples of which are in the *Code Noir,* is a means to ensure sanctity of the principles. The "obvious" is fungible, as are standards of "reasonableness" in contemporary jurisprudence. *Declaration* precepts function similar to today's International Convention on Civil and Political Rights: their effect in civil and political society is contingent on ratification in the legislatures of states.

Jews, black slaves, and women across the color line, included within the abstract language of the *Declaration,* were excluded from its terms by the French state.[17] Even free *gens de couleur* in Saint-Domingue, who distinguished themselves as a social group from both slaves and black *affranchis* and did not lobby actively as a whole for slaves to receive their similar privileges and immunities, were not granted full declaration provisions. Two months after the *Declaration* became state doctrine, people of color in Paris addressed the French National Assembly regarding the plight of *gens de couleur* in the West Indies. The petitioners professed, "Born citizens and free, they live as foreigners in their own fatherland." People of color "find themselves enslaved even in their liberty."[18] They spoke passionately and cited sections of the articles, all to no avail.

The quelled Ogé revolt was another sign of unease among people of color in colonial Haiti. A wealthy merchant from Le Cap, Vincent Ogé orchestrated fellow *gens de couleur* to demand that France honor the *Declaration* principles. He went initially to France to plead his case, traveled clandestinely to England and the US South, and then returned to Saint-Domingue. Ogé intimated in a series of letters that France's ongoing betrayal of the promise of freedom would have dire consequences.[19] In response to the threat, Ogé was taken into custody, put on trial, and executed. The juridical paradox remained until the upheaval of August 1791.

There were four possible responses to the gulf between theory and practice in the *Declaration*. Options one and two were blanket acceptance or rejection of its principles. The third option, which Toussaint espoused, was the hope of ensuring universalization of its core tenets with modifications specific to abolition and sovereignty. Option four was not merely the negation of the *Declaration* and a break from the modern social contract tradition; it was adoption of non-sovereign types of marronage, with mass-oriented flight being optimal. Let us return to marronage vis-à-vis Saint-Domingue to grasp the dimensions of flight obtained in response to the juridical paradox.

Typology of Marronage in Saint-Domingue

Petit marronage is one of the two normative notions of flight documented in historical records since the sixteenth century, described by ethnographers, and an object of jurisprudence and the law of slavery. By *petit marronage*, I mean freedom understood as fleeting ontology, a temporary flight from slavery by an individual or small group through fugitive acts of truancy away from the zone of enslavement. In the Caribbean, petit marronage refers to flight from the plantation.

An agent engaging in short-term fugitivity does so for a variety of reasons. For some, it is to visit relatives and loved ones on other plantations. For others, it is an act of desertion meant to relieve momentarily the everyday horrors of the plantation order. Theft and the search on both cultivated land and in the wilderness to acquire food and water denied by masters are among the rationalizations. Absenteeism to a cadre is tied to a desire for brief avoidance of forced labor.

Episodic flight provides space for an agent on the run to organize clandestine rendezvous with those in separate plantation zones in order to coordinate collective flight, rebellion, or revolution in the long term. Petit marronage was the type of flight that posed the greatest problem for planters on a daily basis, and it is an activity of subjectivity, not intersubjectivity, for it revolves around an individual agent attaining control of property and being of self. It is an imminent philosophy that does not have on its cartography of freedom the vision of collective agents. Although petit marronage is neither a state of war nor revolution, it can cause them. Causality and purpose are intertwined, and petit marronage is a micropolitical causal mechanism for the macropolitics of revolution and freedom.

Slaves in Saint-Domingue before and during the insurrection embarked upon such flight.[20] Often their absence lasted anywhere from a few hours to a week, and the distance from the plantation was generally close. The proximity of flight from the plantation correlated with the rationale for fugitivity. The geography of the Northern Plain, west, and south was a mixture of flat lowlands and mountainous terrain, suitable to episodic escape. The boundary region established in 1697 by the Treaty of Rhyswick, dividing Saint-Domingue from Santo Domingo, had a more difficult expanse, populated more by inhabitants of maroon communities than planters or transients in petit marronage.

The dangers of petit marronage were immense. Whites used dogs to hunt down fugitives. *Maréchaussée*, paramilitary units made up almost entirely of *gens de couleur*, were tasked with catching deserters, further exacerbating tensions among the racial order. Runaways caught were subject to qualified protections in the *Code Noir*, but planters frequently did not follow the rule of law. Punishments of repeat runaways took place across Francophone colonies: whipping, branding, the wearing of dehumanizing collars, the threat of death. But in Saint-Domingue the invention of the *nabot* allowed for a particularly severe punishment. The *nabot* was a large circular device made of iron and weighing six to ten pounds. It would be affixed to the foot of a slave through a grueling process of cold-riveting.[21] The risks were clear: secretly flee to receive the existential benefits of short-term desertion or face punitive measures.

The act of grand marronage distinguishes itself from the petit modality in terms of time, space, scale, and purpose. *Grand marronage* refers to the mass flight of individuals from slavery to form an autonomous community of freedom emphasizing physical escape, geographic isolation, rejection of property relations associated with a slavery regime, and avoidance of sustained states of war through compacts, treaties, and negotiations for political recognition. These "maroon societies," as Richard Price notably calls them, work against a fleeting temporality. They are forged through flight intended to sustain an ongoing community with defined borders.[22]

Spatialization is essential to the project of grand marronage. We can understand spatialization to mean geographies of distance, denotation of territorial boundaries, and capacity for movement inside the isolationist zone. Economies of scale are a component of spatialization. This refers to the population and obtainable resources of a maroon community. The teleology of maroon societies is unequivocal in spite of challenges to their formation and longevity: freedom as existence away from slavocracy in the farthest, hardest to reach expanses of states.

Grand marronage is ultimately a conception of freedom premised upon recognition of the maroon community. While the notion of recognition here differs from formulations made prominent by and after Hegel due to its emphasis on sovereign territorial recognition rather than self-consciousness, grand marronage nevertheless faces similar limitations as a model of freedom within in a world of difference. This is because forms of flight based in recognition lead to junctures of asymmetrical acknowledgment that truncate freedom. Let us be more specific.

The phenomenon of marronage in Saint-Domingue evolved from the pre-revolutionary to revolutionary period. During this time, there materialized what I ascertain to be two types of grand marronage. The first involved acts by individuals and bands of fugitives not associated with a singular maroon community who moved throughout maroon spaces across the island, engaging in raids, cross-plantation meetings, and other actions external to the plantation zone aimed at igniting rebellion. Maroon leaders emerged. There were the courageous, the hungry, the discontented, the utopians, and the mythologized. The second type, most pertinent to the late colonial and revolutionary phase, gave rise to the isolationist maroon communities.

The myth of the maroon began as long ago as grand marronage itself, and it applied to both modes. Repeated folklore about maroons often led discursively to discussions that inflated by the hundreds and thousands the numbers of actual runaways. Maroon leaders were also portrayed as having superhuman capabilities. For example, the famed Windward Jamaican maroon leader, Nanny of the Maroons, was said to be able to catch bullets in her buttocks shot by British soldiers unsuccessfully invading maroon towns. Two centuries later, Nanny was named a Jamaican National Hero and her image presently appears on the Jamaican five-hundred-dollar bill. Zumbi, the decorated maroon leader of the Brazilian *quilombo* Palmares, has achieved a similar mythos. Until his death, many believed him to be immortal.

In the postcolonial Caribbean, maroons have been the subject of literary tropes, nationalist politics, and *noirism*. Michelle Cliff's heroine, Clare Savage, in *Abeng* and *No Telephone to Heaven*, Marlon James's *The Book of Night Women*, Patrick Chamoiseau's *Texaco*, Maryse Condé's *Crossing the Mangrove*, Alejo Carpertier's *The Kingdom of This World*, the writings of Simone-Schwarz-Bart, Haitian dictator François Duvalier's decree to build a statue of the Unknown Maroon in front of the Haitian National Palace, and the late-modern construction of maroon memorials in Fort-de-France, Saint Esprit, and Diamant, Martinique are a representative sample. Miguel Barnet's *Biography of a Runaway Slave*, a testimonial of the 105-year-old Cuban runaway slave Esteben Montejo, intensified the maroon lore. Although the line between fact and fiction was sometimes blurry, the valuable philosophical import of grand marronage's freedom has carried on.

From 1764 to the early days of the revolution in 1793, advertisements containing the names and descriptions of nearly forty-eight thousand maroons appeared in the Saint-Domingue press. Estimates have put at a higher number the total runaways to account for those unmentioned in print media. Unquestionably, the figure whose idea of freedom then exemplified the first category of grand marronage was the one-handed maroon François Makandal.[23]

Makandal was an eloquent orator originally born in Guinea and reputed to have been raised Muslim. He had a command of Arabic, was captured as a slave, sent to Saint-Domingue, and ended up on the plantation of Lenormand de Mézy in the northern district of Limbé. In Saint-Domingue, he adopted the vodou religion.

Makandal took flight from the plantation and engaged in marronage for the next eighteen years until his execution in 1758. He distinguished himself through an orchestrated campaign of poisonings, enlisting both maroon women and men in his cause. The maroon bands joining Makandal did not merely target white masters; that was in many respects less important to them than the other object of their campaigns, which was poisoning planters' resources—their animals, food, and produce. Being one-handed might be construed as a disability. For Makandal, it was a virtue and constant reminder of the conditions under which the accident and resulting amputation occurred. European philosophers and litterati prophesied the romantic appearance of a rebel slave and utopian future world, but none foresaw the philosophy of Makandalism.

If Makandal was feared when alive, he became even more of a threat to masters after death. Makandal claimed that he could transform into a fly, and cries of "Makandal saved" were shouted during his execution ceremony. That public speech act created the image of Makandal as a transcendent resister to slavery, forever reappearing throughout space and time like a specter, heralding a freedom to come.

Women did not simply follow men in marronage, though women were sometimes abducted by male maroons, and women and men sometimes formed their own maroon bands. Although on average in Saint-Domingue men aged 17–35 represented the majority of maroons during the pre-revolutionary and revolutionary periods, men outnumbered women on the island by two to one.[24] It is significant that an estimated 15 to 20 percent of maroons there were women. Unlike later grand marronage, however, Makandalism's philosophy of freedom and racial politics sought the elimination of slavery without crafting a viable programmatic vision of the political to follow the slave regime. Makandalism was too fixated on negative dialectics.

The second category of grand marronage, pronounced during the revolutionary period, exhibited the privileging of its isolated community and desire for freedom in recognition. The Le Maniel maroons in the mountainous border region of Bahoruco typified this archetype. For decades, Le Maniel had residents born and raised in the elevated forests with little to no interaction with those outside the community's boundaries. Maroons would occupy these mountains for nearly ninety years.[25]

Inside Le Maniel maroons demarcated a social space with set borders to cultivate an agricultural economy, defense, rudimentary home building, legal codes, gender mores, modes of governance, and hidden transcripts. The French, British, and Spanish longed for its frontier, only to be repelled at critical stages. Proto-anarchist to the extent that it was masterless, the frontier still had rules and conventions. Le Maniel's maroons privileged acquisition of legal recognition as a maroon society distinct from the slave society of French colonialists, *gens de couleur*, and plantation slaves. In this sense, they entered into a trajectory seen in the registers of Jamaica's Hansards, Brazil's *quilombos*, and countless other maroon communities.

While Haitian maroons did not follow the more common pattern of overwhelmingly signing conciliatory peace treaties with colonial authorities, as did other maroons in the Caribbean and Latin America, they did compromise nonetheless. Le Maniel residents existed as "border maroons" who moved very close to the extreme conciliatory position, making volte-face decisions on the signing of treaties with the colonial power requiring them to return future runaways to the French for a bounty of fifty *écus* each in exchange for remaining on their bounded spaces, unobstructed by the threat of invasion.[26]

Political recognition by an exogenous power signaled endogenous freedom for a chosen group. The desire for acknowledgment of a community's legal right to exist without advocacy of slavery's systemic implosion or establishment of petitions to end slavery came at a price. Political recognition has been a philosophy of the limit, a finitude whose freedom is Janus-faced and involves strictures deeper than the parameters of spatialization. The unintended negative consequences of Le Maniel maroons' brokering to reach a peace-deal compromise were a function of recognition processes.

The Southern Kingdom of the Platons was exceptional in its attempt both to avoid political recognition and maintain a qualified isolationism. Located in a high-altitude mountain frontier very difficult to access, the kingdom had between ten and twelve thousand residents at its height. As Carolyn Fick details, what began as a provisional military encampment grew into a fortified maroon outpost. Community members were transformed into "agents of their own freedom."[27] Platons elected a titular king. They confronted the benefits of spatialization alongside emergent inhabitant interest in lowland slave emancipation. The Kingdom also exhibited conflicting visions of freedom that would lead to its collapse and the unfortunate massacre of primarily women, children, and elderly who could not evade attack: flight as escape to secluded territorial sovereignty, freedom in a sovereign's agency, and flight through revolution.

By the time the maroons of the Platons forged their overarching mission, the isolationist grand marronage ideal was no longer sustainable, as the revolution spread to all the corridors of the island. The problem with grand marronage in Saint-Domingue was its abridged radicalism. Isolationism and recognition could only take the political community and its dwellers so far.

In spite of its blemishes, grand marronage's depiction of community emphasizes intersubjectivity and how persons imagining freedom relate with one another. Sovereignty through the lawgiver, interpreted as distinct from statecraft and the will of peoplehood, is flight shunning the trappings of recognition.

Toussaint's Sovereign Marronage

The desire for sovereignty often mirrors freedom visions. Sovereignty has a range of expressions: monarchical absolutism, sovereignty as self-mastery, popular sovereignty, the general will, and state sovereignty, the last being prominent in late modernity. Spatialization, territoriality, metaphysics, and movement differ among them. Sovereign flight occurs beyond state-centrism, monarchical authority, atomism, and collective generality.

Sovereign marronage is a philosophy of freedom referring to non-fleeting mass flight from slavery on a scale much larger than grand marronage. Its goal is emancipation, its scope is social-structural, its spatialization is polity-wide, its metaphysics includes the individual and community, and its medium is the lawgiver. Sovereign flight is a rejection of isolationism and popular will. Freedom is understood top down instead of bottom up. It is the singular lawgiver, or sovereign, to whom agents look for guidance to achieve freedom for self and community. Unlike other typologies, the lawgiver here is neither a foreigner nor an agent who leaves a polity forever after imparting an epistemology. The lawgiver is a supreme leader, member of society, decision-making authority, and architect of the free life.

The sovereign has several experiences shared by followers, and those commonalities produce empathy between leader and mass. Sympathy is a yearning for affection toward another whom an agent cannot empathize with because of dissimilar experiences. The lawgiver is transformative through the capacity to inspire and to both empathize and convert sympathy into empathy among a group of people with whom she does not share all experiences in common. The more charismatic the lawgiver, the higher the allure and the probability that a sovereign succeeds in these tasks. Masses' response to inspiration and the lawgiver dictate the ordering of actions by masses.

François Dominique Toussaint L'Ouverture's freedom epitomized the appearance of sovereign marronage during the Haitian Revolution. Son of a petty chieftain in Africa, he was born Toussaint Bréda in slavery outside Le Cap. Toussaint would become *affranchis* later in life, released from bondage at the request of a white plantation manager bearing the ironic last name Bayon de Libertat. He entered politics in his fifties, a relatively advanced age.[28]

Toussaint rose to legendary standing at home and abroad during his lifetime in ways few figures attain after death. Slaves, revolutionaries, and military personnel held him in high regard. Toussaint was written and spoken about in the contemporaneous discourses of Founding Fathers and antislavery activists in the United States; in theatrical tropes in Saint-Domingue and France; by Romantic poets; in the histories of Beaubrun Ardouin, Moreau de Saint-Méry, and Marcus Rainsford; in a novella by Heinrich von Kleist; in recalcitrant memoires by white eyewitnesses to the revolution such as Gros, Leonora Sansay, and Michel-Etienne Deschourtilz; by South American anticolonialists at the dawn of the Bolivarian revolution; and in nascent circles of black internationalism across the Caribbean and Atlantic. Admirers and naysayers alike followed Toussaint's every action.

Legends notwithstanding, Toussaint was human, and his life was full of contractions and reversals. He owned slaves for a period when free and fought on the side of the Spanish against the French until the early stages of the revolution. Two years into the insurrection, Toussaint altered course, proclaiming unambiguously his aspiration: "Brothers and Friends: I am Toussaint L'Ouverture. My name is perhaps known to you, I have undertaken to avenge you. I want liberty and equality to reign throughout St. Domingue. I am working towards that end. Come and join me, brothers, and combat by our side for the same cause."[29]

Toussaint never experienced whipping as he was growing up, despite the plethora of injustices in plantation society. His godfather, Pierre Baptiste, provided him a gift few slaves and ex-slaves enjoyed: lessons in reading and writing. Voluminous letter-writing from Saint-Domingue to top officials in France would serve as an integral means to voice Toussaint's opinions in the public sphere. The letters also have become a valuable resource to interpret his archeology of freedom. Aimé Césaire accurately noted that after the

Boukman moment launched the revolution, it was the *Toussaint moment* in Saint-Domingue.[30]

Toussaint allegedly read vociferously sections of the iconoclastic French Jesuit Abbé Guillaume-Thomas Raynal's famous ten-volume treatise, *Histoire des deux Indes*, of which Diderot was the most prominent ghost coauthor.[31] The *Histoire* was written nine years before the storming of the Bastille, and it called for the rise of a "black Spartacus" to lead a revolt against slavery. As with Louis-Sébastien Mercier's *L'An deux mille quatre cent quarante*, Raynal's text echoed existing prophecies of the imminent emergence of a black revolutionary leader who would avenge New World masters. Raynal's treatise separates itself from other prognostications in promulgating notions of natural rights that Toussaint would transform in his political imagination.

Raynal, via Diderot, wrote "Natural liberty is the right which nature has given to every one to dispose of himself according to his will." "If self-interest alone prevails with nations and their masters, there is another power. Nature speaks louder tones than philosophy or self-interest." Raynal's revolutionary slave leader would "appear, doubt it not; he will come forth and raise the sacred standard of liberty." Toussaint himself wrote in "Self-Portrait" that, after hearing a secret voice speak to him, he concluded, "It is I who must be the chief predicted by the Abbé Raynal."[32]

Toussaint, stepchild of the Enlightenment, heeded the omen and supported the universalistic underpinnings of the French *Declaration*. However, he was aware of the juridical paradox that the *Declaration* was unable to solve. Toussaint sought to apply the document's precepts on natural rights and freedom throughout Saint-Domingue. In a letter to the French Directory, he declared, "Whatever their color, only one distinction must exist between men, that of good and evil. When blacks, men of color, and whites are under the same laws, they must be equally protected and they must equally be repressed when they deviate from them. Such is my opinion; such are my desires."[33] Ethics was to determine judgments and differentiation, and race was to shift from the nucleus of the experience of social structuring to the epiphenomenal.

In time Toussaint changed his last name to L'Ouverture, meaning *the Opening*. The name change gestured toward elements of Toussaint's freedom that aimed to provide the enslaved a wider range of possibilities for flight. Flight was not to be atomistic and fleeting, nor a secluded retreat from the realities of an order in need of systemic repair. In Toussaint's estimation, flight had to match the scale of macropolitics, and he believed that a singular leader could effectively achieve freedom for all. Toussaint's thought blended an early obedience to the master in public, the usage of certain

French universal republican principles in practice, commitment to the rule of law, and a brilliant military wit. This was the context of Toussaint's sovereign marronage.

Abolitionism, hybrid constitutionalism, and militarized agriculture are the fulcrums of sovereign flight for Toussaint. Whereas the first two are noteworthy ambitions, the weaknesses of the latter exceed the benefits of the former. Toussaint's speeches, political writings, and 1801 Constitution depict this sovereign, legalistic vision.[34]

The seventy-seven articles of Toussaint's Constitution are arranged in thirteen Title sections. Positioned under Title 2, "Of Its Inhabitants," article 3 declares, "There can be no slaves in this territory; servitude is abolished within it forever. All men who are born here live and die free and French." Article 4 allows persons, regardless of skin color, to be eligible for all employments. Furthermore, the fifth article states that "there exist no distinctions other than those based on virtues and talents" and that the "law is the same for all, whether it punishes or protects."

Abolishing slavery outright marks a radical move that the *Code Noir*, *Declaration*, and adherents of both petit and grand marronage in Saint-Domingue avoid. Toussaint is the lawgiver who overturns several legal precedents of the law of slavery, foremost being the rights of humans not to have the state impose bondage on an agent without recourse. Greater control over movement and property in one's being are acts of flight that the sovereign affords the mass through rewriting *stare decisis*. The moral logic of paternalistic humanism and all juridical provisions of the law of slavery are not subject to scrutiny.

The Constitution upholds a cosmopolitan notion of ontological Frenchness that Toussaint speaks favorably of in his numerous letters and speeches. Metropole and colony are formerly separate political orders, united only by the economies of subsistence supporting the central power. The Francophone epistemology shatters the partition. Spatialization of land, ocean, and sea has no effect on what it means to be French. At the same time, the Constitution outlines pillars of local governance endemic to Saint-Domingue. Self-determination is a principal attribute in Toussaint's balancing of particularity and universality.

Cosmopolitan nationalism, as we might call it, is symbolic of the sovereign flight. It denotes forging indigenous national solidarity, pride, and nation-building within a polity while simultaneously constructing a nationalizing project with universal ideals embraced by other nations scattered across the globe, sharing the same principles. The state here denotes territoriality, and the nation denotes a people. This view of nationalism does place territorial boundaries on the state, but does not claim these boundaries to be forever fixed. For Toussaint, transnational ontological Frenchness is the axis of this outlook.

Cosmopolitan nationalism is palpable in the description of mores, the function of armed forces, courts, municipal legislation, general dispositions, and Toussaint's upholding of the Catholic Church as the only state religion. Public display of vodou is blasphemy and illegal. Toussaint already declares espousal of this philosophy in the "Address to Soldiers for the Universal Destruction of Slavery": "Let the sacred flame of liberty that we have won lead all our acts. . . . Let us go forth and plant the tree of liberty, breaking the chains of those of our brothers still held captive under the shameful yoke of slavery. Let us bring them under the compass of our rights, the imprescriptible and inalienable rights of free men. [Let us overcome] the barriers that separate nations, and unite the human species into a single brotherhood."[35]

With this statement comes a caveat. In refuting charges brought against him by the conservative planter Viénot Vaunblanc and French General Danatien Rochambeau, Toussaint issues a warning. Expressing emergent black transnationalism, Toussaint looks toward the maroons of Jamaica. The model of grand marronage is not the reason, for Toussaint's thought is a sovereign vision. He argues that, if tested, blacks in Saint-Domingue will fight for their freedom when colonial powers do not respect it. For Toussaint, violence is not intrinsic to the human condition. Violence, or the threat of its employment, can be an instrument:

> May France be just toward its children of the colonies, and soon its commerce and its inhabitants will no longer resent the riches taken from it during its greatest prosperity. But if the French government is influenced by Vaublanc's projects, it should remember that in the heart of Jamaica, in the Blue Mountains, there exist a small number of men so jealous of their liberty that they have forced the proud and powerful English to respect their natural rights, which the French Constitution still guarantees us.[36]

Think what a large number coveting freedom might undertake.

Yet by announcing four years later in the same third article of the 1801 Constitution that to be "free" means to be "French," Toussaint falls into a double bind on allegiances rooted in the problem of sovereignty. This mires the relationship between the French and Haitian Constitutions. The dangers of constitutional patriotism and natural rights republicanism compound the dilemma. Toussaint's mature political philosophy is antithetical to how the majority of slaves and ex-slaves view their flight.

Emancipation is Toussaint's act of abolitionism, a liberation whose metaphysics are internal to agents and whose external social-structural policies advance local self-governance under French rule of law. Toussaint's emancipation is a release into assimilation all the way down. The founding of a republic detached from France is a distinct project from this abolitionist agenda. Saint-Domingue is still a "colony" of the "French empire," and this is Toussaint's constitutional prescription. It is to be a beacon, a part of a unified whole. To describe the philosophy of Toussaint as the search for universal emancipation is consistent with the leader's pronouncements. However, it is simply not *the* philosophy of the Haitian Revolution.[37]

Toussaint stops short of declaring political independence from France. Jean-Jacques Dessalines, the actions of slaves, and the first Haitian Constitution after the revolution have that distinction. Toussaint's idea of emancipation is a metaphysics of liberation, not a declarative political prescription. Even if Toussaint had pushed for independence, it would have constituted an integral component of freedom, but a single component nonetheless. Toussaint's cosmopolitan nationalism is the proto-departmentalization architecture of statecraft that undergoes transmutation in the French Antilles. The twentieth-century islands pondering departmentalization status wrestle with Toussaint's foible.[38]

Militarized agriculture (*caporalisme agraire*) is what C. L. R. James refers to as Toussaint's "ultimate guarantee of freedom." That alone introduces "the change from the old to the new despotism."[39] Not only are military hierarchy and political economy under Toussaint cynical obstacles blocking the acquisition of resources and power for the vast majority of ex-slaves, as Laurent Dubois observes, but the authoritarian roots of postrevolutionary Haitian presidential monarchism and the predatory republic are located in the aftershocks to this mutation of despotic rule.[40]

Toussaint's promotion of militarized agriculture is evidenced threefold, first in a forced-labor decree a year before issuing the Constitution, wherein Toussaint announces that agriculture supports government, is the bedrock of commerce and wealth, and requires that, "to secure our liberties, which are indispensible to our happiness, every individual must be usefully employed, so as to contribute to the public good, and the general tranquility," for "liberty cannot exist without industry"; second, in the constitutional clauses of Title 6, "Of Cultivation and Commerce"; and third, in the stipulation that ex-slaves are to be paid only one-quarter of the value of their produce.[41]

An arduous system of wage slavery replaces chattel servitude. Punitive measures for violation of constitutional protocol are less toxic than the

Code Noir, yet severe nevertheless. Additionally, to ensure oversight of the economy, its inhabitants, governance, and final decision-making authority, the twenty-eighth clause of the Constitution instructs that Toussaint be governor for life and commander-in-chief of Saint-Domingue with full sovereignty and police powers to suppress any actions judged contrary to public order. To black masses, this reproduces some of the worst elements of colonial racial slavery, couched under a different subject heading.

The inability of Toussaint to enact a cosmopolitan nationalism that would satisfy the freedom envisioned by revolutionary slaves reveals the edges of sovereign marronage's valuation. Toussaint's natural rights republicanism reproduces the miscalculations regarding freedom and inverted foundations that we encountered in chapter 2. As with the *Declaration*, it is unable to resolve the juridical paradox of the age. It has endearing rhetorical force whose discursive language is at odds with the phenomenology of slavery between past and future.

Toussaint affirms an irreconcilable contradiction: flight is to occur alongside an inalienable freedom that, as his own descriptions attest, is actually not a given but struggled for and fought over. Toussaint conceives freedom to be inalienable once acquired, but this admission disturbs the freedom as natality narrative. Freedom is not immutable. Flight is first experienced after bondage and is not an originary naturalism. Toussaint has a late realization of the nonuniversal quality of revolutionary republicanism, the rift between the self-reflexive hero and the crowd desiring the hero to put them ahead of the sovereign self, and conflict between the Haitian state and the Haitian nation with the latter's non-sovereign conception of freedom.[42]

In the posthumously published "Lectures on *The Black Jacobins*" delivered at the Institute of the Black World, C. L. R. James reflects on how he would rewrite his influential study of Toussaint. He opines, "I would write descriptions in which the black slaves themselves, or people very close to them, describe what they were doing and how they felt about the work that they were forced to carry on."[43] Such a move, however noble, belies the intentionality behind the first two editions of the text, the second of which has the added appendix, "From Toussaint L'Ouverture to Fidel Castro." The revised edition situates the pertinence of the Haitian and Cuban Revolutions for Caribbean Independence and nationalist movements, but it does so through the prism of sovereigns. James's "The Haitian Revolution in the Making of the Modern World," for a long period unpublished, also favors the vantage point of sovereign leaders over masses.[44]

James writes a *black Jacobin* philosophy, a history centered on the sovereign agency of a charismatic leader who tried to indigenize the thought of a

French revolutionary faction. Black Jacobinism is freedom from above, not New World Dantonism, Girondism, Thermidorianism, the peasant-oriented ethnologies of Jean Price-Mars and Trouillot, or the view from below. Incisive philosophical correctives since James on the popular revolution, its slaves, and their dreams of freedom abound. However, the status of sovereign marronage persists as the eclipsed macropolitical oversight.

Trunk, Roots, Freedom

At the height of the Saint-Domingue insurrection, France's First Consul, Napoléon Bonaparte, sent his brother-in-law, General Leclerc, to the island. Accompanied by more than twenty-one thousand troops, Leclerc's mission had two purposes: eliminate Toussaint from leadership and quell the revolution. Although Leclerc failed the second objective, he did apprehend the sought after lawgiver.

When Toussaint, captured and in bondage once again, boarded the ship at Gonaïves bound for France, he declared famously, "In overthrowing me, you have cut down in Saint-Domingue only the trunk of the tree of the liberty of the blacks; it will grow back from the roots, because they are deep and numerous."[45] Former Haitian President Jean-Bertrand Aristide would employ Toussaint's maxim in Haiti's bicentennial during a coup d'état that unceremoniously ousted him from power and sent him into exile in South Africa.[46]

Although Toussaint erred in associating his idea of freedom with that of the black masses, he accurately predicted that the Haitian revolutionaries would enact a radical marronage. The late Toussaint viewed himself to be the trunk of liberty, not liberty's Alpha and Omega. In other words, Toussaint abdicated the philosophy of sovereign agency without premeditation, albeit far too belatedly. In the second major volte-face following his switch of cosmopolitan, nationalist alliance from the Spanish to the French, it would have been more precise for Toussaint to situate the masses as the trunk of liberty and himself one its branches.

Freedom indeed has multiple roots. In Saint-Domingue, freedom is not singularly arboreal. There are manifold sites of roots, branches, and flight, united by the activity of revolution and enriched by differences from above and below. A comprehensive understanding of the psychodynamics and metaphysics of flight elude Toussaint. We will see next the stakes of interpreting their significance.

Toussaint died like an exiled maroon less than a year before the revolution's end, passing away in the French Fort de Joux prison within the depths of the Jura Mountains. As his case shows, sovereign marronage as an ideal expands freedom's scope in ways that petit marronage and grand marronage cannot by addressing normative structures of unfreedom intrinsic to slavery and an alternative typology of flight. Its efficacy falls short, first due to cross-purpose constitutionalism unable to disentangle entirely the juridical paradox of concomitant paternalistic humanism and legal subordination; second, as a result of perpetuating a natural rights philosophy that the masses reject; and third, because of the lawgiver's ultimate reliance upon achieving sovereignty. The desire for sovereignty collapses the vision of the lawgiver into a form of dictatorship.

FOUR

Sociogenic Marronage in a Slave Revolution

We must, with one last act of national authority, forever ensure liberty's reign in the country of our birth; we must take any hope of re-enslaving us away from the inhumane government that for so long kept us in the most humiliating stagnation. In the end we must live independent or die. . . . We have dared to be free, let us be thus by ourselves and for ourselves. Let us imitate the grown child: his own weight breaks the boundary that has become an obstacle to him.
—The Haitian Declaration of Independence[1]

While Dessalines and other Haitian leaders eloquently articulated a passionate refusal of slavery, it was the people of Haiti who truly gave content to that refusal.
—Laurent Dubois, *Haiti*[2]

There is a zone of nonbeing, an extraordinarily sterile and arid region, an incline stripped bare of every essential from which a genuine new departure can emerge.
—Frantz Fanon, *Black Skin, White Masks*[3]

Introduction

"Beyond the mountains there are mountains." The words of this venerable Haitian proverb proffer the transparent and submerged. The geographic image suggests a broad, limitless terrain. The interstices of a trek through a rugged topography present a countervailing difficulty, mobility a reflection of a finite reality. A journey is not only possible but also probable. It can have moments of peaceful fluidity and ominous stagnation, together a sign of a crossroads. The junction marks an opportunity, what Edwidge Danticat calls the site of dangerous creation.[4] The outcome: an experience of friction, resistance, and movement. The traversing of future frontiers brings with it efforts to imagine and experience freedom irreducible to self or sovereign.

We have covered the trials and tribulations of sovereign marronage in Saint-Domingue through the embodiment of Toussaint L'Ouverture. The analytical reduction of the idea of freedom to sovereign, masculine, Founding Father figures by Toussaint's heirs and in the popular imagination did not end following Toussaint's deportation from the island and the subsequent declaration of independence. What did vanish was Toussaint's constitutional vision of ex-slaves as "free and French," a disposition that his successors felt was as nonsensical as the phrase "free and British" would have been to legislators of the early, postcolonial American state.

Jean-Jacques Dessalines, Alexandre Pétion, Henri Christophe, Jean-Baptiste Sans-Souci, and Jean-Pierre Boyer were heirs to, but not imitations of, Toussaint's legacy, who transformed structures of leadership, governance, and statecraft in the Haitian postcolony. They have been as frequently referenced as George Washington, Thomas Jefferson, James Madison, Alexander Hamilton, and John Adams were during the American revolutionary and post-revolutionary periods. Dessalines and Jefferson had the added roles of drafting Constitutions and declarations for their respective new polities, truncating more the significance of an already short list of dignitaries.

Jefferson considered America an "empire of liberty" and underlying his authorship of the American Declaration of Independence were claims to natural law and axiomatic truths regarding the human condition. The self-revelatory superseded performative speech acts.[5] As Jefferson wrote in the second clause of America's most famous founding text, "We hold these truths to be self-evident, that all men are created equal, that they are endowed by their Creator with certain unalienable Rights, that among these are Life, Liberty and the pursuit of Happiness."[6] A section stricken by Congress from the final version of the US Declaration pointed to Jefferson's awareness of likely insurrection against slaveholding regimes, specifically that of Great Britain under King George III vis-à-vis the American colony. Jefferson stated, "That this assemblage of horrors might want no fact of distinguishing die, he [George III] is now exciting those very people to rise in arms among us, and to purchase that liberty which *he* has deprived them, by murdering the people upon whom *he* also obtruded them; thus paying off former crimes committed against the *liberties* of one people, with crimes which he urges them to commit against the *lives* of another [orig. emphasis]."[7]

A well-known contradiction was that Jefferson professed a public philosophy of freedom and was a long-term slaveholder in the private sphere. His *Notes on the State of Virginia* exposed this tension. Equally significant to the dialectic of Enlightenment was the irony that the words excised from the draft could easily have been leveled against Jefferson once he assumed the power of the presidency near the apex of the Haitian uprising.[8] In Saint-Domingue, Dessalines and Haitian revolutionaries made factual in their own context its intuitions.

While doubtful of assertions such as Jefferson's about intrinsic human universality, Dessalines believed in the ability of human agents to be free. What Dessalines and Jefferson respectively contributed to, as did other early leaders in their states, was a commitment for the young Haitian and American governments to establish republican empires wherein forms of freedom would emerge and be cultivated or suppressed.

A common problem facing Haiti and the United States in the immediate post-revolutionary moments was the incompatibility of republicanism and empire, the former notion suggesting the desire to establish representative government, and the latter the expansion of state territoriality and absorption of newly acquired frontiers into a preexisting state unit. The charismatic authority of sovereign presidential and monarchical leaders was unable to hide daily acts of insubordination, law-breaking, and disorders of state occurring among inhabitants of these empires of freedom.[9] There were several indications that inhabitants within these polities resisted inertia through their activities.

In Haiti and the United States, as in societies across time subject to popular revolutions, revolutionary masses outnumbered the leadership elite and were the bulwarks of insurrection. Observers of the Saint-Domingue uprising, writers in the immediate decades after independence such as the positivist Joseph Anténor Firmin, and contemporary philosophical treatises have interpreted freedom on a macro-level as sovereign flight. The actions, beliefs, and ideals of slave masses, good and bad, are, in a repeating circular logic, habitually ignored. We must remove the epistemological cataract. Understanding the actions and events of people, particularly peasants, during the Haitian Revolution rather than sovereign leaders alone is required to accomplish this.[10]

We must first understand the type of flight referred to herein as sociogenic marronage. Prior interpretations of marronage and the Haitian Revolution indeed describe elements of flight. Yet they have done so by reifying a long-standing false binary in studies of social and political orders within large-scale slave societies: flight *or* structural reordering, whereby acts of flight are separated from inquiry into revolutionary politics and the corresponding transformations indicative of the shifts between the previous order and the ensuing sociopolitical system. Sociogenic marronage allows us finally to understand how revolutions are *themselves* moments of flight that usher in new orders and refashion society's foundations.

Frantz Fanon's philosophy illuminates facets of the sociogenic and reaffirms the importance of the psychological to the lived experience of freedom. Naming, imagined blueprints of freedom (vèvè architectonics), the state of society, and constitutionalism are the nucleus of sociogenic marronage. Subsequent explanation of these principles, only implicit in Fanon, demonstrates the contours of sociogenic flight, and explication of their manifestation in the Haitian Revolution underscores their ongoing significance for the politics of revolution and the meaning of freedom.

The act of naming, considered banal prematurely by some, has catalytic repercussions for the process of becoming free. Our imaginaries of freedom for self and mass have integral effects as well. Our conceived designs of the free life are not reducible to the theological or the secular, though in the context of revolutionary Haiti, there is a symbiosis between architectures of freedom and political theology. Attention to peasants' longings and actions, both the centripetal and the centrifugal, reveals as well the intersecting valences of gender that are often submerged discursively and how enslaved women demanded provisions emblematic of the reconfigurations in the state of society. Documents of the revolution and constitutionalism offer throughout additional insight into revolution, flight, and epistemic vistas. The post-revolutionary sustainability of sociogenic marronage matters less than the experiences and ideals stated. The failure to maintain its phenomenology of freedom is a consequence of abandonment by sovereigns, not its vision from the underside.

Romanticizing revolutionary Saint-Domingue is not the aim. Our objective is twofold: first, a refutation of conventional analysis reducing the project of freedom during the Haitian Revolution to the vision of Toussaint; and, second, comprehension of the trans-historical, macropolitical, sociogenic conception of flight. What follows highlights a fundamental quality of marronage philosophy: attempts at actualization of flight, of the ability of individuals to become free and to exit from that condition, and perpetual acts of attainment and restructuring are part and parcel of what it means to be human.

Sociogenic Marronage

Sociogenic marronage denotes macropolitical flight whereby agents flee slavery through non-fleeting acts of naming, vèvè architectonics, liberation, reordering of the state of society, and constitutionalism. It is a non-sovereign state of being whose conception of freedom is shaped by cognition, metaphysics, egalitarianism, hope for refuge, and the experiences of masses in a social and political order. Condition, not place, is vital to its phenomenology.

In the beginning of our study, we discerned how marronage operates against the presumption that slaves exist in a state of "social death." In the language of vodou, social death is the life of a zombie, a being roaming the earth with glazed eyes, lacking the ability to control its actions, an entity neither dead nor alive. Social death is compatible with maintaining that all slave revolts inevitably enter into a maroon dimension and that freedom is the slave's response to powerlessness, dishonor, and natal alienation under mastery. The idea of social death denies the significance of psychology to freedom, rendering it unable to explain how slaves are able to become free physically outside the actions and intentions of enslaving agents. It also cannot explain the metaphysics of freedom, thereby offering an incomplete account of becoming free as it relates to the constitution of the self and drastic alterations of social structures.[11]

Prominent nineteenth- and twentieth-century European thinkers, including Friedrich Nietzsche, Sigmund Freud, Anna Freud, Alfred Adler, and Jacques Lacan, opposed the bracketing of the psychological in interpretations of child, adolescent, and adult behavior and actions. Nietzsche went so far as to categorize psychology as a *prima philosophia* and the foremost human science beyond good and evil.[12] Before the Martinican philosopher and psychiatrist Frantz Fanon, the fields of psychoanalysis and psychopathology shared a common limiting epistemology inherited from the Enlightenment: the reduction of individual psychological experiences to universal human attributes.

In the mid-twentieth century, Fanon reshaped psychological inquiry by placing it alongside the traditions of existential phenomenology and Caribbean thought. This would shatter the assumptions of European human sciences and leave, well into the twenty-first century, residual questions for the philosophical conjectures of adherents of the social death trope who have sought to overturn Western bifurcations of negative and positive theorizations of freedom while subordinating the psychological to statistical insignificance. Fanon once wrote of composing ideas that were not to be construed as timeless truths. But his revelations turned out to be of transhistorical import, and they can be read for our purposes backward into the Haitian Revolution.

Fanon argues in *Black Skin, White Masks* that the unfree exist in a "zone of nonbeing" (*zone de non-être;* see fig. 1). This hellish cartographic space is physical and psychological, and it structures personal expression as well

Figure 1. Visual representation of marronage. (I thank Mika Hirai for graphics assistance.)

as the state of society. Rather than an inert state of social death, the zone of nonbeing is "an extraordinarily sterile and arid region, an incline stripped bare of every essential from which a genuine new departure can emerge."[13] As loathsome as life inside this zone of enslavement might be, it is a zone of hope and natality.

Flight always exists as a potentiality constrained by circumstance. The experience of the unfree in the zone of nonbeing, which Fanon likens in his final treatise, *The Wretched of the Earth*, to that of the *damnés* (the damned), foments the trepidations and aspirations of the enslaved. The famous fifth chapter of *Black Skin*, mistranslated into English for decades as "The Fact of Blackness," is properly translated "The Lived Experience of the Black" (*L'expérience vécue du Noir*). Fanon detects there how the experience of the black Antillean under slavery and the racial gaze during and after slavery and colonialism structures her unfreedom, choices, and vision of an alternative future. He laments an experience of a walk in France when, after having departed Martinique for the metropole, a young white child, fearful of Fanon's presence by virtue of his blackness, points to him and shouts: "Look, a Negro (*Nègre*)!" The child's parent replies, "Ssh! You'll make him angry. Don't pay attention to him, monsieur, he doesn't realize you're just as civilized as we are."[14]

The "Look" fixes Fanon, the black over-determined externally because of the epidermal racial schema, the black unable to avoid the effects of another's learned language rooted in the political philosophy of white supremacy. Fanon details unfreedom and the phenomenology of antiblack racism not only in late colonialism, but also in transatlantic slavery. His point, though, is to exhibit an edict that transcends periodization. Fanon examines the zone of nonbeing, determining that, however counterintuitive or nauseating, the zone "prepares [the human] to act," can "induce man to be *actional*," and is a region ripe for an authentic upheaval.[15] Whether through négritude, Marxism, sources of the self, or another system beyond Fanon's considerations in *Black Skin*, the axiom is clear: The zone of nonbeing harbors the prospect for revolution among the unfree who ascertain dissatisfaction with existing life options.[16]

In weighing exit options from the zone, Fanon proposes in *Black Skin* the sociogenic turn. Fanon observes that some schools of thought propose phylogenetic worldviews that classify different beings on the ordering of species, and some espouse ontogenic explanations of the individual that frame the human self as having universal attributes, tendencies, dreams, and psychological dispositions, regardless of lived experiences. Fanon introduces a third worldview beyond species-beings and the Freudian turn in psychoanalysis: sociogeny.[17]

Sociogenesis is the idea that lived experiences fashion our social world and structure our civil and political orders. It is the notion that humans bring the state of society into being through objective and subjective measures. Human procedures and appraisals occur in a world embedded in language, its meaning, and resistance to inertia. Sociogenesis is, in short, the prism that captures the process of flight from the zone of nonbeing.

Against the de-raced, de-gendered, universalizing rhetoric of documents decreed by colonial and racial orders that nonetheless inscribe Manichaean, epidermal-based, biocentric theories of statecraft premised on human difference, Fanon deploys a way to see and value our differentiated lived realities in the face of bad-faith assertions by those in positions of mastery. What he develops further after Frederick Douglass's enunciation of comparative freedom and Édouard Glissant later homes in on with philosophical poetics is the fundamental relationality of flight, evident in the Saint-Domingue revolution.

The white and the black, functioning as master and slave in the Antilles, are far from bracketed ontological subjects. They exist in relation to each other. While not a mutual struggle for self-consciousness within a slavocracy, flight in Fanon's estimation entails awareness of lived experiences informing reflection on our situations, options, life chances, responsibilities, and humanity.

History is the silhouette that posterity gazes upon and that we limn to clarify our current walks of life. But history is never to fix the future wants of the human. Nor are humans to be permanent instruments of artifices supplanting flight with acts of unfreedom. This, Fanon argues, is apparent during, prior to, and after Saint-Domingue.[18]

Understanding our cognitive states is the first phase in liberation, constitutionality, and order realignments. Whereas *Black Skin* presents the sociogenesis of the individual black Antillean in a world of difference, *Wretched* extends the logic of flight to human collectivities, states, and mass revolution.

Wretched is a manifesto on the metaphysics of violence, the grandeur and weaknesses of spontaneity in revolution, the misadventures of national consciousness, the function of culture amidst coloniality and racial states, the cognitive dissonance of persons subjected to torture and war, the pitfalls of anticolonial cosmopolitan nationalisms, such as Toussaint's, unable to imitate Europe and maintain postcolonial, local self-determination, the interconnectedness of revolution and freedom, and the new humanism required for freedom to materialize. Its final words capture the aims of revolution to "make a new start, develop a new way of thinking, and endeavor to create a new man (*un homme neuf*)," and they echo Aimé Césaire's injunction that processes of revolution "invent souls."[19]

Inherent to natality are invention and innovation, even when retaining traditions. "If we want humanity to take one step forward," Fanon states, "if we want to take it to another level than the one where Europe has placed it, then we must innovate, we must be pioneers."[20] This proclamation evokes the spirit of the Haitian Declaration of Independence, of daring to be free "by ourselves and for ourselves,"[21] of the disentangling of the juridical paradox left unresolved through sovereign marronage, and the countless unknown revolutionaries in Saint-Domingue whose imagined dreams and institutional designs of the free life disown stasis. Sociogenesis is a pluralistic sanctuary, relational, intrinsic to revolution, and a humanism. Naming, the first of sociogenic marronage's principles, which is only implied by Fanon, begins to elicit a justification.

Naming

A name defines our individuality, our groups, our institutions, organizations, nations, states, and transnational bodies. It is one of the most intimate qualities of a human being. A name can be a label, categorizer, designation of identity and difference, formal, informal, legal, secular, religious, alias, familial, inherited, or invented. It is the way we call and respond to one another, how we get others' attention. Names are conveyed through letters, figures, writings, sounds, and sign language. In all mediums, a name is symbolic of who we are.

Naming is the voluntary or imposed act of entities receiving and giving names. People are often named around their birth. Time is always a variable, its pendulum indicative of the circumstances under which naming occurs. A parent, guardian, and secular calendar-based traditions or divine right, cosmology, and theologically grounded traditions are channels sanctioning modes of naming. Context matters for interpreting meaning, and language is the conduit of naming, meaning, and their symbolism. Ludwig Wittgenstein describes naming as a "remarkable act of mind, as it were a baptism of an object." For George Lamming, a "name is an infinite source of control," and it is a product of the "eternal conflict between the naming of a thing and a knowledge of it."[22] Our use and understanding of language affects our perceptions, knowledge, movements, actions, and interactions. The experience of naming is no exception.

Naming can be political and controversial.[23] For example, as Mahmood Mamdani discerns, the invocation of disparate terms to refer to the same phenomenon can have significant geopolitical outcomes. Referring to civilian casualties in the contemporary Western Sudan region of Darfur as "genocide" and those in Iraq as a "cycle of insurgency and counter-insurgency" leads to unequal judgments and valuations by participants and observers. Language shapes and transforms the interpretation of meaning for the mind, self, and collectivities.[24]

The process of naming ranges from the uncontested to the fraught, most instances tied to the phenomenology of flight. The circumstances surrounding the rendering of a name as a procedure of statecraft are substantiation. The coining of state names is frequently a *re*naming, a label reflecting the polity's imagined future and a distancing from the attributes of the past of which the discarded appellation was a reminder.

Think of the language and meaning behind the modern state renaming of the Gold Coast to Ghana, Rhodesia to Zimbabwe, the kingdom of Holland to the Netherlands, East Germany and West Germany to Germany, New Holland to Australia, New Spain to Mexico, Abyssinia to Ethiopia, Palestine to Israel, West Bank, and the Gaza Strip, Burma to Myanmar, Persia to Iran, states of the former Incan Empire, Russia after the USSR's collapse, Santo Domingo to the Dominican Republic, and last, but not least, Saint-Domingue to Haiti. The intrastate renaming of towns, principalities, and cities also follows a similar logic, be it the shift from Bombay to Mumbai, Saigon to Ho Chi Minh City, Constantinople to Istanbul, Leningrad to Saint Petersburg, Edo to Tokyo, New Amsterdam to New York, and Cap-Français on Haiti's northern coast to Cap-Haïtian.

The official naming of Haiti (Haïti) occurred with the reading of its Declaration of Independence on January 1, 1804, at Gonaïves. Dessalines composed the Declaration with the assistance of Louis Boisrond-Tonnerre, a *gens de couleur* (person of color) who was his personal secretary.[25] While shorter than Haiti's first constitution, promulgated in 1805, the Declaration still embodied core principles formulated by black ex-slaves during the revolution. This is notable, given the anxieties over and strain between the mass-based conception of freedom and Dessalines's increasing assertion of sovereign authority that would persist until his assassination a year later in 1806. Although there was a document dated shortly before, on November 29, 1803, allegedly signed by Dessalines, Christophe, and Augustin Clerveux and republished across the Atlantic world—especially in the written press of Great Britain—proclaiming the independence of Saint-Domingue "In the Name of the Black People, and Men of Color of St. Domingo," there is no known record of its existence within the island, and it is thought to be a likely fabrication.[26] The Declaration has endured as Haiti's acknowledged announcement of a new order to a local and global audience.

The name "Haiti" derives from the original, precolonial, indigenous Taino appellation for the land of Saint-Domingue, *Ayiti*. Its translations include "mountainous," "rugged," "mountainous land," and "land of mountains." The choice of the name Haiti continues to be a subject of debate and conjecture.[27] In spite of competing rationalizations, we can deduce a few points about the new state's appellation through the Declaration's announced addressees and their imagined function in the postcolony.

First, Dessalines refers to his audience, Haitians, throughout the Declaration, as "Citizens." Rather than "Subjects" or "Ex-Slaves," Dessalines chooses as his first word "Citizens," thereby intimating a swallowing of hierarchical divisions in order to afford an egalitarian new beginning. Citizens are beings able to make claims to state along with those in their respective communities and relations over the self. Dessalines will decree elsewhere that citizens are to live the new life, starting with "Year 1" in place of the Gregorian calendar year, 1804. The idea of calendar resetting is one of the few principles of Jacobinism accepted by Haitian revolutionaries, whose actions, ranging from mundane tasks of maintaining daily food provisions to a soldier's acquiring artillery for battle, can be understood as a critique of cosmopolitan nationalist philosophy.

Second, Dessalines uses the pronoun *your* repeatedly to orient clauses meant to appeal to the perspective of the formerly enslaved, not simply cadres of the Haitian people belonging to the military class, economic gentry, and political elites. Near the beginning of the Declaration of Independence, Dessalines conveys admiration for courageous revolutionary soldiers and generals. "These generals," however, "who have guided your efforts against tyranny have not yet done enough for your happiness; the French name still haunts our land."[28] The use of *your* is, at the same time, suffused in its meaning with an aversion to all things French and a chiding of elite soldiers, whose service to the Haitian state is appreciated while contextualized as one of the many ways to contribute to the new society.

The third signal of the selection of the state's name is the deployment of "Native" language, thereby renaming as indigenous the people residing in the new society. The Declaration displays a worry over the specter of France: the French presence, the French name, and the French women, men, children, and customs that implacably pervade the terrain. Dessalines refers to Haitians as natives, nonforeigners, and the people who are the rightful heirs of a space that was and should be their own. By renaming Haitians "natives," the newly endowed citizens are able make demands of freedom, accountability, and responsibility on the state and one another. Their recently acquired capacity to *believe* in that authorized capability itself is an agency of flight.

"Native citizens, men, women, girls, and children, let your gaze extend on all parts of this island," exhorts the author. Later on, Dessalines proclaims in the Declaration:

> Natives of Haiti! My happy fate was to be one day the sentinel who would watch over the idol to which you sacrifice; I have watched, sometimes fighting alone, and if I have been so fortunate as to return to your hands the sacred trust you confided in me; know that it is now your task to preserve it. In fighting for your liberty, I was working for my own happiness. Before consolidating it with laws that will guarantee your free individuality, your leaders, who I

have assembled here, and I owe you the final proof of our devotion. Generals and you, leaders, collected here close to me for the good of our land, the day has come, the day which must make our glory, our independence, eternal.[29]

Our land. Our. Land. The Declaration notes the contributions of various actors in the revolution: the generals, the soldiers, the commander in chief, the women, men, and children who are an essential part of the day's celebration. Military leaders must prove their devotion to the cause of the people rather than the reverse. But it is the renaming and indigenizing of a land and a people in the mind and political imagination of the ex-slave population, gens de couleur, and cadres of whites who fought on behalf of the revolution's ideals for the ability of the affranchis to till it that has meaning.

Haiti announces its entrance into the comity of states as the first "Black" Republic in the New World. As the subsequent discourse on constitutionalism indicates, Haiti introduces a racial republicanism in which *biological* does not function as an ascriptive designation. Race mutates from the biological into the political. Politically, *black* becomes the new *native*. The native is free. Haiti indigenizes blackness, an accomplishment previously nonexistent in the Americas.

From the Declaration's opening dispensation against "the barbarians who have bloodied our land for two centuries"[30] to its conclusion, the meaning of *our land* has much to do with distance, movement, property, and purpose. Although the Declaration of Independence does not prescribe the comprehensive contours of freedom, it locates freedom in two interrelated ways, one being an *imperative to interiority*, about peering into our own minds and souls, and reminding ourselves who the individuals tasked with the naming and construction of another world are; and the other an *imperative to exteriority*, the evaluative mechanism whereby we ascertain the persons for whom freedom in the realm beyond the self is to be acquired. The imperatives to interiority and exteriority ground an additional adage of the Declaration: cherish independence, but do not confuse it with freedom.

Dessalines implores citizens of Haiti to "vow before me to live free and independent and to prefer death to anything that will try to place you back in chains."[31] Only a few months later on April 28, 1804, Governor-General Dessalines bolsters this maxim in a blistering address to the inhabitants of Haiti entitled "Liberty or Death! A Proclamation." Dessalines's words display a hemispheric awareness, invoking events of the time in Guadeloupe and Martinique to dissuade Haitians from taking paths that lead in his view, unsurprisingly, to quelled rebellions and stunted self-governance. For Dessalines, the act of independence means that he and the revolutionaries have not only abjured France. They have "avenged America."[32] After avenging comes the promising, yet difficult, task of constructing a future world. In a caveat with Fanonian resonances, Dessalines warns that decolonization in the early postcolony does not end with the introduction of new national flags, anthems, songs, and renaming. Independence affords a nation and its peoples the context for the emergence and shaping of the free life. As Dessalines implores in the Declaration, "We have dared to be free, let us be thus by ourselves and for ourselves."[33]

Renaming Saint-Domingue Haiti was not a disavowal of its Taino past but homage to a people who were once free and no longer able to inhabit their land because of enslavement, conquest, and decimation. Land was, and still remains, a critical factor connecting names and naming to other aspects of flight. The second principle of sociogenic marronage is an architectural envisioning portraying its significance.

Vèvè Architectonics

There is a long-standing saying that Haitians are 90 percent Catholic and 100 percent vodou. Whether estimates are accurate or inflated, the integral nature of vodou in Haiti is undeniable. The inauguration of the Haitian Revolution at Bois-Caïman was even done through a vodou ceremony.

Vodou (vodun, vaudou, voodoo) developed in Saint-Domingue as a religion incorporating elements of West and Central African worship with tenets of Roman Catholicism. In addition to the Supreme Being, Bondye, and deities (*lwas, loas*), who have unique attributes as extensions of the creator, ancestors are said to function in the daily lives of persons, mediating human interactions with nature, one another, spirits, and the Supreme Being. In vodou, the body is believed to wither away with time, but the soul never dies. Dead ancestors communicate with the living through signs, divination, and rituals.[34]

The utterance of *lwa* in Kreyòl phonetically sounds indistinguishable from the French word *loi*, meaning "law." Yet a *lwa* has an organization of law higher than human jurisprudence. To experience the wisdom of a *lwa* and channel a connection to Bondye, an individual must become possessed, and the body mounted by a deity. The embodied agency of spirit possession can lead to bodily convulsions and rapid movements.

Witnesses to mounting clap hands and drum. Preparations for mounting require consideration of the lwa's characteristics: its clothing preferences, colors, symbols, special days of the week, method of possession, and ritual offerings. Regardless of its qualities, the *lwa* can mount women and men, adult and child alike. How the lwa knows when to mount a human and the human when to expect the lwa and the unfolding of knowledge of future life paths is a consequence of a ritual specific to each deity: *vèvè* (pronounced veh-veh).

A vèvè is a ceremonial image drawn on the ground with coffee, cornmeal, or flour. Its intricate aesthetics depict on the land geometric shapes, hearts, animals, serpents, earth, water, and the faces of the deities in Rada and Petro, Rada being the worship of spirits originating in Dahomey, and Petro the veneration of creole deities from Saint-Domingue. Vèvès are conduits calling to appear lwas such as Baron Samdi, Damballah, Ezili, Agwé, Sobo, Zaka, Gédé, Ogou Feray, and Legba, deity of the crossroads, the liminal sphere straddling nonbeing and being. A vèvè is the symbolic architecture of the deities whose guiding principles are reputed to structure actions of the good and the bad, the free and the unfree.

Borrowing from the idea of a vèvè, we can understand *vèvè architectonics* to mean the blueprint of freedom that an individual or collectivity imagines in an ideal world. Vèvè architectonics within polities is a pictogram of mass flight that resists sovereign decisionism and institutional design conducted by the state without authorization, advice, and input from the citizen. It is the design and structural roadmap beckoning the construction and refashioning of cognitive, physical and political orders. Orders of state, from planned rational systems to irrational decrees requiring forced popular submission, are commands and routes of formation that it obviates.[35]

The Bois-Caïman ceremony is alleged to have begun with a sacrifice, a vodou chant, and a speech. A pig was offered as ritual, its blood sucked and engulfed by those secretly convened. The chant was uttered in Kikongo. In the two decades prior to revolt, African-born slaves, or *bossales*, from the Kingdom of Kongo were the majority of enslaved blacks in Saint-Domingue. Before their capture, many of these slaves were highly skilled soldiers, veterans who fought in a civil war that was tearing the Kongo apart. In the 1780s nearly 60 percent of the slaves, both in Southern Saint-Domingue and the North Province region of the insurrection's beginning, were Kongolese. On the eve of the Haitian Revolution, the Kongolese were the most powerful of the bossales and a significant force among all revolutionaries, bossales and creole.[36]

Canga, a central word in the chant, is an imperative at the start of four of the five chant lines. It derives from the verb *Kanga*, which can be translated in multiple ways, including "to hold back" or, in a literal sense, "to stop or bind." But the most compelling idiom with *Kanga* is "to protect," "to save," and "to deliver."[37] *Canga*'s meaning ("Protect!" "Save!" "Deliver!")

has content premised on the intentionality of the believer, a form based on an agent's image of the free life, and linguistic force evocative of the calling of spirits to the body and the land. It proved catalytic in Haiti's peasant-driven, popular revolution.

The speech has been passed down among the short list of prominent works in Haitian letters. Boukman Dutty, the speech's author, was a slave from Jamaica, whose subsequent experience as a maroon in Saint-Domingue led to his initiation into the vodou priesthood. He presided over Bois-Caïman along with an elder, African-born priestess. Boukman acknowledged the inspiration of faith, his God, his political theology, and his frustration with the inadequacies of the governing racial order, which was causing entropy. Boukman's speech went beyond political theology, challenging those nearby to realize that their unfreedom, their nonbeing, was a resource in the realization of genuine upheaval. It defended having vèvè architectonics as an essential facilitator of the activity of flight. *"Couté la liberté li pale coeurs nous tous,"*[38] Boukman exhorted—"Listen to the liberty that speaks in all our hearts." Our hearts. Our land.

The slave revolution was launched.

State of Society

Peasants were a decisive force, and the rural peasantry was its fulcrum. In this respect, the revolution begun in Saint-Domingue mirrored other modern revolutions. As prescient as Karl Marx was, he erred in viewing urban agents as the primary catalysts for these upheavals. The Chinese, Russian, Cuban, French, and Haitian Revolutions began in the mountains and countryside. Revolutions may have had their crescendo in cities, but their beginnings were outside those zones. Popular revolutions have been centripetal, not centrifugal.

Where Saint-Domingue had a distinguishing mark was in the existence of a sizable enslaved peasantry comprising the great majority of island dwellers. Its revolutionary peasants, especially those disgruntled with Toussaint's substitution of cosmopolitan nationalism for their vèvè architectonics, sought land. Gender equity, unrestricted private and public worship, and grievances over equal pay for equal work were also essential to freedom.

Flight involves negotiating the third principle of sociogenic marronage, *the state of society*: the dominions of the civil order, the sphere of the nation; the political order, the governance structure of the state; and the space of the citizen in those coextensive orders. Freedom is not a consequence of the triumph of individual wills, sublation into ethical life, and rigid separation of disproportionate zones from one another. Flight occurs within the always existing orders of civil and political society, each zone comparable and overlapping with the next. It is in the overturning of asymmetries internal to the respective zones and the departure of unfreedom that the experiences of flight take place.

The Haitian Revolution erupted in a colonial state system differentiating the metropolitan governance of citizens from the local governance and administration of subjects. The colonial state was a compartmentalized world ravaged by the bifurcation of native and colonizer (*colon*). Rather than categories of the human, native and colon were considered different species with dissimilar conditions of being.[39] The colonized native was, according to Achille Mbembe, an *animal*, domesticated through acts of conviviality and venality during colonization.[40] The native was able to live when adequately instrumental to the goals of the colon. The colon annihilated and replaced the native once the latter was superfluous and of no instrumental value.

Civil society and political society in Saint-Domingue were racialized, each zone protecting the White colon. Bracketed off from the political order as a result of the juridical designation as slave, enslaved peasants were also not part of the civil order, because slaves were constructed as uncivilized. Civil society and civilization were indistinguishable. The idea of black civil society was an oxymoron.

The dual revolutionary project of anticolonialism and antislavery ostensibly required deracialization of the state of society in flight, but it was only in the order of civil society that this would take effect. The creation of an indigenous civil society whose associational life and institutions fostered pluralism, delimited hierarchy, and eliminated racially inscribed access prerequisites was a premium. Instead of a racialized state governed by the biocentrism of the colon, who folded the words *white* and *citizen* into synonyms, political society was to be rethought. The new order was to be predicated on the activities of people in the zone of the Black Republic, a postcolonial state whose name, modes of rule, and definition of the citizen were to signify a political, rather than biocentric, notion of blackness.[41]

Land is integral to the civil order. This is true for individuals residing in rural, suburban, and urban domains. Land is a space of cultivation. It is where one can work and rest. Land is the foundation for schools, roads, tenements, assemblies, trees, vitamins, food, markets, lodges, large edifices, artistic performances, government buildings, and places of worship. The experience of communion between an agent and the land generates flight.

From the earliest phases of the revolution, peasants associated land with freedom. They deplored the forced tilling of land as slaves under the plantation political economy of the colonial state. In Toussaint's regime, affranchis continued to deny the efficacy of imposed work based on the plantation model. Agrarianism was valued, yet tilling the land in obedience to a sovereign decree was abhorred. Creole slaves and bossales from the Kongo kingdom, Dahomey, Oyo Empire, and other regions of Central and Western Africa exhibited antagonism to inegalitarian land arrangements.

The right to proprietorship of land is an element of actually existing civil society. Even in the period of the revolution, when emancipation was declared temporarily, and ex-slaves had to remain working on plantations, the emancipated organized themselves in brigades as a precondition of freedom. Every brigade had persons assigned to sections of the land, and those individuals could sell the produce not needed for their basic subsistence.[42] Land could be for private, personal use, economic capital, social capital, networking, nongovernment agencies, or the public good. Peasant revolutionaries argued that civil orders were strengthened where shared access to land was realized.

Enslaved women demanded gender equality, normalizing standards for conditions of work, and the evanescent moments of leisure throughout the insurrection, as they did egalitarian pay for the revolutionary years of qualified emancipation. By *gender equality*, black women slaves meant the same norms for hours on the plantation, rest at night, compensation for work, and qualifications for leadership positions in clandestine revolutionary enclaves across the island. While it is speculative to reduce all actions of revolutionaries to specific bossale traditions, what is undeniable were common retorts raised by creole and bossale slaves pertaining to the status of women and their capacity to participate in civil society.

Assemblies were sites where discourses affected the civil and political orders. Slaves had no control over how many hours per day they had to report to the plantation and a master's home. Under Toussaint's 1801 Constitution, ex-slaves had greater control of the self, but no input into the compensation received for their plantation activities. At plantation assemblies, adult slaves and ex-slaves frequently voiced support for a five-day work week. The free life, they argued, could materialize with caps on the number of mandatory day and work hours.

Where plantation assemblies affected imaginings of an indigenous civil order, the vèvè architectonic of postslavery Haitian constituent assemblies was thought to be a stabilizing mediator of any entropic forces of the political order. What we can call *proto-constituent assemblies* existed in the immediate aftermath of temporary French abolition. These embryonic civil assembly spaces allowed for pluralistic participation. Unlike in the colonial state, ex-slaves were full members under this civil body. One could be a speaker, a delegate, and seated in the audience.

Discourse was intersubjective, whereby a speaker on the docket asserted claims, and constituents responded. Decisions were a product of discussion, not *a priori*. These assemblies were "proto" because of the nonactionable nature of certain petitions under the regime. That made them civil as opposed to political orders. Nevertheless, the logic of their organization would be applied subsequently for reimagining the body politic.

Black women used the proto-constituent assemblies to protest against inegalitarian recompense for tilling on Saint-Domingue plantation fields. Although they worked the same schedules as men, save absences due to pregnancy and childbirth, women received one-third less pay.[43] Women declared their discontent in the presence of peers and the body tasked with listening to the grievances, conveying unhappiness to persons in positions to make changes and reaching agreement. Comprehensive freedom required equal pay for the same duties performed.

The experience of the interrelated elements of gender and race, referred to in the late modern language of black feminism as a human's intersectionality, mutually structure the phenomenology of enslaved women.[44] Those experiences, proto-constituent assemblies, activities of children and adults, and land claims help us refine the macro-philosophy of flight. Haitian constitutionalism is the realm where the peasant vèvè architectonics of political order becomes more apparent. It replicates the justification for rethinking in the sphere of politics an agent's place in the state of society.

Constitutionalism

Constitutionalism is the foundation of freedom, and it is contingent on the interconnected process of liberation. Whereas liberation and its cognates, emancipation and independence, can pertain to one or more agents, constitutionalism is an act of forming principles, articles, and structural mechanisms applicable to a mass in a political order. Constitutionalism is the fourth precept of sociogenic marronage, and it has explicit implications for the macropolitics of revolution and freedom.

New constitutions are a consequence of revolutions, but revolutions are not the only channel for constitutional change. Violence is not an inherent preconstitutional attribute. In polities shifting from colonial to postcolonial states, violence is an intrinsic facet of anticolonial activities, the thorny procedures of decolonization, and the natality of constitution making.[45]

1805 was Haiti's first act of constitutionalism following the revolution. Promulgated a year after the Declaration of Independence, the Imperial Constitution of Haiti (*Constitution Impériale d'Haiti*), has endured as a tantalizing document full of engrossing prose and linguistic innovations. It was a hybrid constitution, fusing the languages of abolitionism, domestic jurisprudence, international law, republicanism, creole royalism, and indigeneity. It maintained an outright denunciation of slavery, as did Toussaint's 1801 Constitution. However, it came into being under an order that Toussaint's regime would not decree: a political state independent of France. While post-revolutionary Haiti would institute several replacement constitutions, the 1805 text echoed most the constitutionalism principle of the philosophy of flight, expressed by those revolting from bondage.[46]

Four elements of the constitution reflect this. The first pertains to the announcement of the polity as the "Empire of Haiti." Initially asserted in the Preliminary Declaration, developed in the following section, "Of the Empire," and continued periodically henceforth, the constitution restates its creation of a state that is dually a republic and an empire. "The Haitian Empire," according to article 15, "is one and indivisible; its territory divided into six military districts." The word "Imperial" in the constitution's title refers to the polity's regal status rather than a doctrine of state expansion through external invasion, occupation, and assimilation associated with imperialism. The thirty-sixth clause, though, prevents the actions of the commander in chief and citizens from "any project with the idea of conquest" that would "disturb the peace and internal regime of foreign colonies." The royalism of Haiti's state name has overtures of other avowed empires of the age, including Napoleonic France and pre-Victorian Great Britain, but it must not overshadow the anti-imperialist republicanism contained in several of Haiti's constitutional provisions. Haiti is to exist as an *imperial empire* resistant to *imperialism*.

The second component is the anointing of Dessalines as Emperor Jacques I: Dessalines as "His Majesty" (Preamble), "avenger and liberator of his fellow citizens" (Article 20), supreme chief of the army (Article 37), and head of state, himself a supporter, like Toussaint, of agricultural plantation political economy. The mixture of state-as-empire and leader-as-creole-royalist bears a strong resemblance to sovereign marronage and its discontents. The hybridity of the constitution is a point of strain indicative of contrasting pillars of macro-flight. In spite of this, as Vicki Hseuh maintains, New World hybrid constitutions contain contradictory clauses within which those who were formerly subjugated through slavery and colonialism can have pronounced juridical claims on their behalf in natal states.[47]

A third feature supports this outlook. The trilogy of articles 50–52, in the section "Of Worship" (*Du Culte*), espouses unencumbered belief systems. In Haiti, "The law admits no dominant religion [*religion*]," and the "freedom of worship [*des cultes*] is tolerated." The constitution employs in its division heading the word *culte*, meaning "worship" (primarily) or "religion," instead of *religion*, the same spelling in English as French. While *cult* in English suggests a quasi-religious entity whose practices are held under suspicion and strict scrutiny among nonadherents, *culte* denotes a mode of worship that practitioners and nonfollowers must hold in mutual respect. *Culte* includes formal religious groups, rituals, and the metaphysical convictions of individuals.

The constitution did not mention atheists. Inferences about the worship protections of those who did not believe in a supreme being are speculative, as were protections and constraints under the law of slavery for practitioners of vodou, which was not named in the body of the 1685 *Code Noir* but was implicitly held in contempt and fear as a form of worship other than that of the Roman Apostolic Church. The 1805 Constitution's pluralism of *culte* sanctioned by the state radically alters previous Francophone jurisprudence, diverging from the law of slavery and the stipulations of the L'Ouverture regime. Where Toussaint decreed Roman Catholicism the official state religion, the constitution protected multiple beliefs, whether vodou and Catholicism, Protestantism, and other religious and nonreligious worship.

It should also not be forgotten that until this constitution, Judaism was outlawed. The dogma of the *Code Noir* barred the practice of Judaism and the presence of persons identified as Jewish and of Jewish descent on the island. Where constitutionalism in revolutionary times at best submerged Judaism to the private sphere, public acknowledgement of Judaism was not tolerated. The constitution overturned this.

More than Judaism, it was vodou, "the medium of conspiracy" for the revolution in the words of C. L. R. James,[48] the religion with the largest percentage of peasants subscribing to its tenets, that the 1805 Constitution emboldened. Something is missed when observers polarize the constitutional projects of the French and Haitian Revolutions by reducing the former to the genesis of a bourgeois separation of church and state, a product of modern secularization, disenchantment, and secularism, and the latter to the unity of state and religious doctrines, the theological determining the architecture of the body politic.

That interpretation is inaccurate, for neither revolution results in theocracy, and political theologies exist in the respective postrevolutionary states despite what has been called by Hans Blumenberg, Saba Mahmood, and Charles Taylor a secular age. It also neglects a phenomenology at the heart of all acts of flight, before, during, and after the Age of Revolution: the enabling of an agent to participate in private, public, and social life without the coercion of another agent, whether an individual, an institution of the civil order, or the state apparatus. *Non-sovereignty* defines this condition of directed movement, enabled participatory action, and absent external decisionism.

Notwithstanding the torture of the collar, the four-post tying of a slave's hands and arms to the grounds, mutilation, and the master's death drive, enslaved peasants "remained, despite their black skins and curly hair, quite invincibly human beings, with the intelligence and resentments of human beings," as James put it.[49] The implosion of slavocracy, humanism, and non-sovereign channels of participation are signs of an agent's entry into the political order.

The citizen, rendered male and isomorphic with the white under the biocentrism of colonialism, is inverted and transformed in Haitian constitutionalism. In the prior system, where the epidermalization of and antipathy toward blackness were constituted in bad faith, "BLACKNESS is trouble. Blackness is Absence. Blackness is a hole. Blackness is *that which has gone wrong*," as Lewis R. Gordon said.[50] Haitian constitutionalism mutates blackness beyond biological ascriptions of race and mummified designations of culture tied to race. The citizen becomes *black*, as do land proprietors, property holders, the women and men jointly classified under its label, and, by the act of renaming, the Republic. Blackness is now a presence, an attribute buttressing the self and the state of society whose visibility is associated with principles instead of phenotype.

And this brings us to the final mainstay of the 1805 document: the idea of political blackness. According to article 14, in the new society, "Haitians shall henceforth only be known by the generic appellation of Blacks." We know from the preceding article that there are persons considered white in biocentric racial terms included under the denomination black. These include naturalized white women married to citizens, and German and Polish mercenaries who reneged on their agreement with Napoleon to kill Haitian revolutionaries in order to quell the uprising. We also know from the twentieth article of General Dispositions that the national colors of Haiti were to be black and red, marking the elision of the color white from the former French tricolor flag.

To be black means to subscribe to the vèvè architectonics enshrined in the constitutional clauses, to be, as the Independence declaration decreed, "by ourselves" and "for ourselves." It is to be a citizen, to be Haitian, to be independent, and to be free. Freedom materializes only when we act to "constitute a free people." As the framers signing the Imperial Constitution of Haiti decree at the document's end, "We recommend it [the Constitution] to our descendents, and present tribute to the friends of liberty, to philanthropists in all countries, as a signal pledge of divine goodness, who, in the course of immortal decrees, have given us an opportunity to break our chains (*nos fers*) and constitute a free people (*nous constituer en peuple libre*), civilized and independent."

This introduction constituting the flight of blackness foreshadows the rise of other political conceptions of blackness, such as Négritude and sur-realism in the Caribbean, Rastafari, Womanist black feminism in the United States, Steve Biko's black consciousness movement in South Africa, Walter Rodney's postulation of black power, and Sylvia Wynter's idea of the Human after Man.

The metaphysics of violence intrinsic to the decolonization process, when coupled with the traces of sovereign decisionism left unexcised from the late revolutionary period, unleashed a sinister underside to an otherwise progressive constitutional project. Not long before Dessalines adhered to the constitutional provision folding cadres of whites into the category black, he ordered the island-wide massacre of whites considered to be political enemies. Exterminate or be exterminated was Dessalines's recourse.[51]

Land and property-holding privileges of whites surviving the massacre were revoked soon thereafter. Dessalines conceived of Saint-Domingue as an inoperative community, a fractured polity whose societal claims to com-munity were at best a façade on the level of the state and authentic only in terms of subnational groups and nations within the colonial polity.[52] Re-birth and the functional operation of postcolonial Haiti came at the expense of presupposing the annihilation of the Other.

Another consequence was the imposition of juridical restrictions on measures requested by enslaved women in the proto-constituent assem-blies. The former bondswoman became a citizen more than a century before women in the United States. The citizen had the right to own land, conduct commerce, exercise private and public speech, tribunals by a judge, bodily comportment, self-determining relocation inside the republic, work, and play. Adult citizens were entitled to suffrage. The masculinist language of the 1805 constitution, however, decentered woman and made the realities of women's citizenship status ambiguous.[53] The end of the Haitian Revolution and emergence of Haiti was the naissance of freedom.

Revolution, Freedom, Epistemic Vistas

In "Children of the Sea," Haitian-American writer Edwidge Danticat tells the riveting story of a young, late-modern couple separated by water.[54] One is a passenger on a tiny boat that has left Haiti and is bound for the United States. There are thirty-six other persons aboard the vessel, "boat people" in the colloquial parlance of G-8 member states, each aspiring to gain asylum from the brutal regime of President François "Papa Doc" Duvalier. Passengers give offerings to the lwas to protect them during the journey. They enter into Kreyòl storytelling, in which the narrator utters "Krik?" and the audience responds "Krak!" in order to hear the tale. And they dream of what might be.

The other is stuck in the Duvalier state and subject to the excesses of the Tonton Macoutes, a paramilitary terrorist unit created by Papa Doc to instill fear and carry out summary executions on command. The Macoutes are torturers, "dew breakers," known to revel in their authority, intruding into homes unannounced, holdings machetes and guns to the heads of residents, forcing parents to commit incest with their children at the threat of death, and decapitating persons deemed enemies of state.[55]

Among the boat people is Célianne, a nearly twenty-year-old pregnant woman who joins the crew after recent despair resulting from a gang rape by Macoutes and the murder of the child's father. The narrator on the vessel observes Célianne and writes of her actions in a notebook, a travelogue of existence. Born on the boat with the help of a midwife, Célianne's baby does not utter a single cry. The baby does not survive. Célianne reluctantly tosses the child overboard. The last person she throws overboard to the bottom of the sea is herself.

Time fluctuates as the separated couple describes the lifeworlds around them. The woman in Haiti is unable to avoid Duvalierism and the dangers of a state that has gone from authoritarian to totalitarian. The system of the sea ultimately engulfs not only the stillborn child, but also the partner whose experiences we come to know. Derek Walcott remarks that the "sea is history," and Edward Kamau Brathwaite says that the "unity is sub-marine." The same body of saltwater through which captives from Africa are transported and thrust into Saint-Domingue's slavocracy is thought in a later era to be an escape route. That assessment of freedom is premature.[56]

The man who never makes it ashore envisions the sea as symptomatic of the quandary surrounding the options of flight available to an agent living in unfreedom. He wonders if he "was chosen from the beginning of time to live there with Agwé at the bottom of the sea." To be submarine might mean being "among the children of the deep blue sea, those who have escaped the chains of slavery to form a world beneath the heavens and the blood-drenched earth where you live."[57]

Perhaps escape from the state is warranted, and refugees successful in escaping to another territory are significant in their entrance into diaspora.

It does not, however, foreclose the marronage of those bound to the land, those neither fleeing offshore nor to the bottom of the sea, whose flight is conditional rather than geographic, domestic rather than occurring under the limited rubric of the diasporic.

We should not read these events as tragedy, since the real import of Danticat's story is located in a consideration of Haitian daily experiences in the struggle for freedom. We must think through how inhabitants under the regimes of Papa Doc and his son, Jean-Claude "Baby Doc" Duvalier, do not give up hope in achieving their vèvè architectonics, as the enslaved of Saint-Domingue do not bury their visions of the future in chains. This requires assessing how a domestic macropolitics of flight is possible, the function of refugees and diasporas in the internal structural reorderings of the state of society, and how the local and the global are intertwined in the macropolitics of flight. None of this is without debate.

Discussions of Haiti from the immediate postrevolutionary period through today are predictable and often unsavory. Authoritarianism. Dictatorships. Witchcraft. Campaigns against superstition. Power struggles. Occupations. Departures. Homeless peasants. Color hierarchies. Hurricanes. Lagging restructuring. Earthquakes. More unsettled rebuilding. Freedom-loving nation. Enslaving leaders of state. "Haiti is the poorest country in the Western hemisphere." Global isolation. The financially crippling indemnity paid by Haiti to France after Haiti became independent an afterthought. Causal explanations abound.

While our aim has not been to decide on a single rationale, the legacy of sovereign marronage in the postcolony provides a key explanatory variable. Peasants in the nineteenth and twentieth centuries repeatedly challenged doctrines of state, only to be repudiated by sovereigns. The Army of Sufferers, a Southern Haitian movement, argued in 1844 for principles of democratic governance to be legislated as beacons of freedom. "The Haitian Revolution of 1946," a moment marking the rise of the Afro-Haitian peasant Dumarsais Estimé and the return of political blackness under Estimé's presidency, also involved attempts at reactualization of the long-suppressed principles of non-sovereign-centered freedom.[58]

Haitian masses enjoyed for nearly a decade a decentering of sovereign agency. The emergence of *noirism*, perversion of political blackness, appropriation of vodou rhetoric, public assertion of masculinity, the onset of rule by Papa Doc Duvalier, and renewed tension between the Haitian state and Haitian nation stunted sociogenic flight once again. The additional international factors of economic isolationism, cooptation, and regional containment forged the perfect storm for the siphoning of freedom.[59]

What competing causal tales generally point toward is a fundamental element of marronage in all its forms represented after 1804: just as an agent can become free, an agent can fall out of the free condition. This does not mean the Haitian revolutionary project of sociogenic flight is flawed. It suggests that flight, sociogenic and otherwise, is inertia-resistant and subject to flux. The Haitian Revolution exhibits radical epistemic vistas whose inability to sustain freedom in Haiti on a macropolitical level in the phenomenal world should not obviate its value for our ways of thinking and knowing. "Beyond the mountains there are mountains."

PART THREE

Freedom as Marronage in Late Modernity

On the notion of modernity. It is a vexed question. Is not every era "modern" in relation to the preceding one? It seems that at least one of the components of "our" modernity is the spread of the awareness we have of it. The awareness of our awareness (the double, the second degree) is our source of strength and our torment [orig. emphasis].

—Édouard Glissant, *Caribbean Discourse*

In the contemporary world, the future of our freedom lies in the daunting task of taming Leviathan, not evading it.

—James C. Scott, *The Art of Not Being Governed*

FIVE

Marronage between Past and Future

... the maroon's vocation, which is to be permanently opposed to everything down below, the plain and the people enslaved to it, and thus to find the strength to survive.
—Édouard Glissant, *The Fourth Century*[1]

The need for this unanimity, not imposed by some prefabricated ideology, and possible in a Caribbean context, dictates the choices made by Martinican militants: there is no alternative to a uniting of all those who struggle for independence. Have I, in saying this, drifted away from the idea of cross-cultural poetics [*la Relation*]? No. It is built on the voices of all peoples, what I have called their inscrutability, which is nothing, after all, but an expression of their freedom.
—Édouard Glissant, *Caribbean Discourse*[2]

The figure of the Maroon as the nonassimilated Antillean will therefore be central to Glissant's oeuvre, to its inscription of the "antithetical values" between the rebellious, "nondomesticated" mountains, based on the ancestral African cultural model, and those of the "tamed landscape of the lowlands," based first on the model of the plantation, then on that of contemporary France—a model which, I hope to show, is itself instituted for both the French and the Martinicans by the Word of "Man" and its related order of discourse.
—Sylvia Wynter, "Beyond the Word of Man"[3]

Introduction

Three vignettes capture an interrelated set of dilemmas that confront those aiming to articulate political freedom in late modernity. The first surrounds the widespread debates in France over the commemoration of the abolition of the slave trade. In 1848, the French government issued the decree abolishing slavery throughout France and the country's colonies. During the months leading up to 1998, heated discussions occurred regarding how France should address the date of abolition one hundred and fifty years later. Among the responses voiced were calls for slavery reparations, the construction of sites of memory, and the ignoring of past historical injustices in order to focus on the present and future.[4]

Under former President Jacques Chirac, France in 2006 became the first Western polity to devote a day—May 10th—to the annual commemoration of a country's prior involvement in the slave trade. Chirac used the announcement of this act to appoint Édouard Glissant as chair of a newly formed Slavery Remembrance Committee, whose task would be to create multiple spaces where future remembrances could occur.[5] President Chirac, in the proclamation, designated slavery to be a crime against humanity and an institution that must be remembered so as to prevent any other national retrenchments into the atrocity. The decision of the Chirac government received both outright denunciations and an ambiguous reception from many across France, including Chirac's successor, President Nicolas Sarkozy.

The second vignette comes from the beginning of 2009, when general strikes erupted across the French overseas *départements* of Guadeloupe and Martinique. The previous year, financial markets collapsed throughout the world, placing even G-8 countries' fiscal status into uncertainty. France has long asserted a universalist national policy of assimilation such that residents of *départements*, whether within the former metropole or overseas territories, retain the same status as French citizens, regardless of one's self or imposed ascriptive characteristics. Despite this policy, residents in overseas *départements* felt a neglect occurring that belied claims to universalism. Island citizens suggested that ascriptive markers of class and race actually signaled rampant inequities.[6]

Guadeloupe and Martinique at the time were also at the very top of the list of territories with the highest unemployment in the European Union. The prices of commodities and living expenses increased exponentially as work continued to disappear. Disgruntled residents eventually took to the streets, picketed, demanded accountability and attention, and yet simultaneously faced the reality that their islands had neither advocated for independence from, nor enacted a revolution against France. The paradox of asserting particularity amidst being a part of a universal French body ensued. Only after the French government conceded to a series of demands did the general strikes end.

The third key moment, beyond solely the Francophone world, is still unfolding. From December 2010 into 2013, revolutions against authoritarian rulers erupted in the Middle East and North Africa. The revolutions in Egypt, Tunisia, Libya, Syria, and Yemen have been especially noteworthy. Although the specifics of each country's uprising have differed during the Arab Spring, there are commonalities that have confounded scholars who had not probed closely enough into the meaning of freedom. Most of the uprisings have been organic, without premeditated planning. Most situate the activities of masses against the rule of a leader who has spent decades usurping power for personal benefit at the expense of the collective. Most challenge *realpolitik* assumptions of the War on Terror after September 11th, whereby the actions of a limited number of violent, non-state actors become proxies for the views of an entire citizenry thought neither to value nor understand the idea of freedom.

Perhaps the largest commonality among the revolutions is in the utterances and billboard signs of individuals and groups—a significant number of whom are young adults—who conceptualize themselves as slaves who desire to be free. That the Egyptian Revolution centered on Tahrir Square (Tahrir meaning "liberation") is noteworthy. The imagined structures of governance following the revolutions and Libya's decentralized civil war, however, are where commonalities no longer cohere. Moreover, liberation is but one aspect of the complex process of becoming free.

All three examples underscore our late modern impasse on thinking about freedom. The recently deceased Martinican thinker Édouard Glissant, I contend, provides a system of thought grounded in the concept of marronage that offers a useful framework for attending to the problematics of our late modern times. Not only does Glissant propose solutions to issues presented thus far in our inquiries into Hannah Arendt through the Haitian Revolution, but he also asserts a notion of freedom that completes a deferred objective of Orlando Patterson: to bring negative and positive articulations of freedom into a unified whole.

Glissant's political theory integrates the poeticism and historicism of Afro-Caribbean thought, scholarship on creolization, reflections on the post-plantation American South, the nuances of Francophone theorizing, and the contours of French and German Continental philosophy.[7] In early works such as the epic poem *The Indies* (1956), the novel *The Ripening* (1958), the play *Monsieur Toussaint* (1961), and the theoretical tract *Poetic Intention* (1969), Glissant explores the impact of Columbus's voyages and the rise of Toussaint L'Ouverture for revolutionary politics in the Caribbean and Americas. The middle phase of Glissant's oeuvre interrogates postcolonial Caribbean political solidarity movements and the meaning of freedom for agents in different nation-states who are seeking to reconcile language,

culture, politics, and conceptions of the political. The late Glissant—
exemplified in monographs and essay volumes such as *Poetics of Relation*
(1990), *Faulkner, Mississippi* (1996), *Traité du tout-monde* (1997), *Une nouvelle région du monde* (2006), and *Philosophie de la relation* (2009)—has a
preoccupation with modes of Relation and organizing in a world of a dual
political paradox—heightened interconnectedness and global becoming, *la
mondialité*, alongside the building of walls to demarcate borders between
peoples.[8] Glissant, thus, probes the possibility of Martinican and Caribbean
nationalisms as well as the global interrelations across nation-state borders.
Glissant's founding of the Martinican Institut Martiniquais d'Etudes (IME)
in 1967 and the Institut du Tout-Monde in Paris after the turn of the millennium were think-tank corollaries to the aforementioned body of work.

Most importantly, more than any other major thinker in the last half
century, Glissant situates both the figure of the maroon and the idea of
marronage (flight) in its multiple types—petit, grand, sovereign, and sociogenic—at the center of his entire work, from poems, plays, and novels
to numerous volumes of philosophical essays.[9] Contrary to the critics who
posit *Poetics of Relation* as a radical break in Glissant's thought—a shift from
the national to the global—I argue that Glissant is consistent throughout
his oeuvre regarding marronage and that the late writings merely reflect a
worldly extension of the singular concept underlying Glissant's work.[10]

The core of this chapter provides a philosophical reading of two Glissant
texts from the early and middle phases that engage the interrelated historical
and imaginative valences of marronage: Glissant's 1964 novel, *Le quatrième
siècle* (*The Fourth Century*) and his 1981 magnum opus, *Le discours antillais*
(*Caribbean Discourse*). References to Glissant's *La case du commandeur* (*The
Overseer's Cabin*)—also published in 1981—*Poetics of Relation*, and select
writings from the early to late Glissant are included in order to supplement
the overall claims. In articulating the valences of marronage within the
works, Glissant develops key notions such as *le retour* and *le détour*, prophetic
vision of the past, *Antillanité* (Caribbeanness), and creolization as Relation
(*la Relation*). The contours of these concepts frame what I contend is Glissant's four-stage blueprint for sociogenic marronage.

The next section explores the utilization by Glissant of the concept of a
rhizome. It considers how lines of flight explain modes of marronage as an
economy of survival, state of being, and condition of becoming, from fugitive acts of truancy and attempts at liberation to the constructive constitution
of freedom. The chapter concludes with a discussion of marronage as a vocation and the practical implications of Glissant's system for contemporary
politics. I indicate throughout amended translations and, where pertinent,

citations from original French passages deleted in the English-language editions. To fully understand freedom as marronage in Glissant, however, it is necessary to examine first Glissant's interpretation of creolization and the creolizing of political theory vis-à-vis alternative creolization accounts.

Glissant and Creolizing Political Theory

The discourse on creolization emerged in Caribbean and Latin American thought, and it has since become an important framework in forms of thinking around the world.[11] Although notions of hybridity, *mestizaje*, and douglarization have a family resemblance to creolization, creolization itself has a particular lineage grounded in the slave ship, the plantation, and post-plantation politics, out of which debates have ensued concerning its meaning and utility. The English word *creole* (*criollo* in Spanish, *créole* in French, each derived etymologically from the Latin verb *creāre*, "to create") originally referred to Europeans born in the Caribbean and Americas, then to slaves brought from Africa who were born in the post-Columbian New World, and later to foods, gumbo representative of the latter. *Creolization*, by extension, came to refer to a discourse concerning mixture, identity, and the concomitant intersecting processes of language, culture, religion, race, indigenization, and the political. Theories of creolization challenge fixed, absolutist conceptions of being, although disagreements exist over the nature of identity in a world of ongoing processes of change.

According to Paget Henry, creolization is "a process of semio-semantic hybridization that can occur between arguments, vocabularies, phonologies, or grammars of discourses within a culture or across cultures." This process allows those previously limited in the exercise of agency to accumulate the "capacity for ontological resistance."[12] For Antonio Benítez-Rojo, three recurring words encapsulate creolization: *plantation, rhythm, and performance*.[13] In "Creoleness: The Crossroads of a Civilization?" Wilson Harris probes elements of voluntary and involuntary associations that lead to creolized ways of life. Harris questions certain claims to racial authenticity while at the same time demonstrating the backward-looking and forward-looking implications of the Haitian vodou lwa Legba, the deity of the crossroads. "Legba's creolization makes visible," Harris argues, "an insecurity in the pantheons of the gods around the globe. Such insecurity is a kind of arrival in tradition: it runs counter to secure ideologies or dogmas in which immortality is described as the grain and blood of hierarchical privilege."[14]

There are two competing positions on the meaning of creolization that traverse Anglophone, Hispanophone, and Francophone thought. The first positions creolization as an encounter from which new identities and attributes result and create novel, fixed essences that cannot be reducible to notions from the prior order. The rejection of Africanness, blackness, and artifacts of coloniality in the Antilles in favor of a creole identity and creole languages by members of the *Créolité* movement is exemplary. As the opening line of the *Créolité* manifesto by Jean Bernabé, Patrick Chamoiseau, and Raphaël Confiant states, "Neither Europeans, nor Africans, nor Asians, we proclaim ourselves Creoles. This will be for us an interior attitude—better, a vigilance, or even better, a sort of mental envelope in the middle of which our world will be built in full consciousness of the outer world."[15] A criticism of this camp, expressed by Maryse Condé, is that *Créolité* merely asserts another orthodoxy that banishes future difference outside the parameters of what defines being creole.[16]

The opposing position to *Créolité* acknowledges in the present the retentions of races, cultures, and peoples from prior orders in addition to embracing aspects of newness that have arisen in transplanted environments. The work of Kamau Brathwaite is within this camp.[17] Brathwaite, for instance, argues that one can—and should—speak of a rooted Afro-Caribbeanness, Indo-Caribbeanness, blackness, whiteness, nationality, and cultural roots in the region and around the world. Critics, however, similar to the detractors of the *Négritude* movement, question the metaphysical presuppositions of this model of creolization.

Between these poles, Stuart Hall questions the longing for origins and whether humans can retain facets of a premodern past that can no longer be accessed for historical and geopolitical reasons, yet might still positively condition how we currently imagine ourselves, late modernity, and our relations with others.[18] Édouard Glissant provides a comprehensive answer to Hall's query that also specifies a third alternative beyond the gulf in contemporary political theory between intellectual-historical scholarship and normative methodologies. Intellectual-historical work foregrounds contextual periodization at the expense of conceptual clarity, and normative political theory veers toward history-transcended methods in order to elucidate the pillars, scenarios, and propositions of concepts including freedom, rights, order, equality, and justice. Postmodernism sought to eradicate the false divide, but the turn to ending grand narratives of thought yielded a retreat away from the political, which left the divide in place. The exposition of creolization necessitates the bridging of this gap.[19]

In Glissant's view, creolization is neither reducible to mixture (*métissage*) nor to a system espousing desire for the atavistic. "If we posit *métissage* as, generally speaking, the meeting and synthesis of two differences, creoliza-

tion seems to be a limitless *métissage*, its elements diffracted and its consequences unforeseen."[20] By *atavism*, Glissant means the search for Genesis,
origin narratives, and founding myths. Atavistic societies seek recognition
in past myths and sameness without emphasizing alternative visions of the
future and acts of novelty in the present.[21] Composite, creolized communities acknowledge difference, inclusion, and multiple visions of the political.
"If we carefully observe the situation in the world today," Glissant opines,
"we can see that within most atavistic cultures, identity is an exclusionary
concept, whereas in composite cultures, that possibility is almost nonexistent."[22] Furthermore, creolization—what, as I shall explain later, Glissant
calls "Relation"—is ongoing, never fixed, and ever changing.

Glissant, however, does not dismiss claims to blackness or other forms
of identity, culture, indigenization, and concepts within the political, such
as freedom. He is insistent, nonetheless, that our interconnectedness forges
countless, unpredictable acts of newness that require careful attention. As
Glissant observes in "Creolization in the Making of the Americas,"

> This experience of diversity, and the long-unnoticed process it spawned, I
> label "creolization." Creolization is not an uprooting, a loss of sight, a sus-
> pension of being. Transience is not wandering. Diversity is not dilution. . . .
> Creolization is unpredictable, whereas the immediate results of crossbreed-
> ing [*métissage*] are more or less predictable. Furthermore, creolization opens
> on a radically new dimension of reality, not on a mechanical combination
> of components, characterized by value percentages. Therefore, creolization,
> which overlaps with linguistic production, does not produce direct synthesis,
> but *resultants*, results: something else, another way.[23]

Marronage is the key to understanding concretely what these manifold
results entail for Glissant's idea of freedom. Words and their conceptual
meanings move across landscapes, space, and time.[24] If creolization involves
ongoing natality, then the process of creolizing political theory indicates
moving words, moving concepts, and moving theory. Marronage, for Glissant, is a creolized notion occupying this terrain. Glissant's texts offer greater
supporting evidence.

On *The Fourth Century*

Glissant's novel *The Fourth Century* demonstrates how poeticism can serve
as a medium to specify principles of freedom that historicism alone cannot accomplish. The term *poeticism* refers to the spheres of poetry, fiction,

playwriting, music, sculpture, painting, and the physical and imaginative arts more broadly. It may include aspects of the historical, as Glissant's work shows, but poeticism differs from historicism in the style and form of the expressions of ideas. Glissant composes fiction that integrates mythic thought and phenomenological accounts of characters' lived experiences, going against a subsequent communicative turn in critical theory that posits rationality and reason outside the realm of myth.[25] The rational and the irrational—whether premised on metaphysics, myth, or individual belief—are each compatible with reason.

Reading Glissant's text requires awareness of disparate interpretations of the relationships among politics, the political, and literature. The "arts of the imagination" allow us to escape narrow notions of the political. The novel, in particular, provides insights into what Harris calls visions of consciousness and potential models to navigate the tragicomedy and realism of everyday life. As a specific form of literature, the novel can be generative for solutions to endogenous and exogenous factors facing individuals and society.[26] The political is an arena of actions, processes, and states of becoming between agents, and politics, at a meta-level, is the plane wherein a system of interactions acquires a name and logic to define its systemic order of things. Flight occurs at the level of the political, for flight is processual. Discourse on freedom as a concept of the political is an interactive discourse of becoming.

Poeticists capture archetypes of politics through political representations of becoming. The genre of poetics conveys becoming and is an avatar for alternative visions of the world. "Thus essence is to birth as relation is to becoming."[27] Poetics has a dynamic temporality that, unlike the purely historical, reflects and refracts the actions of its authors, thereby eclipsing inert time. For Glissant, the Platonic axiom to banish poeticists from the *politeia* should be shunned.[28] Poetics represents the tripartite elements of community, individual intentionality, and the relation between individual and community.[29] Inquiry into the maroon, fugitiveness, and marronage provides an intellectual space to articulate these pillars, out of which norms of politics coalesce.

As Michael Hanchard argues, fiction is especially able to illuminate the micro- and macro-dimensions of quotidian political analysis.[30] Furthermore, Jacques Rancière suggests that the politics of literature is not reducible to the beliefs, ideology, and personal commitments of a writer. A connection exists among politics, ways of doing and enacting the political, and literature as the art and practice of writing. "The politics of literature thus means that literature as literature is involved in this partition of the visible and the sayable, in this intertwining of being, doing and saying that frames a polemical common world."[31] Glissant deciphers a polemical world inhabited by multiple agents who inextricably rely on one another even when plotting to extricate themselves from the enslaving lifeworld of an opposing agent.

The Fourth Century is set on the island of Martinique. The story takes place from the latter portion of the eighteenth century until the mid-twentieth century and centers on two family lineages, the Longoués and the Béluses. The additional family lines—the Targins and Celats—trace their members to the Longoués and Béluses, and all four families become integral to Glissant's novels as a whole. The Longoués are descendants of a long line of maroons, and the Béluses' lineage comes from slaves on one of the earliest Martinican plantations.

The start of the novel describes an exchange between the last living Longoué maroon, Papa Longoué, and a boy named Mathieu Béluse who, in 1940, sought out Papa Longoué in the elevated forest hills. The Longoués and Béluses have developed a deep antipathy for one another, and Mathieu desires to find out from the elder Papa Longoué, a quimboiseur (seer), the details of the past and omens for the future. Papa Longoué's parentage is heretical in that his mother Stéphanise was a Béluse who ended up living with a Longoué named Apostrophe, going to the hills, and bearing a child, Papa, who possesses the gift of sight across space and time. In the course of the story, The Fourth Century explores petit marronage, grand marronage, plantation politics, the political after emancipation, land and landscape, and the dilemmas confronting both maroons and non-maroons alike in the post-emancipation period who come to the realization that emancipation and freedom are not synonyms.

We learn that in July 1788, on the eve of the French and Haitian Revolutions, two ancestors from Africa are taken against their will on the slave ship Rose-Marie. These men witness the atrocities of the Middle Passage, unsure of what their future shall hold. On board the ship, a fight breaks out, and one captive nearly kills the other. The ancestors eventually arrive on Martinique, immediately part ways, and decide on competing visions of how best to survive. The first approach, by the "Negro maroon, the one they hunted one whole evening with the dogs: Longoué," is to escape from the sands on the shore and run as far away as possible, taking flight to the hills and mountains to inaugurate a lineage of generations of maroons. The original Longoué is a "Maroon from the first day. Maroon from the first hour."[32] In the eyes of the plantocracy and slave population, the maroon is "the personification of the devil" because she or he is "the one who refuses."[33] Perspective, however, is Janus-faced. The maroon for Glissant is heroic, the ultimate negator (*Négateur*), who institutes a negative dialectic that, in the act of Great Refusal, rejects everything associated with slavery, the plantation, and creolization.[34]

The second survival approach, enacted by the first Béluse, is to become a slave, a creolized African in the Antilles on the Senglis plantation. Slaves lack the maroon's capacity for movement. "Motionless" is thus a word of fear uttered frequently in the text. Senglis slaves are all "motionless in the stagnating hours, walled inside white, motionless death," says the narrator.[35] Béluse becomes "the procreator of slaves for the Senglis estate," "watching days then years go by," pondering ever so often, despite hatred of Longoué, the choice made to opt out of flight.[36] Béluse presents us with the question of whether the slave is a potential future negator or the archetype of political assimilationism.

Papa Longoué uses his powers to transport Mathieu back in time to observe select scenes from the site of entanglement on the slaver, and Mathieu repeatedly refuses to acknowledge what has transpired concerning these two modes of existence and what it means to be free. Glissant, via the omniscient narrator, expands the boundaries of dialectical analysis on slavery and freedom through examination beyond the bi-directional framework of the worlds of masters and slaves. Glissant describes a third-tier of complexity: the distinction between slaves and maroons. In *The Overseer's Cabin*, Glissant shall introduce a fourth-tier agent—the black overseer—who, in the language of Caribbean interpretations of Shakespeare's *The Tempest*, occupies a liminal, spectral role similar to that of Ariel.[37]

Names and the act of naming are critical to Glissant's explication of freedom. Whereas Béluse is *given* a name by his plantation mistress, Longoué *chooses* one. "I named you Béluse for the good use I could make of you."[38] Longoué deplores the reduction of humans to utility and instrumental reason. Longoué's act of taking his name is demonstrative. "He took the word [*dongré*] and said it his way: 'Longoué, Longoué.'"[39] The name Liberté Longoué is chosen in *The Fourth Century* first for one of Longoué's sons and second for his granddaughter, in requiem for the murder of that son:

> Liberté the ancestor's second son, who was given that name because his father had refused to crouch to slavery on the Acajou estates; and so on for all the others, there was always some explanation for the names. The names appeared out of the dark, it was just a matter of seeing them and grabbing them.[40]

In *The Overseer's Cabin*, the Liberté Longoués reappear with a note on the meaning of freedom (*liberté*) as a program of becoming:

> We had remarked that Liberté was not a name but a memory: that of Liberté
> Longoué, Melchoir's brother, the man whose laughter was in centipedes, in-
> spired by wind and leaves—whose name had not been a name but a program:
> "Liberty," in the language of those very men who enslaved at the same time
> as they proclaimed that they liberated. . . . We thought Melchoir had, so to
> speak, dedicated his daughter to beginning his brother anew. . . . She had
> black maroon blood in her, something we know nothing about.[41]

These "Names of freedom," as Priska Degras notes,[42] underscore both the
promises and difficulties of living a life of refusal, for Liberté the granddaughter, like her deceased uncle, "suffered from her name: from the confu-
sion into which she had dissolved."[43]

Liberté the granddaughter and the Longoué line face an ambivalent
emancipation. France's abolition proclamation declares freedom for slaves
during a time when the maroons had been fleeing both slaves and masters to
preserve their space in the hills. Freedom is *given*, not taken. There were scattered revolts and no revolution equivalent to Saint-Domingue. At the same
time, emancipation mutates temporality, forcing the Longoué maroons to
interact openly with ex-slaves and former slave masters for the first time in
nearly sixty years.

The narration of these tiers of personages meeting at the name regis-
tration bureau is evocative. The post-emancipation state catalogues the
identity of island residents, recording in law a segment of the population
that rejected state legalism. The maroons have dignity in already possessing
names of their choosing, but they experience alienation when confronting
the creolized subjects whom they have fled for so long.[44] The remainder of
the text explores whether episodic acts of petit marronage and larger-scale
grand marronage are either feasible or desirable and if we can ever be truly
autonomous agents in a world of heightened interconnectedness.

Glissant poses in stark terms the benefits and limitations of freedom
for existence in state versus non-state spaces. The lowland areas, comprising plantations, valleys, and apparatuses of modern statecraft, are *zones of
appropriation*. Such zones are territories of governance premised on fiscal
legibility, hierarchy, the idea of the state as a self-liquidating entity, and the
unfreedom of slavery. Modern states, colonial and otherwise, invent the
political vocabulary of development, progress, and civilization in order to
distinguish the civilized from unruly barbarians who do not subscribe to
the dictates of the state.

Non-state spaces, in contrast, are what James Scott—in reasoning similar
to Glissant's—defines in *The Art of Not Being Governed* as "shatter zones,"

or *zones of refuge*.[45] Marshes, swamps, mangroves, hills, and mountains are sites of resistance and sanctuaries away from the enslaving norms of the state. Flight from the zone of nonbeing to zones of refuge results in keeping states at a distance.[46] Escape from state legibility and the enactment of local forms of lawmaking, epistemology, organization, agriculture, and relations is a mechanism to avoid the appropriating dynamics of state power. The psychodynamics of qualified autonomy affects as well the worldview of the inhabitants of non-state spaces. Glissant's portrait of maroon existence in the first model of survival reflects these characteristics. It is unclear, though, if maroon communities can fully maintain autonomy from the state, as shown by the acts of raiding plantations for provisions unavailable in the hills. Moreover, there are problems with grand marronage that Glissant recognizes in the novel's denouement.

Martinicans have a saying that a black man is a century. A corollary to this is the meaning of the "Fourth Century" of Glissant's title, which is neither a sum of years nor a marker of patriarchal right. Instead, it is symbolic of stages in the attainment of freedom. "'The sea we cross is a century." "And the coast where you debark, blinded and with no soul or voice, is a century. And the forest . . . is a century. And the land . . . is a century.'" Blood, death, suffering, naming, hope, and natality are knotted together.[47]

This, then, brings us to the novel's conclusion. Following the death of Papa Longoué, Mathieu Béluse marries Marie Célat—known also as Mycéa—an ancestor of the Liberté Longoué the second and a descendant of maroons who did not adhere to a maroon existence throughout the generations. Mycéa is the central figure in Glissant's *The Overseer's Cabin*, for she shall be deemed mad and consigned for a period to an insane asylum, despite being the most lucid of commentators on the human condition.

Earlier in *The Fourth Century*, however, Mycéa and Mathieu marry in 1946, the year in which Martinique becomes a *département* of France.[48] Glissant presents Mycéa and the post-World World II Martinican landscape "after having escaped from that duality—hills and valleys—" which produced perpetual moments of tension and uncertainty. Mycéa and Mathieu ruminate on temporality and processes of becoming, and whereas Mathieu has a preoccupation with past time, Mycéa implores that "it is action" and the construction of a future vision for a mass society comprising hills, valleys, and interstitial spaces that must be forged.[49]

Maroons' resistance and power of political imagination are admirable, yet their aversion to creolization is a flawed inertia valorizing a bygone past.[50] Maroons undergo a metamorphosis in the denial of private property for individuals and retreat to frontiers that situate the earth as the material basis for a common humanity. They retain in their newer expanses static, nondomesticated notions of epistemology, metaphysics, and ontology that deny creolization. At the level of language, this is the difference between ontological stasis (*l'Être*, to be) and evolving being (*l'étant*) with new epistemic vistas.[51]

Martinique has become a part of France, and late modern challenges to its ambivalent status as an overseas territory have arisen. *The Fourth Century* is a meditation on how petit and grand marronage cannot offer complete extrication from slavery and how granting emancipation and *département* classification to former colonies is not equivalent to freedom. Glissant's *Le discours antillais* points to a path forward.

On *Le Discours Antillais*

Le discours antillais is Glissant's magnum opus and a marker of a definitive shift in both Afro-Caribbean thought and Francophone philosophy.[52] It is a work of historicism, in that it utilizes written and oral texts for means of documentation, evaluation, and examination of previous occurrences. Historicism is compatible with political imagination, may be complementary to poeticist treatises, and can be either solely backward-looking or both backward- and forward-looking. Late modern Afro-Caribbean historicism has been dominated by Pan-Africanist and Marxist thinking, which are often are in conflict. Glissant traverses stalemates, introducing a unique perspective to prior intellectual traditions. As is not the case in his novels, Glissant integrates lived experience into the phenomenological analysis of the essays without allowing it to overdetermine the evaluative claims rendered.

Intellectual Formation

Le discours antillais responded to a lacuna in Martinican thought that had existed since the writings of the island's two best-known figures, Aimé Césaire and Frantz Fanon. Glissant grew up in the landscape of the *mornes* (hills). In 1939, Glissant changed schools after gaining acceptance to the prestigious Lycée Schoelcher in the lowland capital city, Fort-de-France. There, he was influenced greatly by Césaire, who returned from Paris to teach modern languages and philosophy at the school after publishing the founding work of the Négritude movement, *Cahier d'un retour au pays natal*, in the same year.[53]

Fanon, another student of Césaire at the lycée, stated in "West Indians and Africans" the radical nature of Césaire's arrival. In Fanon's estimation, it was the first time that a lycée teacher "was seen to announce quite simply to West Indian society 'that it is fine and good to be a Negro (nègre)'" and that "the 'big black hole' was a source of truth."[54] Fundamental to coining of the neologism négritude was a conscientious shifting of the accent on the e in the French word nègre, meaning both "black" and "nigger," from a demeaning è to a prideful é to denote the consciousness of valuation of black self-worth when an agent looks into the mirror.

Glissant joined the Franc-Jeu and campaigned on behalf of Césaire in the mayoral election of 1945 as a result of the rise in black consciousness, the critique of white supremacy, and the increased inequalities instituted during Vichy-occupied Martinique. Following Césaire's election on the ticket of the French Communist Party—a party Césaire would resign from in a decade—, Glissant went to Paris on scholarship to attain higher degrees in philosophy at the Sorbonne under Jean Wahl and ethnology at the Musée de l'homme. In France, Glissant maintained ties with Fanon and met other Francophone scholar-activists. Glissant, though, adamantly opposed Césaire's endorsement of Martinican departmentalization status. The act of making Martinique a département, Glissant argued, was the "most concrete form of fear and self-denial, marking the extreme edge of alienation, the limit of self-expression as well."[55]

The 1959 riots in Fort-de-France, coupled with this ongoing political and philosophical disagreement, led Glissant to co-found the Front-Antillo-Guyanais pour l'Autonomie (FAGA), the primary unrealized goal of which was the achievement of Martinican independence from France. General Charles de Gaulle banned Glissant because of this activism, relegating Glissant to travel within France.[56] De Gaulle's decision is perhaps unsurprising given his stated position on a visit to Martinique: "Between Europe and America I see only specks of dust."[57] FAGA would fold in the year of Fanon's death and the posthumous release of The Wretched of the Earth. Glissant published The Fourth Century in exile shortly before the lifting of the travel ban, and he returned to Martinique in 1965. It is from this moment through the next sixteen years that Glissant forged the intentional concept of the political contained in Le discours antillais.

Glissant acknowledges the vital contributions of Césaire to black consciousness and Fanon to theorizations of racial identity, revolutionary violence, and the psychodynamics of coloniality. Glissant states unequivocally that it "is difficult for a French Caribbean individual to be the brother, the friend, or quite simply the associate or fellow countryman of Fanon. Because of all the French Caribbean intellectuals, he is the only one to have acted on his ideas."[58] Freedom, in Glissant's view, nevertheless requires another vision that incorporates flight from unfreedom, the call to action, *and* a blueprint (vèvè architectonics) for existence in refashioned modern states.

Stages of Freedom

I argue that Glissant develops the blueprint for sociogenic marronage in four stages. The first stage is *rearticulating a philosophy of history*. The enslaved inhabit a world that characterizes much of the evidence of their existence as irrelevant. The start of enslavement and forms of slave trading create a dislocation between a slave's surroundings, nature, and accumulation of experiences, that is, culture. The nature-culture divide ruptures a slave's historical consciousness and impedes an agent's desire to flee from unfreedom. The totalitarian philosophy of history imposed by masters eradicates slaves' individual and collective memories, which are essential to upholding a people's consciousness and the formation of communities. The psychological wage, the "ideological blockage," is as damaging internally to agents as physical coercion and the economic blockades of states deemed heretical to global powers. Glissant refers to the lack of an agent's capacity for collective consciousness as *nonhistory*.[59]

Glissant resists G. W. F. Hegel's framework in the *Philosophy of History* and *Philosophy of Right* that situates African peoples and their descendents as unhistorical, Amerindians as prehistorical, and Europeans and their progeny within the realm of History and the march of *Geist*. Teleological philosophies of history produce the illusion of a lone root History. What Walter Benjamin only intimates in the eighth and twelfth propositions of "Theses on the Philosophy of History," Glissant explicates with precision.[60] Multiple histories exist, and this is why Glissant writes of human behavior in terms of *transversality* rather than a singular *generalizing universality*.[61] It is acts of merging nature and culture, uncovering and/or preserving abyssal histories, and prophesying the political between past and future that must foreground projects of flight:

> That means also that our history emerges at the edge of what we can tolerate, this emergence must be related immediately to the complicated web of events in our past. The past, to which we were subjected, which has not yet emerged as history for us, is, however, obsessively present. . . . This exploration is therefore related neither to a schematic chronology nor to a nostalgic lament. It leads to the identification of a painful notion of time and its full projection forward into the future, without the help of those plateaus in time from which the West has benefited, without the help of that collective density

that is the primary value of an ancestral cultural heartland. That is what I call
a prophetic vision of the past.[62]

There are notable landmarks in Martinique of dispossession, illusion, and
the failure to enact a prophetic vision of the past, the stakes of which pertain
to the local and global. Glissant's periodization begins with the masking of
the conquest of the island by Columbus under the name "discovery"—a
theme explored elsewhere in Glissant's *The Indies*—and continues through
the phases of colonization, the extermination of the Caribs, introduction of
the slave trade and settlement, the world of the slaves, the plantation system
and plantation political economy, the appearance of the elites in bourgeois
life, the triumph of beet sugar over cane sugar, departmentalization and
the Schoelcherist doctrine of political assimilation, and the threat of the
implosion of Martinique with the advent of economic assimilation. There
is a discontinuity between the chronology of events and the advancement
of a people. The paradox of emancipation exacerbates the complexity of this
nonlinear temporality.

Glissant's diagnosis of the nineteenth-century letter addressed to Martinican field slaves from the provisional director of the interior of the French
Republic regarding abolition is indicative. The director announced that
"Freedom will come! Good luck, my children. You deserve it. It is the good
masters who requested it for you." "You must prove that you understand
that freedom is not the right to wander aimlessly, but the right to work for
oneself. In France, all free men work harder than you who are slaves, and
they are far less happy than you, for over there, life is more difficult than
here." The letter ends: "Until the time when I come to say to you: 'The law
is official. Long live freedom!'" The document disturbs, Glissant notes, because it mirrors the dilemmas of dispossession and enslavement in the present. The breakdown of solidarity, the futility of post-departmentalization
sectoral planning, the urge to imitate, and the weakness of responding to
mainland state power maps the phenomenology of the dispossessed.[63]

Glissant responds to the director's letter, asking, "What has changed since
then? The good news still comes from elsewhere. Today it deals with the
publication of the figures for *official aid.*"[64] Emancipation not only foreclosed
freedom for ex-slaves; it inculcated an illusory liberation from bondage that
implanted systemic neurosis. "Political freedom has been only a constant
lure."[65] The double consciousness of being Martinican and French stifles.
The ex-slaves are aided instead of being the cultivators of local economic
provisions. They are the potentially underdeveloped if economic assistance
does not come from Paris. They are assimilated de jure and fractured de

facto. Glissant's normative assessment is a prognostication of the contemporary politics of neoliberalism and critiques in documentaries such as *Life and Debt*. But why? A prophetic vision of the past requires locating the neurosis's source and then building another world.

The second stage in the process of becoming free is acknowledgment of two contrasting models for reconciling history and future action and the choice to privilege the latter route over the former: *retour* (reversion/return) and *détour* (diversion/detour). *Retour* is the yearning to return to a single origin and fixed state of being. Glissant argues that individuals and groups who have been transplanted by force from one location to another develop an obsession with finding strategies to recreate lost primordial customs and ways of life and to return to an original ancestral locale. *Retour* is the negation of contact and creolization inside the boundaries of a new land and the reification of an imagined permanence. Glissant recognizes the appeal of the reversion impulse. The trauma of enslavement, the loss of cultural artifacts, the denial of public expression of language and religion after capture, the separation of family units, and relegation to the nonhistorical are reasons for agents to seek reconstitution. *Retour*, however, becomes impossible the longer a population has insufficient knowledge of its past. Prolonged distance from an ancestral land dissipates the insidious effects of the desire to imitate the unattainable.[66]

Détour is the desire to acquire freedom in a place or medium other than your transplanted homeland. Glissant conceives of *détour* to be both a trickster strategy and camouflage. *Détour* cannot occur when a people's consciousness as nation, within a state, is already formed. Creole languages are a signal initial *détour*. For Glissant, with the exception of Haitian Kreyòl, creole languages across the Caribbean and in polities worldwide remain inextricably tied to the language of conquerors and the written form in spite of their inimitable intonations and syntax. This interpretation posits Creole as a derivative language, a *forced poetics* that fails to emerge organically as a *free or natural poetics*.[67] At the level of political movements, the most prominent early manifestation of diversion in the black world and Caribbean thought is the advent of Marcus Mosiah Garvey, Garveyism, and the Universal Negro Improvement Association and African Communities League (UNIA-ACL). Other political programs of *détour* are Négritude and the grand and intoxicating political acts of Fanon in Algeria.[68] The political thought of Trinidadian communist and black feminist Claudia Jones could be added to Glissant's list.

The rhetoric of political mobilization outside the confines of Western nation-states, education in a foreign land leading to consciousness of iden-

tity from your native land, reassertion of valuation of the racial self, and utilization of philosophical and political categories of the West to project back
a critique of Occidentalism define political *détour*. Glissant's assessment of
Creole languages and Garveyism is debatable, as Garveyism, for instance,
is not simply defined by the escape to another land—the Back-to-Africa
pillar—but by the simultaneous rebuilding of the political domestically
and transnationally. Glissant's larger point, though, is provocative: political
projects that either obsess over fixed being in a new land or the search for
freedom away from an agent's home state without realizing the dynamic
possibilities of natality on an agent's current landscape are projects destined
for implosion or partial actualization.

The land, landscape, and the resources therein are sites of flight, restructuring, action, and prophetic historicism. "Our landscape," Glissant writes,"
is its own monument: its meaning can only be traced on the underside. It
is all history."[69] Fanon has already established that for "a colonized people,
the most essential value, because it is the most meaningful, is first and foremost the land: the land, which must provide bread and, naturally, dignity."[70]
Glissant enlarges the scope of the Fanonian injunction threefold in structure
and content, first in applying the significance of land to the category of the
unfree; second, by the elucidation of the interrelatedness of land and landscape; and third through emphasizing the role of landscape in a peoples'
historical reconceptualizing of themselves. Space is an overlapping attribute,
but Glissant does not conceive of space in landscape one-dimensionally as
sovereign place. By *landscape*, I take Glissant to mean then the domains of
physical environment, embodied cognition, and the metaphysical presuppositions of agents in an order.

The physical environment is geographic locale, objects grown from the
earth, and the contents of the sea. Northern Martinique is where the maroons
sought refuge, central Martinique the location of cane fields and plantations,
and the island's south is the realm of beaches and tourism, exhibiting the
distress of the late modern present. Embodiment is the cognitive result of
a people's inability to access entirely the function of the landscape they
inhabit. Slaves walk *on* land, unable to be *of* the land or to recollect how to
benefit from its resources. Alienation from the land and the past inhibits the
prophetic recreating of history.[71]

The metaphysics of landscape are the gods, deities, and secular *a priori*
interpretations of the landscape's relevance to the structuring of our past,
present, and future conditions. Myths and mythic discourses of reason are
essential here. Myths are neither tales nor folklore. They are stories of the
environment and environmental actors, and their rationalizations of the

environmental order of things affect the rationale of political governance. Myths bend time, producing history in their premonitions of the past and future prognostications even when positing narrative acts better shunned than repeated in human history.[72]

Conflicting conceptions of landscape among masters, overseers, and slaves engender disparate basic structures of societal conditions for the unfree and the free. The astute critic of Glissant, Sylvia Wynter, notes the significance of landscape for marronage and the central archetypal figure in Glissant's oeuvre, the maroon.[73] Wynter's own political philosophy is useful in discerning the stakes of Glissant's image of landscape for *retour, détour,* and sociogenic freedom.

For more than five hundred years after Columbus's 1492 arrival in the Caribbean, shifts in Western orders of knowledge (*epistemes*) corresponded to different representations of "Man." These regional notions of Man attained, at distinct periods, the global status of orthodoxy. Such normative orders masked themselves as generalizing universals of what it meant to be Human. Prior to the Columbian moment, the Christian idea of unfreedom in medieval feudal Latin-Christian Europe inherited from Saint Augustine was enslavement to original sin. Freedom and the route of entry into the City of God (*civitas dei*) lay in spiritual redemption from lust, desires, heretics, and temptations repeated since Adam and Eve's fall and departure from the Garden of Eden. The clergy became intermediaries between God and Man, showing the latter the way to exit unfreedom.

The late fifteenth to eighteenth centuries marked a new episteme. The advent of Renaissance humanism, the *studia humanitatis*, the acceptance of Copernican science over Ptolemaic astronomy, and the concept of races led to the emergence of the political Man (*homo politicus*). The disenchantment with religious explanations for human well-being in polities accompanied the rise of secular politics based on the faculty of rationality. The *homo politicus* conception of freedom was rational redemption from the mad, the racialized *indios* and *Negros*, and the irrational that did not succumb to the secularizing reason of state.[74]

The current order of Man that over-represents itself as "the Human" emerged in the late eighteenth century. Wynter defines this as the era of *homo oeconomicus*, bio-economic Man, wherein the normative order classifies the unfree as the genetically "dyselected," in Wynter's terms, in a time of natural scarcity. Biodicy has replaced theodicy as slavery's supreme source of legitimacy. Genetic difference, economic apartheid, and the biocentric identity of Man are the new normal. Freedom is the state of breadwinners with selected genes, and one acquires freedom through material redemption. The poor, dispossessed, and the purportedly underdeveloped evolve inversely with time.

In each episteme, the unfree experience liminality. Liminality is a fringe existence, a lack, a marginality in an order that nonetheless relies upon liminal figures to buttress a normative agent's way of life.[75] Epistemes naturalize cultural constructs to the advantage of normative agents' structuring of rules, regulations, and laws of governance. The liminal being, naturalized, is an organism with a metaphysical lack. Specific mythic discourse, like other facets of one-dimensional philosophies of history, contributes to the consolidation of political naturalization, particularly the discourse of origin narratives.

When political orders decay, *liminal agents* are the catalysts in epistemic reorderings of polities. Slaves are an order's most liminalized group. Liminal agents have their own metaphysical myths, secular views of social ordering, and embodied phenomenology of comparative freedom vis-à-vis the landscape. They are the potential revolutionaries.

Wynter petitions for the founding of another ceremony of knowledge, a new order. Glissant's thought invites a new discourse of the Antilles beyond the "Word of Man," accomplishing this with more nuance than Wynter attributes. Although the periodizing of regimes of freedom fundamentally contradicts Glissant's trans-historical framework, Wynter explicates a compatible organizing conceptualization of slaves on a landscape. Slaves are liminal agents who perform duties against their will because masters justify acts using the language of natural scarcity, thereby proscribing slaves from land access. Glissant would argue that this dynamic transcends the era of *homo oeconomicus*. It is a human problem.

Slaves must reconcile *retour* and *détour* on the present landscape. The environment, physical and embodied, metaphysical and mythic, is where the transformative in freedom begins. But marronage cannot occur until the slave, as the most liminal agent in an order, confronts a submerged, abyssal history. To understand political freedom and embark upon sustainable rather than fleeting flight, we must revisit the site of enslavement, to the *point of our entanglement* in unfreedom, and ascertain the processes of relation at that moment and thereafter in the landscape. As Glissant observes,

We must return to the point from which we started. Diversion is not a useful ploy unless it is nourished by reversion: not a return to the longing for origins, to some immutable state of Being [*l'Être*], but a return to the point of entanglement [*au point d'intrication*], from which we were forcefully turned away; that is where we must ultimately put to work the forces of creolization [*la Relation*], or perish.[76]

Stage three in Glissant's system of flight is the method of liberation: *resistance*. The essay, "Resistance," deleted from the English translation of *Le discours antillais*, is the primary locus for this examination. Jorge Luis Borges opines that the problem of translation is consubstantial with the study of literature.[77] A task of a translator is negotiating the original literal and contextual factors of a work to prepare for a mode of translatability to an audience in another language.[78] An equally important aspect of translation, when invoked, is the choice not to include sections of an original text. Translators are conduits with linguistic bridge-making authority. Mistranslations and sizeable abridgements of original works frequently distort an author's intentions, whether or not there is a political agenda behind the translation architecture.

Think of the effects of the first English translations on the meanings of the chapter titles in Fanon's *Black Skin, White Masks* and *The Wretched of the Earth*, the entirety of Max Horkheimer and Theodor Adorno's *Dialectic of Enlightenment*, and the substantial abridgement of Michel Foucault's *Folie et Déraison*, released originally as *Madness and Civilization* and comprehensively reissued as *History of Madness*. The motivations of J. Michael Dash, who translated *Le discours antillais*, to omit large portions of the original book are uncertain. The translator's *Créolité* politics, his personal and professional knowledge of the author, or, more modestly, a wish to introduce a truncated Glissant to an audience previously unfamiliar with his philosophy are potential incentives. What is transparent, however, is that most of Glissant's extensive examinations of marronage underlying his theory of freedom are absent from *Caribbean Discourse*. A recovery of Glissant on resistance is thus paramount.

If liberation is the negative dialectical release from bondage prior to the constitution of freedom, then resistance is the means through which an agent achieves this condition of emancipation. Glissant argues that popular resistance is an *economy of survival*.[79] In classifying marronage this way, Glissant notes that acts of resistance are sometimes violent, entail movement, and result in distancing between regimes of political order. He asserts further that marronage as a means of survival contradicts statist policy prescriptions of macroeconomics.[80]

I interpret spatially Glissant's explication of resistance along two axes: vertical and horizontal. The vertical y-axis of resistance refers to the differentiation between overt resistance and covert acts of resistance as well as conscious versus unconscious resistance. The horizontal x-axis denotes modes of resistance that can be physical, psychological, violent, nonviolent, individual, and collective; they may involve music, paintings, theater, gestures, speech, written texts, grassroots, and/or electoral-political action. Resistance may be overt/conscious, overt/unconscious, covert/conscious, and covert/unconscious, and acts of resistance may occur in non-state and state spaces. All these modes of resistance are embedded in the cultural and in lived experience. Wynter, echoing Glissant, correctly states in *Black Metamorphosis* that marronage has become synonymous with a cultural conception of resistance. The situation of resistance, in existential terms, produces an oath to self and to others to negate the impositions of unfreedom.[81] Mastery and slavery should not be understood otherwise.

The fourth stage in the process of freedom is what Glissant calls *Antillanité*. Glissant develops this positive dialectical notion in book 4 of *Le discours antillais*. In "The Dream, the Reality," Glissant opens with a proposition:

> The notion of *antillanité*, or Caribbeanness, emerges from a reality that we will have to question, but also corresponds to a dream that we must clarify and whose legitimacy must be demonstrated. A fragile reality (the experience of Caribbeanness, woven together from one side of the Caribbean to the other) negatively twisted together in its urgency (Caribbeanness as a dream, forever denied, often deferred, yet a strange, stubborn presence in our responses). This reality is there in essence: dense (inscribed in fact) but threatened (not inscribed in consciousness). The dream is vital, but not obvious.[82]

The content of Glissant's statement appears initially opaque and implicitly interrogative, but it serves as the essential foundation for the vision of *antillanité* that he will concretize in the remaining chapters of the text. Like Glissant's conception of creolization, *antillanité* is ongoing and never finished. *Antillanité* is the link between liberation as resistance and freedom as constitution. It is necessary, therefore, to specify its parameters.

To *become* Caribbean and, by extension, to become free, agents must cultivate collective experiences and convert them into conscious expressions.[83] The situatedness of individuals to nation, nation to state, and the land respective to all is important to decipher. Glissant ruminates briefly on the collapsed project of forming a regional Caribbean federation of states that in many respects was the progenitor for the European Union. Federation was a dream rather than a reality, because individuals within polities did not begin with an understanding of their placement vis-à-vis their nation. Elites constructed the contours of federation without input from the masses of people.

A nation is a collectivity of persons who share beliefs, experiences, languages, and culture. Territoriality does not define a people, since nations can exist either outside a homeland or without an extant physical territory, as the case of Armenians in the twentieth century attests. The characteristics and composition of nations change with time, and with creolization comes diversity that expands the norms of a people. The input of the people is paramount in expressing the consciousness of a collectivity that desires to construct another world.

Glissant's inquiry into theater as a space to voice the consciousness of a people is an example of this stance. Performance is merely one element of theater. Theater is a representational venue that transcends folklore while preserving the mytho-poetics of the political.[84] "All political activity is theater (just as all caricature of political life becomes a circus). If politics for us gives meaning to that which is being represented, theater can be considered as representation (or the signifying expression) of politics."[85] Theater rearticulates the history of a people, expresses the inventory of a nation's ideals, is dynamic, is an arena of action, is a disalienation catalyst, and is a site of resistance that relies upon expression to convey a message.[86]

Marronage, of course, exceeds the theatrical. Peter Hitchcock accurately indicates how marronage, for Glissant, offers an "aesthetic/political strategy" to critically evaluate the late modern Antillean condition.[87] Marronage also provides a critique of the operations of the state form. The state is the apparatus of govermentality. States may comprise the belief systems of a single nation, in the manner of the post-Westphalian nation-state model; of multiple nations, as in the United States; or they may de-align with the nation, as in the instances of Haiti under the Duvaliers, Israel after World War II, and South Africa under apartheid.

Whereas *The Fourth Century* narrated the excesses of lowland modern states as zones of appropriation, *Le discours antillais* posits a notion of statecraft that constructs the state—not the hills—as the region of refuge. Eradicating the valley-hill dichotomy is necessary to accomplishing this task. This does not mean preventing agents from populating the hills. Instead, it is an acknowledgment of unanimity through supporting differences within the state, from the cities to the frontiers.

Glissant restates in the closing paragraphs his view that the "independence of Martinique is vital to this process" and a pre-condition of political freedom.[88] However, to reduce *antillanité* to a normative principle of nationalism is reductionistic. Glissant's choice of the word *pays* (land, country) is, therefore, telling. Two main sections of book 1 end with chapters that have the title *"Pays,"* as does the fifty-eighth chapter excised from *Caribbean Discourse*. Book 2 bears the heading *"Paysages, pays"* (Landscapes, Land), and the iconography of the land features prominently throughout the text.

Glissant abstains from regular usage of *patrie* (country, homeland), *nation* (nation), *état* (state), and *terre* (earth, ground, soil). These are crucial terms, but not in isolation. *Pays* connotes the intersections of country, nation, state, and soil with the landscapes of a people. Revolutionary nationalism often produces slogans rife with the language of generalizing universality, chauvinism, and ethno-racial exclusions. *Pays*, the land, is the sum total of physical territories, spatial zones, diversity, collective expressions, and political strategies. No single person or place is sovereign over others.

A wider conceptual issue that Glissant probes is the context within which agents of the land living amidst multiplicity can found a sustainable political order. Any condition less than independence is at best better than a proclaimed emancipation and at worst a scenario in which symbiosis shall forever remain the fate of a people. Participatory democracy, Glissant notes, is fundamental to freedom. The ability of each agent to contribute to nation formation, statecraft, and the body politic is possible and achievable, even those in small islands. Glissant includes in the appendix a table of the diaspora that diagrams the interconnectedness of continental America, the Caribbean, and Africa.[89] The table could easily have been expanded to include other regions of the world. Glissant's point here is that one must situate Caribbean discourse among the myriad discourses and activities that have shaped the creolized landscape of Martinique and all modern landscapes.

Responsibility is the last attribute of freedom. Existentialists describe freedom and responsibility in terms that either ignore slavery or assume that we are born free instead of enslaved. Glissant rejects these premises, arguing that the constitution of freedom stipulates responsibility to the actions of an agent emerging out of unfreedom and founding the new society. Responsibility originates in liberation, and individual and collective responsibility cannot be the purview of those in power who seek to exercise power over agents. Similarly, agents previously existing in the zone of nonbeing who become free through flight and then abdicate responsibility are themselves held to the same standards. Those agents would thereby relinquish free existence. This dictate is not for Martinicans alone. Responsibility "is built on the voices of all peoples, what I have called their inscrutability, which is nothing, after all, but an expression of their freedom."[90]

Unaccounted Vistas

Le discours antillais is masterful work asserting the generative qualities of marronage. There is, however, a twofold limitation in its account of freedom. First, the text elaborates on petit marronage, grand marronage, and sociogenic marronage—the latter the most radical form of flight—and does not detail the strengths and weaknesses of sovereign marronage—what we established in the third chapter as the desire for mass flight by a populace through locating freedom in the sovereignty of a singular lawgiver. Sovereign marronage opposes isolationist geographic flight. It is collective flight within the contiguous land—high and low, near and far—from a previous order to a political order where slaves and ex-slaves defer to the idea of freedom asserted by the lawgiver-leader.

Glissant assumes prematurely an audience that has read his critique of sovereign marronage in the play, *Monsieur Toussaint*. Toussaint L'Ouverture inspired large numbers of Haitian revolutionaries to resist French colonial and imperial rule. He did so despite remaining throughout his capture, deportation, and imprisonment an admirer of the French cosmopolitan principles and supporter of a postcolonial model of plantation politics amended to local self-governance conditions. Glissant's Toussaint is a tragic hero, haunted in his Fort-de-Joux prison cell by the gods, the dead, the people, and the excesses of his sovereign decision making.[91]

The play is a temporal anomaly, for the setting moves between Toussaint's prison cell in France and revolutionary Saint-Domingue, with the specters of deceased figures iconic in Haitian political history visiting Toussaint.[92] Only Toussaint can see and hear the voices of the dead. Prison guards wonder if Toussaint is delirious. One of the dead is Moyse, a Haitian general and Toussaint's nephew, whom Toussaint had executed for insubordination out of fear of a challenge to his rising power. Mackandal, another among the dead, is the critical character in the play besides Toussaint. Importantly, Mackandal was a one-handed maroon whose name was synonymous with marronage in pre-revolutionary Haiti. Mackandal's conception of freedom was starkly at odds with Toussaint's.

Mackandal has dialogue with Toussaint up until the play's end, appearing to Toussaint as a *primeval conscience*.[93] Through Mackandal's advisory discourse, debate, and forewarning, Glissant highlights Toussaint's accolades while expressing doubts about the sovereign marronage model of freedom. Sovereign dictatorship, even if resulting from the imaginings of L'Ouverture's strategies of dual anticolonial and antislavery resistance, is not tantamount to freedom.

Le discours antillais continues to receive criticism as a putatively regional work in spite of its global implications. The late Glissant attempts to remedy this second weakness.

Rhizome, Relation, and Lines of Flight

For Glissant, freedom is a condition of becoming and Relation. *Becoming* is a state of emergence in which the processes operationalizing an agent's aspirations are the site of natality. Becoming signifies the core dimensions of flight: distance, movement, property, and purpose. Growth and expansion, whether qualitative or quantitative, are attributes of becoming, as is the denial of linear and homogeneous teleological systems. Human and nonhuman vitalistic agents have the capacity for becoming, and human agents can emerge or devolve from antecedent conditions.

Relation is Glissant's term for creolization, and it defines how agents link to one another between past and future. There are various beings in the world, not one Being. "Beings remain, as long as Being dissipates." "Being is relation," Glissant asserts, "but Relation is safe from the idea of Being." "That is why it is not: (of) Being, but:—(of) beings."[94] Glissant previously ascertained in *The Fourth Century* that peoples of the hills and valleys exist in dialectical Relation irrespective of mutual antipathies, a point reiterated by James Scott.[95] In *Poetics of Relation*, Glissant broadens the epistemic horizon, arguing for modes of Relation uniting the local and global in addition to intrastate and intranation relationships.

Relation mitigates the contradictions of chaos.[96] We do not exist in a vacuum, and our individual intentions produce actions affecting other agents and vice-versa. Glissant reexamines his long-standing use of Relation and supplements the idea with notions of the rhizome and lines of flight formulated by Gilles Deleuze and Félix Guattari.[97] Whereas Deleuze and Guattari are interested in rhizomic thought to criticize schizophrenic actions caused by global capitalism, Glissant employs the rhizome as a metaphor for Relation and lines of flight to explain further the act of marronage as a continual process of becoming in order to underscore freedom as a relational concept.

Totalitarian philosophies have singular root genealogies. The image of a tree encapsulates this rooted narrative. An arboreal root goes into the ground with a sole source that locates its genesis. The rhizome "as a subterranean stem is absolutely different from roots and radicals." A "rhizome ceaselessly establishes connections between semiotic chains, organizations of power, and circumstances relative to the arts, sciences, and social struggles."[98] Multiplicity, heterogeneity, deterritorialization, and myriad decentered roots are the bulwark of a rhizome. Like a plateau, a rhizome has no absolute beginning or end, but situates itself in the interstitial spaces of becoming between extremes.[99]

Lines of flight are ruptures in the segmentary spaces within the rhizome, wherein strata and assemblages enact movements of flight from deterritorializations. Lines of flight form between entities in a nonlinear fashion, and these lines, ostensibly nomadic, connect back to one another much as a boomerang circles back to its thrower.[100] Unlike vectors in mathematics that follow in straight lines, lines of flight are multiplicities with expanses that bend and meander in their extension into space, often erupting out of the abyss.

The *abyss* is a realm of the unknown and zone of nonbeing that paradoxically is a source of knowledge and world-building. Representations of the abyss at the point of entanglement in slavery are the womb abyss on the belly of the slave ship, the abyss in the depths of the sea, and a reverse image of all that an enslaved agent leaves behind in the savannas of the imagination. An experience in the abyss shapes who an agent will become, and it creates a shared experience of Relation with others and a body of knowledge that is a key source of exchange in any reconstructive process of freedom before, during, and after liberation.[101]

Maryse Condé narrates elements of this rhizomic freedom in the character of Xantippe in *Crossing the Mangrove*, and Glissant, in documentary collaboration with Manthia Diawara, retraces the abyssal landscapes of the Middle Passage in a cross-Atlantic journey from South Hampton, United Kingdom, to Brooklyn, New York, on the ship *Queen Mary II*.[102] The voyage vessel is posh, incommensurate with the slaver the *Rose-Marie* of *The Fourth Century* and the real-world carriers of human cargo. All the same, unsettling evocations of slavery distill in front of the viewer who joins in the crossing of waters before the appearances of mangroves, marshes, and sites of industrial building smoke. The inferences from Glissant's journey to the locale of entanglement resonate with Condé, Edwidge Danticat, and Derek Walcott's aphorism given as the first textual epigraph to *Poetics*: "Sea is History."[103]

There is a historical consciousness that the sea affords, as there is Relation of human to ship, sea, and new beginnings. It is fitting that the complementary verse component to "The Sea Is History" in Walcott's *The Star-Apple Kingdom* is "The Schooner *Flight*," a verse tale of the multiracial Shabine, a Caribbean sailor, married and a father, dreaming of his transgressions and aspirations, traversing St. Lucia and regional republics and encountering facets of the Middle Passage. *Flight*, the name of Shabine's vessel, is evocative of actions and experiences to come. Shabine faces an arduous storm out of which it is uncertain whether he and his crew will survive. Shabine lives through the maelstrom, confronting the depths of the sea as a way to experience rebirth.[104]

The philosophy of the rhizome applied to marronage is significant for Glissant insofar as it accentuates the *concurrent* modalities of flight from slavery occurring in the world. The fugitive's episodic running away from a plantation for a day, mutineers on a slaver, maroons in the hills, suppressed slave rebellions, the Haitian revolution: each is a different scale of flight that can transpire in overlapping temporality. Epistemologically, flight spans former and future bodies of knowledge. Access to historical knowledge is critical for the liminal agent. To rearticulate a philosophy of history involves multiple lines of flight and abyssal passages as nuclear components.

Glissant's essay "To Build the Tower" provides a historicist account through the examples of language and relations of contagion, subservience, intolerance, and fascination to bolster this contention.[105] Language is as essential to freedom as the clauses that govern a legislature's proceedings. Glissant favors multilingualism over monolingualism, but he also differentiates *langue* (the language one speaks) from *langage* (how one speaks a language).[106]

A *langue* is the uttering of a voluntary national language , such as Spanish, or the imposed language of French in Martinican schools and government. *Langage* is the use of a language such that authors, theorists, and politicians from Martinique, Jamaica, and Barbados, including Édouard Glissant, Sylvia Wynter, George Lamming, Kamau Brathwaite, Errol Barrow, Raphaël Confiant, Aimé Césaire, Michael Manley, and Portia Simpson-Miller can be said to utilize the cadences and intentionalities of a language even if their type of language differs. This argument applies to the interpretation of documents, including Haiti's first post-revolutionary Constitution, which, while written in French, contains creolized cadences and principles that both resemble and reject central articles of the French revolutionary *Declaration*. Attention to language-voice and language-use affects how agents build a polity and the Relation of agents across borders. Lines of flight from unfreedom fortify in the fractures sparked by the phenomenology of the abyssal.

Poetics of Relation considers the political ramifications of freedom as marronage. Our present age fluctuates between the illusions of freedom in neoliberal globalization and *mondialité*, a worldly disposition of freedom in Relation.[107] The late cosmopolitan turn of Glissant neither disavows local Martinican politics nor eschews the challenges facing national territories around the world. The Relation of agents to landscapes in *le monde* (the world), not simply *patrie, nation, état*, or region, is Glissant's fixation. World-echoes, world-chaos, and the totality of world ebbs and flows have moments of rupture that transform normative orders.

Poetics is prophetic in foretelling of one of the most significant contemporary political issues following September 11: immigration. Flight occurs within and across state boundaries, and yet numerous G-8 countries are implementing policies curtailing the right of persons to relocate within their polities. Land and territory are objects of contention in immigration policies. For Glissant, Relation identity "does not think of a land as a territory from which to project toward other territories but as a place where one gives-on-and-with rather than grasps."[108] Relation operates "against those who deal out generalizing lessons. Against ideology content with its own company. Against petty local masters. Against an intolerant, nationalist seclusion. Against those who erect borders."[109]

Glissant returns to the imagery of the *mornes*, the forested hills of Martinique, the site of a form of marronage in that island's New World plantation political economy. But Glissant warns that recreations of the plantation are happening right now. Tourism, neoliberal economics, ghetto communities, home foreclosures, the abandoning of villages, barrios, and other territories are emblematic.[110] Glissant is an optimist, make no mistake. He does, though, wish us to remember that freedom, lines of flight, and threats to the free life are a Relation, imperative of struggle, perennial work, and in constant metamorphosis.

Marronage as a Vocation

In the foregoing, I examined texts by Édouard Glissant to present evidence by a rare contemporary thinker who interrogated the negative and positive polarities of freedom and joined them into a unified whole. The idea of marronage was the central principle Glissant utilized as an epistemological bridge throughout the early, middle, and late phases of his writings. The choice of poeticist and historicist texts was deliberate, and the chapter suggested that a comprehensive analysis of political ideals would be insufficient without the knowledge drawn from poeticist and historicist mediums. The chapter explored the notion of creolization vis-à-vis identity formation and how creolization applies to wider concepts, including freedom, a notion that includes but is irreducible to the political. Additionally, by positing freedom as a condition of becoming, I challenged conventional scholarship denying the levels of lines of flight that define what it means to be free.

The three vignettes I began with reveal the present impasse on freedom. Let me conclude with a discussion pertinent to each case—Glissant, and freedom in late modernity. In 2007, Édouard Glissant and Patrick Chamoiseau publish the political treatise *Quand les murs tombent* (*When the Walls Fall*) in response to French President Sarkozy's proposal to create a Ministry of Immigration, Integration, National Identity, and Codevelopment. The treatise is based substantively on Glissant's philosophy. While its audience is primarily observers of Francophone politics, the stakes of its assertions are global, inclusive of debates on the Golan Heights and the Gaza Strip in Palestine, Arizona Senate Bill 1070, the United States-Mexico border, gypsies in Germany, Somalis in Kenya, and agents seeking asylum upon arriving via boats and on foot. The increase in migrants seeking relocation to France after 9/11, the War on Terror, and the rise in Islamophobia lead to trenchant discourse on security and freedom.

Glissant and Chamoiseau find meaning in the building of walls— physical structures, public policies, and the walling of rigid identities. Walls result from a longtime reification of the sameness of identity and the fear of difference. The manifesto criticizes the nation-state as a form, arguing that we do not belong exclusively to a country or a nation. We, the *tout-monde*, belong to places in *mondialité*, linguistic places, places of the imagination, landscapes of the political through which we have movement around the world *within and across* borders.[111] This stance complements Glissant's assertion that "we are not the owners of the earth, we are the custodians of the earth" who must espouse "an attitude of inclusion rather than exclusion."[112] Glissant's dismay with Europe's retrenchment to border policing is coupled with a belief that Europe, like the Caribbean before it, is transforming into an archipelago. Europe, Glissant argues, must develop into an "island-region": "Official, administrative life still takes place through nation-states. But quotidian and cultural life has already gone beyond this stage and has put regions in contact with one another."[113]

The *refugee-immigrant* is a late modern maroon straddling the outward flight into diaspora of genres of grand marronage and macro-visions of another world in the vèvè architectonics of the sociogenic imagination. Refugee immigrants deny isolationism and perpetual domesticity, and they desire movement across borders throughout the island-regions of the globe. Involuntary or stateless immigrants take lines of flight to flee regimes of unfreedom. Immigrants fleeing to another polity may have reasons that justify flight to a place where the act of becoming can expand. Refugee-immigrants, moreover, embody the generative qualities of marronage. Marronage affects agents who are stateless within polities as much as it does on governing apparatuses of the state.

Quand les murs tombent probes the politics of debt relief, the increased ministerialization of the French government, the idea of repentance, and the international development principle of codevelopment.[114] *Codevelopment* is a doctrine that aims to foster immigration that will benefit both the country migrants leave and the one in which they relocate to. The influx of refugee-immigrants and the remittances sent back to the home countries of migrants granted asylum, resident status, and, in some cases, naturalized citizenship can foster human progress in economic terms and in terms of moral philosophy by tempering the tensions among residual liberal, imperial politics of states in the Global North, neoliberalism, and the dilemmas of development.[115]

Cross-border flight opens opportunities to the refugee-immigrant. At the same time, the polities a migrant flees have the responsibility to restructure their states. They must undergo flight between political orders that in the long-term will allow intra-state strengthening and Relation between inhabitants of states and migratory diasporic communities. Freedom in our contemporary world lies not in the permanent evasion of Leviathan, but the taming of Leviathan through these lines of flight.[116]

Codevelopment in practice, however, has been a way to limit quantitatively the number of immigrants permitted into a polity, thereby making it a qualified principle. The word *integration* and the phrase *to tolerate differences* collapse into platitudes. Codevelopment arguably is not a joint venture, but a pretext, under the guise of the political language of toleration, to appease wary citizens, humiliate the immigrant, and stifle freedom. Although they offer only conjectures about debt forgiveness for slaveries, colonizations, genocides, and holocausts, Glissant and Chamoiseau are emphatic in their concluding appeal to humanity to abolish all the existing, menacing walls.[117] The reaffirmation of the humanity of the slave is a consequence of marronage, and freedom can emerge only when mechanisms of enslavement and partitioning are razed. This must be our humanistic vocation.

A vocation is more than a method. It is, as Sheldon Wolin notes, an epic calling.[118] Glissant upholds the dictum of marronage as a vocation. The *maroon's vocation* "is to be permanently opposed to everything down below, the plain and the people enslaved to it, and thus to find the strength to survive."[119] Marronage is neither reducible to fleeing from states nor to movement within state borders. It is perpetual flight from slavery and an economy of survival. Late modernity poses obstacles to the achievement and maintenance of this vocation. But then again, the absence of a struggle to survive on the landscape would mean that we had never experienced the process of becoming free in the first place.

Why Marronage Still Matters

> 400 years
> And it's the same
> The same philosophy.
> I've said it's 400 years
> Look how long
> And the people they still can't see . . .
> Come on let's make a move
> I can see time
> Time has come.
> —Peter Tosh, "400 Years"[1]

In "400 Years," Peter Tosh's haunting lyrical commentary on flight and temporality on the Wailers' album *Catch a Fire*, Tosh chants with a recurrent cadence the inability of masses globally to acknowledge a singular philosophical worldview shaping orders of unfreedom.[2] Tosh bemoans why people cannot decode the transparent. A move, Tosh implores, has to occur. Otherwise, our existence in states whose laws may no longer sanction forcing inhabitants to wear chains will remain forever unfree. Although the four centuries Tosh refers to encompass the duration of New World slave systems, Tosh intends for the point to apply to the state of society throughout space and time. "400 Years" is an example of a "prophetic vision of the past" in Édouard Glissant's terms, "a painful notion of time and its full projection forward into the future."[3] It is a call to reorient our epistemology of freedom around marronage.

We are able to decipher freedom's meaning when we acknowledge a basic precept of the theory of freedom as marronage: freedom materializes in the liminal and interstitial social space between our imaginings of absolute unfreedom and the zone of its opposite. The Hegelian legacy and turn to diaspora studies are two modern attempts to break the rigid bifurcation of negative and positive interpretations of freedom that we encountered at the start of this study, each insufficient for divergent reasons. Whereas the first foregrounds the experiential at the expense of reducing freedom to the awareness of self-consciousness, the second frames flight in purely geographic terms that shroud the significance of the liminal and interstitial. Marronage diverts the double-bind.

Marronage philosophy runs counter to the idea of fixed, determinate endings. This afterword is thus an ending by way of a beginning, the opening up of a conversation on a late modern movement that presents us with the benefits and complexities of the types of marronage in the contemporary moment: *Rastafari*.

Rastafari emerged in the twentieth century as a maroon movement with heretical roots in Jamaica, Garveyism, Ethiopianism, and Pan-Africanism. The movement started in the hills, spread into the urban spaces of Kingston, and reached into rural and city expanses across the island and later the globe.[4] In the late nineteenth and early twentieth centuries, post-emancipation Jamaica was still a British colony. With the end of the 1865 Morant Bay Rebellion, an uprising quelled before transforming into the next regional revolution after Saint-Domingue, there materialized a cadre of charismatic black nationalist preachers, lay intellectuals, and activists prophesying redemption and freedom for a disinherited black majority amid the antagonisms of a state fractured along racial and color lines. The revival cleric Alexander Bedward and Marcus Mosiah Garvey, founder of the Universal Negro Improvement Association and African Communities League (UNIA-ACL), would be most influential in this regard.

During World War II, a major event happened. The year 1930 marked the coronation of Ethiopian Emperor Haile Selassie I. Garvey foretold this in the play, *The Coronation of the King and Queen of Africa*, not long before that a black monarch would be crowned in Africa. *Le premier Rasta*, Leonard Howell, would be the first individual subsequently to proclaim Selassie I divine. In time, other adherents would follow, not without resistance, defamation, and disbelief by those who did not agree.

Although November 2, 1930, signified the formal introduction of Rastafari into the world's religions, members of Rastafari would say they have been Rasta from time immemorial. The first major Rastafari epoch began in 1930, for it was only then that the rest of the world began to understand this rationalization.[5] Other epochs and elements of routinization unfolded over time.[6] In addition to being known by the literal translation of his name,

Power of the Trinity, and by his title as emperor, Haile Selassie was referred to as the King of Kings, Lord of Lords, Elect of God, Light of the World, Conquering Lion of the Tribe of Judah, and as a direct descendent of the Queen of Sheba, King Solomon of Israel, their child Menelik I, and the Solomonic line recounted in the Ethiopian text, *Kebra Nagast*. For Rastas, Selassie was Jah (God), the Most High, His Imperial Majesty (H.I.M.), the medium for *I-an-I*, the dual, self-regarding and other-regarding communion between individual and redeemer.

There has been a mystery surrounding the naming of Rastafari. For a significant portion of cases, as Ludwig Wittgenstein notes, the meaning of a name reveals itself in the name's bearer.[7] Selassie, bearer and namesake of the movement, was born Tafari Makonnen on July 23, 1892, and held the title of *Lidj* (child of a dignitary). From 1916–26, he then received the title of *Ras* (Ras Tafari Makonnen), which is similar to "Duke" in modern European monarchical systems. Between 1928 and 1930, Selassie assumed the position of *Negus* (King). Upon coronation, Selassie was the *Negusa Nagast* (King of Kings). Why the movement is not called NegusaNagastI or another variant instead of Rastafari remains unknown. While the source of the movement's appellation is unknown, naming, language, and grammatical investigations have been central to its precepts ever since formation.

Rastas in the first epoch read Selassie I to mean the pronoun "I" rather than Roman numeral "The First." The interpersonal connection between savior and believer led to an enduring transformation of written and spoken language, the former enshrined by Rastas who write the movement name "RastafarI." The introduction of I-language (Rasta talk, dread talk) and the evolution of Rastafari from a Caribbean theological movement to an international political force were always grounded in flight and remain so.

Rastafari have considered themselves the true Israelites exiled from home, the children of the twelve lost tribes of Israel written of in the Torah and Old Testament, and they regard Selassie as the black reincarnation of Jesus Christ prophesized by both the Book of Revelation in the King James Bible and by Garvey. Although Selassie never professed to be the returned messiah, Rastafari reply that he, like the Christ described in the New Testament, did not know his divine status as the savior and sovereign of a distinct faith while on Earth. Moreover, Garvey denied being the prophet of the movement and was a virulent public critic of early Rastafari doctrines, including the smoking of ganja, the holy herb, as a ceremonial sacrament.[8] This has not precluded the situation of Garvey as a core figure in the Rastafari pantheon among the branches (Houses, Mansions) of the movement. The Rasta artist, Burning Spear, chanted in *Marcus Garvey* and *Garvey's Ghost* that Garvey's words regularly have come to pass, words that at times contradicted Garvey's own writings and speeches.

Rastafari employ the term *livity* to refer to its members' way of life.[9] Livity is a phenomenology; a mode of living involving a saltless diet, a lexicon, a style of attire; a connection to the environment and the *ital* (natural); a manner of interaction with self, sovereign, and other human; and a disposition grounded in mutual love and respect. Love and respect apply to one's family and friends. Those who deem you an enemy are also to receive your respect and love. According to Rastafari, by loving and respecting yourself and others, you constructively change the psychological and metaphysical dispositions of humans and all forms of life. Rastas follow politics carefully and are outspoken about their conceptions of the political. It is "politricks," the replacement of politics with an unhealthy substitute, notably in the partisan electoral domain, that members customarily evade.

The Houses of Rastafari, including the well-known Twelve Tribes of Israel, Ethiopia Black International Congress (Bobo Shanti), and Nyabinghi Order, acknowledge conflict and violence while disputing the use of violence as a mechanism of flight. The songs "Revolution," "War," and "One Love/People Get Ready" by the most famous Rasta, Nesta Robert Marley, and the contributions of Mortimo Planno, Judy Mowatt, Marcia Griffiths, Mutabaruka, Maureen Rowe, Ras Daniel Heartman, Ras Dizzy, Black Uhuru, Inner Circle, Morgan Heritage, Yasus Afari, Sizzla Kalonji, Damian "Junior Gong" Marley, Alpha Blondy, Lucky Dube, Lauryn Hill, Queen Ifrica, and Empress Barbara Makeda Blake Hannah through lyrical thought, writing, painting, and documentary films illustrate this. Nevertheless, the fear of the violent Rasta, first expressed by colonial administrators and later spread by indigenous postcolonial elites, presents a false image of Rastafari livity and how Rastas view freedom.

The razing of the Rasta commune at Pinnacle in St. Catherine parish, the forced shaving of Rastas' beards and dreadlocks by the police, state repression of Rastafari leading to the noted 1960 University College of the West Indies study, *Report on the Rastafari Movement in Kingston, Jamaica*, and the torture and imprisonment in 1963 of more than one hundred and fifty Rastafari at Coral Gardens, outside Montego Bay on Good Friday (what Rastas call "Bad Friday"), sanctioned directly by Jamaican Prime Minister, Sir Alexander Bustamante, a year after independence point to the discursive perpetuation of inaccuracies.[10] The unfreedom that Rastas experience in the wake of reggae's emergence and the slow but growing circulation of information about Rastafari tenets among non-Rastas further signals this distortion. Rastafari are not immune to fault, sin, and contradiction. Their discourse holds them responsible for actions, and it indicates imaginings on the multiple valences of flight.

The early Rastafari consider Jamaica to be Babylon and themselves strangers in a strange land. Rastafari are slaves exiled from a home they have never known. Their flight is a departure from Babylonian captivity, an end to a protracted unfreedom. Babylon is not the construction of diffuse individual actions. It is a system, and its organization is highly structured. Rastas strive to "chant down Babylon" from within, hoping Babylon's system will fall one day. As in the scriptural story of Jews enslaved in Egypt seeking escape from the confines of Pharaoh, Rastafari aim to exit a Jamaican state thought to reify alienation.

Zion is the Promised Land and region of refuge. In a shift of space and place from Jewish and Christian scripture, which interpret Zion as Palestine, Zion for Rastafari is Ethiopia in the original conception; later it is Africa broadly, and in more recent formulations, it is the achievement of domestic structural transformations of the Jamaican state, and in all interpretations it signifies cognitive realignments of the self.

Freedom for Rastafari, however, defies reduction to Exodus stories of a people returned from diaspora and geographic fugitive escapes documented in the Hebrew Bible, the Old Testament, and African-American narratives of flight from the South to the North. Popular receptions of the ballads on *Rastaman Vibration*, *Babylon by Bus*, and *Survival*—what Marley dubs in "Redemption Song" songs of freedom—and the tracks with the Wailers on *Exodus*, *Time* magazine's album of the twentieth century, usually constrict the wider meanings of flight rooted in Rastafari epistemology. While having less popular currency, Tosh's *Mystic Man*, *Mama Africa*, *Wanted Dread and Alive*, *No Nuclear War*, and *Talking Revolution* have a common knowledge convergence. These albums are outgrowths of texts integral to Rastafari: Howell's *The Promised Key*, *The Philosophy and Opinions of Marcus Garvey*, *The Holy Piby*, and Planno's *The Earth Most Strangest Man*. The association of freedom and Zion with place, condition, or communion with Selassie is a reflection of the Rastafari movement's metamorphoses over epochs.

The three Rs—reasoning, reparations, and repatriation—are notions as inseparable from late modern Rastafari discourse as livity, Babylon, and Zion. Reasoning is the mode of discursive, intersubjective exchanges whereby an individual testifies to a collectivity and offers input into vital personal, social, and political issues; reparations the twofold acts of public apology and rectification to persons experiencing a historic injustice and to the living descendants of the unrepaired. Repatriation means the physical and psychic modes of acquiring freedom either never experienced or lost.

Reasoning often occurs in circular and ritualistic "groundation" spaces and presents speech acts whose habitual rational and irrational logics function as accepted public reason. The atrocities of slavery are the basis for the advocacy of reparations by Rastafari. Whereas reparations claims are not part of original Rastafari doctrine and require mediation between Rastafari and agents of state, repatriation is one of the oldest Rasta tenets that can, yet need not, involve state agencies for realization. Repatriation is a recognizable legacy of Garveyism in the movement.

Dread characterizes the consequences and enabling capacity of unfreedom. If livity describes mores and a desired way of living, then dread defines the existential condition shaping our ability to cultivate those customs. Dread is first "an experience: it is the awesome, fearful confrontation of a people with a primordial but historically denied racial selfhood."[11] Second, dread is not anxiety, for it is more than apprehension of an unnerving impending reality. Dread amounts to trepidation and knowledge of a confining reality. That reality need not be an everlasting circumscription on the human condition. For the unfree, dread is the incessant contemplation of strictures of nonbeing, an encounter with history, and an awareness of the human ability to alter future states and actions.

Although Rastas have become known as "dreads," fearful to some and nonviolent righteous warriors to others, dreadlocks are an aesthetic and spiritual feature of Rastafari that was entirely absent during the movement's earliest decades. The subsequent doctrinal introduction of dreadlocks into Houses of Rastafari signifies the daily reminder of present and past unfreedom and the possibility for a genuine upheaval, an uprising. Dreadlocks are an external signifier, but the dread condition is also an internal embodiment. Uprising against enslavement involves mutations of mind, body, language, and state that must not suppress, disavow, or bend the history shaping who and what we are. Rastas "overstand downpression" instead of "understand oppression," the dread talk a phonological indicator of the refusal to be subordinate to another.[12]

Rastafari suggest an unadulterated confrontation with history and slavery. The heart is where reasoning on this begins. Love and respect coalesce under the dread condition once reasoning occurs and the decision for flight is made. The humanism of Rastafari livity coheres through facing the maelstrom of our past, embracing nature in the present, espousing a culture of love and respect for ourselves and those we interact with, and utilizing the imperative of change to fortify visions of the free life. No wonder the last major record Marley worked on, released posthumously, has the title *Confrontation*.

The current global reach of the Rastafari movement spans from Cuba to St. Lucia, Central and South America, North America, Great Britain, the contiguous countries of Europe, the Middle East, and the African continent from South Africa to Ethiopia, Ghana, and Zimbabwe. It reaches to the islands of the Pacific Ocean, including New Zealand and Fiji, and has notable branches in Asia, especially in Japan. With the internationalization of Rastafari and its emphasis on decentralization comes the pluralization of precepts. Rastafari now has, heterogeneity notwithstanding, overlapping homogenous principles across Houses and practitioners. Its heterogeneous composition proffers competing genres of marronage.

The first Rasta commune at Pinnacle and the original Bobo Shanti domicile in the territory of Bull Bay, which still endures, have their location in the hills. They share with the Jamaican Windward maroon communities of the Blue Mountains, Nanny Town, and Moore Town, as well as the Leeward maroon frontiers of Cudjoe Town, Accompong Town, and Cockpit Country from the eighteenth century a view of flight predicated on geographic separation from the state. The hills are their refuge. Pinnacle and Bull Bay Rastas stop short of creating states within a state, as is characteristic of grand marronage. Yet, in the case of Bobo Dreads, the idea of flight as physical escape extends into their repatriation efforts for relocation to Ghana.

Bobo Shanti adults are subject to a tithe, the sum total of which goes toward a repatriation fund for all members, adults and youth. This includes the performance proceeds of established Bobo dancehall artists. Bobo Dreads utilize clauses of the United Nations *Universal Declaration of Human Rights* (UDHR) concerning the right of stateless peoples in order to justify repatriation claims under international law.[13] As article 13 of the UDHR text states, "(1) Everyone has the right to freedom of movement and residence within the borders of each state. (2) Everyone has the right to leave any country, including his own, and to return to his country." Additionally, according to stipulations of the fifteenth article, "(1) Everyone has the right to a nationality. (2) No one shall be arbitrarily deprived of his nationality nor denied the right to change his nationality."[14] In the Bobo Shanti constellation, freedom is initially domestic separation and subsequently transnational.

Demands for physical repatriation as constitutive of freedom precede the Bobo Shanti. Since the recommendations of the 1960 *Report* on Rastafari, the April 1966 visit of Selassie I to Jamaica, and the land grant afforded to Rastas in the diaspora by the decree of the emperor after the visitation, thousands of Rastas over the last decades have repatriated to Shashamane, Ethiopia. Many revel in the imagined Promised Land, but not all repatriated

Rastafari experience bliss. Shashamane lacks sufficient water and health care provisions to sustain a large community. The repatriated also gain residential recognition without full claims to Ethiopian citizenship.[15] These problems lead to reconsiderations of repatriation, first in terms of the geography and second regarding physical escape as its customary medium.

The status of Selassie across the Houses is undergoing, to a lesser degree, its own transition. The divinity of Selassie, rituals, and dread talk together demonstrate sovereign marronage, the freedom of the individual manifest through the agency of the supreme authority and leader. Whereas Toussaint L'Ouverture has quasi-divinity in the Haitian popular imagination, Selassie as Jah is God on earth, an ambulatory state of exception.

All Rastas, however, no longer hold to belief in Selassie's divinity. Rationalization of this volte-face is explained in part by the coup near the end of his life that successfully toppled his regime, although Selassie was thought to be invincible and everlasting. Another cause for reconsideration is a result of questioning a dogma that Selassie himself never embraced.[16]

Between flight to the hills, escape into diaspora, and sublation into the sovereignty of Selassie lies the final sociogenic overstanding of freedom thought unfathomable to Rastafari at the turn of the twentieth century: the transformation of the Jamaican state along with mind, body, and language. In the new Rastafari millennium, begun September 11, 2007 in the Western Gregorian calendar, Rastafari finds itself at a crossroads. The fleeting flight of petit marronage has had little traction for Rastas through time. Rastafari inside and outside Jamaica, though, are rethinking repatriation, the Promised Land, and their relation to flight.[17] Cuban Rastas today overwhelmingly reject supra-state physical repatriation. They conceive of Rastafari as the mechanism to reinvigorate the ideals of the Cuban Revolution, ideals pertaining to antiracism and revolutionary politics that some factions from Santiago de Cuba to Havana think have been lost and that they seek to reinscribe.[18] Ethiopia, Africa, Russia, Dominica, and any territories beyond Cuba's borders are not regarded as destinations for flight. Cuba is still their Promised Land.

The discursive shifts surrounding repatriation allow for Rastafari in Jamaica to challenge and work with the Jamaican state, preserving simultaneously the non-state and state spaces that Rastafari inhabit. Immanent critique no longer follows a purely antistatist narrative.[19] Until recently, a single, ill-fated Rastafari political party at the beginning of the 1960s was the only sign of Rasta interest in electoral politics one could reference. A growing minority of Rastafari is becoming engaged in state public policy. Rastas continue to shun running for elected office as members of either of the two dominant political parties. There is a change nevertheless toward viewing the state as a partner, not an inhibitor, in the materialization of freedom for Rastafari experiencing the dread condition. What this means for repatriation is questioning migratory overstandings of it. Envisioning repatriation as a condition of the heart and mind has consequences for the political. This does not preclude Jamaican Rastas from demanding international and domestic reparations. It does foster redemption and, ultimately, freedom.

The promise and shortcoming of Rastafari during its present epoch attest to an underlying maxim of marronage: freedom is perpetual, unfinished, and rooted in acts of flight that are at moments evanescent, durable, overlapping. Marronage still matters.

NOTES

INTRODUCTION

1. Orlando Patterson, *Freedom*, vol. 1, 1991, 9.
2. Hannah Arendt, "What Is Freedom?" in *Between Past and Future*, 1993, 143.
3. Aimé Césaire, *A Tempest*, 2002, 60.
4. In contrast to political theorists who adopt John Rawls's stance in *A Theory of Justice* (1971), methodologically privileging what Rawls terms ideal theory—a strict compliance theory abstracted away from the realities of real world conditions—I utilize the perspectives of both ideal *and* nonideal theory. As Charles Mills states, "The best way of realizing the ideal is through the recognition of the importance of theorizing the *nonideal*" ("'Ideal Theory' as Ideology," 2005, 166). For further discussion, see Mills, *The Racial Contract*, 1997, 1–7; Liam Murphy, *Moral Demands in Nonideal Theory*, 2000.
5. Kamau Brathwaite, *Wars of Respect*, 1977; José J. Arrom and Manuel A. Arévalo, *Cimarrón*, 1986; Gad Heuman, ed., *Out of the House of Bondage*, 1986; E. Kofi Agorsah, ed., *Maroon Heritage*, 1994; Richard Price, ed., *Maroon Societies*, 1996; Kenneth Bilby, *True-Born Maroons*, 2006.
6. James C. Scott, *The Art of Not Being Governed*, 2009, 22–26, 40–63, 130–37. See also Scott's *Domination and the Arts of Resistance* (1990) and *Two Cheers for Anarchism* (2012).
7. Aimé Césaire, *Discourse on Colonialism*, 1972, 21. On the geopolitical context in which Césaire wrote many of his anticolonial works, see Robin D. G. Kelley, *Freedom Dreams*, 2002, 172–81.
8. Aimé Césaire, "Poetry and Knowledge" [1944], in *Refusal of the Shadow*, 1996, ed. M. Richardson and K. Fijałkowski, 134.
9. James Clifford, *The Predicament of Culture*, 1988, 175–81; Nathaniel Mackey, "Other: From Noun to Verb," 1992; Maryse Condé, "'Fous-t-en, laisse dire Aragon,'" 2000.
10. Aimé Césaire, "Le verbe marronner" [1955], in *Aimé Césaire*, 1983, ed. C. Eshleman and A. Smith, 368–69.
11. Ibid., 368–71.
12. Charles Taylor conceives of the modern Western "social imaginary" to be an idea distinct from social theory, and he contends that a society's moral order transforms radically the prevailing social imaginary at moments of revolution. We see this in what Taylor calls the contemporary Western world's "great founding revolutions": the American and the French. Taylor states upfront that his conception of the social imaginary is Western, and urges political theorists to take seriously the call by Dipesh

Chakrabarty (2000) to provincialize European thought instead of equating thought from that region as the only site of modern political reflection. This model endorses the language of a social, rather than political, imaginary. See Taylor, *Modern Social Imaginaries*, 2004, 23–48, 195–96. My contention is that a modern "political imaginary" relates inextricably to the question of the social. The Haitian Revolution provides a prime example beyond the theoretical optics of the American and French Revolutions.

13. Sibylle Fischer, *Modernity Disavowed*, 2004, 1–2.

14. Paget Henry argues in *Caliban's Reason* (2000, 1–18) that there are three broad phases in the development of the Afro-Caribbean intellectual and political tradition: the idealism of traditional African religions (1630–1750), the Afro-Christian period (1750–1860), and the phase straddling the late colonial and postcolonial periods (1860–present). This third phase contains two schools of thought: (1) *poeticists* and (2) *historicists*. The poeticists include Aimé Césaire, Edwidge Danticat, Édouard Glissant, Wilson Harris, Claude McKay, Jamaica Kincaid, Derek Walcott, and the early Sylvia Wynter. The historicist school divides along pan-Africanist and Marxist lines in addition to further subdivisions within those categories. Representatives of Caribbean historicism include Edward Blyden, Frantz Fanon, Marcus Garvey, George Padmore, Rastafari movement figures, Walter Rodney, and C. L. R. James.

15. Stephen Best and Saidiya Hartman, "Fugitive Justice," 2005, 1–15; Robert Gooding-Williams, *In the Shadow of Du Bois*, 2009; Cristina Beltrán, *The Trouble with Unity*, 2010; William Connolly, *A World of Becoming*, 2011.

16. *Oxford English Dictionary*, online edition, *s.v.* "freedom" (http://www.oed.com).

17. John Hope Franklin, *From Slavery to Freedom*, 1947. That one of his last books before passing is the coauthored work with Loren Schweninger, *Runaway Slaves* (1999), is a sign that Franklin recognized late the importance of the interstitial processes of flight, although only in the US context.

18. Michael Hanchard, *Party/Politics*, 2006, 33–44.

19. Richard Price's edited volume, *Maroon Societies* (2nd ed., 1996, originally published in 1973), was the first major collection devoted to marronage. With the exception of Orlando Patterson's reprinted entry, the contributors to the volume base their conclusions on anthropological and historical epistemologies. Alvin Thompson's *Flight to Freedom* (2006) and Sylviane Diouf's *Slavery's Exiles* (2014) are the most recent examples of texts that do not break out of the confines of historicism, despite updated perspectives on marronage.

20. Steven Hahn, *The Political Worlds of Slavery and Freedom*, 2009, 26. See also Hahn, *A Nation under Our Feet*, 2003.

21. The interventions into diasporic thought by Theodor Herzl, W. E. B. Du Bois, Hannah Arendt, Marcus Garvey, St. Clair Drake, Stuart Hall, Carole Boyce Davies, Michael Walzer, Rey Chow, and Paul Gilroy, to name a few, all reflect this.

22. J. G. A. Pocock, *Politics, Language and Time*, 1971, 3–41.

23. Ian Shapiro, Rogers Smith, and Tarek Masoud, eds., *Problems and Methods in the Study of Politics*, 2004.

24. Hanna Pitkin, *Wittgenstein and Justice*, 1972.

25. Patchen Markell, *Bound by Recognition*, 2003, 9.

26. Ludwig Wittgenstein, *Philosophical Investigations*, 2001, 90, 36 (orig. emphasis).

27. Laurent Dubois, *Avengers of the New World*, 2004, 52, 55. See also his *A Colony of Citizens*, 2004.

28. Kamau Brathwaite, *Roots*, 1993, 231; Henry, *Caliban's Reason*, 1–18.

29. Edmund Burke, *Reflections on the Revolution in France*, 1969, 123.
30. Guadeloupe and Martinique also have statues publicly dedicated to the Unknown Maroon. The statues recapture the disavowed "flame of liberty" that the realm of the maroon stands for. See Catherine Reinhardt, *Claims to Memory*, 2006, 7, 154–75.
31. Édouard Glissant, *Caribbean Discourse*, 1989, 64; and *Le discours antillais*, 1997, 227.
32. Suzanne Crosta, *Le marronnage créateur*, 1991.
33. Glissant, *Le discours antillais*, 118.
34. Glissant, *Caribbean Discourse*, 248 (orig. emphasis).
35. Thomas Hobbes, *Leviathan*, 1991 [1651], 145.
36. Isaiah Berlin, "Two Concepts of Liberty," [1958], in *The Proper Study of Mankind*, 1997, 194. In "'From Hope and Fear Set Free'" [1978], republished in the same volume, Berlin extends the defense of negative liberty as the primary ideal of freedom (91–118).
37. Berlin, "Two Concepts of Liberty," 206–16.
38. Ibid., 193, 195, 232, 235.
39. While this book does not examine Rousseau because of his proclivity for treating slavery as an abstract ideal rather than a lived experiential phenomenon, I explore Rousseau on slavery, flight, and the dimensions of freedom in a forthcoming essay, "The Fall into Slavery." Jimmy Klausen's *Fugitive Rousseau* (2014) offers another account of Rousseau on fugitivity and freedom's political valence.
40. Homi Bhabha, *The Location of Culture*, 1994, 1, 2.
41. Notable works by Orlando Patterson include *The Children of Sisyphus*, 1964; *The Sociology of Slavery*, 1967; *The Ordeal of Integration*, 1997; *Rituals of Blood*, 1998; and "Freedom and 9/11," 2011, 9–13. For Patterson's self-conception of the interconnections between his early and mature works, see the extensive interview by David Scott, "The Paradox of Freedom," 2013, 96–242.
42. Patterson, *Freedom*, 1. In the Distinguished Lecture commemorating Jamaica's fortieth anniversary of independence, "Emancipation, Independence and the Way Forward," Patterson reaffirms the organizing premise of *Freedom*, which is applicable across geopolitical spaces and time: "If I've learned one thing after all these years it is this: that the link between slavery and freedom is not contingent, not something peculiar to the Jamaican past and that of New World descendants of slaves, but a link that is intimate and constitutive of relevance to all those who claim to cherish freedom" (3).
43. Orlando Patterson, "Slavery and Slave Revolts" [1970], 246–92.
44. Ibid., 279.
45. Ibid., 276.
46. Ibid., 275, 277.
47. Orlando Patterson, *Slavery and Social Death*, 1982, 1–14.
48. Ibid., 39–51.
49. Ibid., 97–101.
50. Ibid., 334–42.
51. Patterson, *Freedom*, ix–xviii, 9.
52. Ibid., 3–5.
53. Ibid., 95–105.
54. Ibid., 203–90, 337–401.
55. Ibid., 405.
56. Vincent Brown, "Social Death and Political Life in the Study of Slavery," 2009, 1231–49. Franklin Knight reaches a conclusion similar to Brown's. For Knight, Patterson's "image of 'social death' is greatly exaggerated" and the concept of social death is unsubstanti-

ated in philosophy and social science. See Knight, "The Haitian Revolution," 2000, 105, 105, n.12.

57. Patterson, *Slavery and Social Death*, 97.
58. Patterson, *Children of Sisyphus*, 1.
59. Ibid., 100.
60. Ibid., 19.
61. Patterson defends this position again in "God's Gift?": "It [freedom] is, instead, a distinctive product of Western civilization, crafted through the centuries from its contingent social and political struggles and secular reflections, as well as its religious doctrines and conflicts" (2006).
62. Hanna Pitkin, *The Concept of Representation*, 1967.
63. Hanna Pitkin, "Are Freedom and Liberty Twins?" 1988; Eric Foner, *The Story of American Freedom*, 1998; David Hackett Fischer, *Liberty and Freedom*, 2004; Aziz Rana, *The Two Faces of American Freedom*, 2010.
64. Scholarship on the state of contemporary political theory includes Roxanne Euben, *Enemy in the Mirror*, 1999; Dipesh Chakrabarty, *Provincializing Europe*, 2000; Jodi Dean, ed., *Cultural Studies and Political Theory*, 2000; Achille Mbembe, *On the Postcolony*, 2001; Fred Dallmayr, "Beyond Monologue," 2004; John Dryzek, Bonnie Honig, and Anne Phillips, eds., *The Oxford Handbook of Political Theory*, 2006; Michael Hanchard, "Contours of Black Political Thought," 2010; Farah Godrej, *Cosmopolitan Political Thought*, 2011; Diego von Vacano, *The Color of Citizenship*, 2012; Romand Coles, Mark Reinhardt, and George Shulman, eds., *Radical Future Pasts*, 2014; Jane Anna Gordon, *Creolizing Political Theory*, 2014; David Scott, *Omens of Adversity*, 2014.
65. Michel-Rolph Trouillot, *Silencing the Past*, 1995. See also Fischer, *Modernity Disavowed*; Susan Buck-Morss, *Hegel, Haiti, and Universal History*, 2009.
66. Stephen Greenblatt, *Learning to Curse*, 1990, 16–39.
67. Walter Mignolo, *The Idea of Latin America*, 2005.
68. William Connolly, *Identity\Difference*, 1991, 36–63; Carl Schmitt, *The Nomos of the Earth in the International Law of the Jus Publicum Europaeum*, 2003.
69. Sylvia Wynter, "1492: A New World View," 1995; Wynter, "Unsettling the Coloniality of Being/Power/Truth/Freedom," 2003.
70. George Lamming, *The Pleasures of Exile*, 1991, 118–50. Moreover, Greenblatt comments on the phenomenology of Caliban's *subhumanity* vis-à-vis Prospero's oppositional gaze: "Caliban is deformed, lecherous, evil-smelling, idle, treacherous, naive, drunken, rebellious, violent, and devil-worshipping. According to Prospero, he is not even human" (1990, 26).
71. Henry, *Caliban's Reason*, 4–5, 11–12.
72. Enrique Dussel, *The Underside of Modernity*, 1996; Dussel, *Ethics of Liberation in the Age of Globalization and Exclusion*, 2013.
73. Bartolomé de Las Casas, *A Short Account of the Destruction of the Indies*, 1992, 23. See also Anthony Pagden, *The Fall of Natural Man*, 1982; Tzvetan Todorov, *The Conquest of America*, 1999; Enrique Dussel, "Origen de la filosofía política moderna," 2005.
74. C. L. R. James, *The Black Jacobins*, 1963, 3–4.
75. Iris Marion Young, *Justice and the Politics of Difference*, 1990; Young, *Responsibility for Justice*, 2011.

CHAPTER ONE

1. Hannah Arendt, "Revolution and Freedom," 1962, 595.
2. Philip Pettit, *Republicanism*, 1999, 32.

3. C. L. R. James, *Every Cook Can Govern*, 1992, 15.

4. Hanna Pitkin, "Are Freedom and Liberty Twins?" 1988. In *The Attack of the Blob*, Pitkin provides a critique of scholars such as Isaiah Berlin who use *freedom* and *liberty* interchangeably in English without careful examination of political language. Whereas *freedom* derives from a Germanic root by way of the Anglo-Saxons, *liberty* has its linguistic origins in Latin and the Old French of the Normans (1988, 523, 544). Investigating the relationships among freedom, slavery, and slave agency at the level of political language offers greater precision into freedom's meaning.

5. On slavery as metaphor, see David Brion Davis, *The Problem of Slavery in Western Culture*, 1966; Moses Finley, *Ancient Slavery and Modern Ideology*, 1980; Dale Martin, *Slavery as Salvation*, 1990; Peter Garnsey, *Ideas of Slavery from Aristotle to Augustine*, 1996; Page duBois, *Slaves and Other Objects*, 2003; Peter Dorsey, *Common Bondage*, 2009.

6. Michel-Rolph Trouillot, *Silencing the Past*, 1995.

7. *Oxford English Dictionary*, online edition, *s.v.* "disavow." (http://www.oed.com).

8. As Sibylle Fischer observes in *Modernity Disavowed*, disavowal "is also a concept that only works if we remain cognizant that it is *something* that is being disavowed; . . . the concept of disavowal requires us to identify what is being disavowed, by whom, and for what reason" (38). For inquiry into the significance of disavowal for race and racial knowledge, see George Shulman, *American Prophecy*, 2008, 131–54; Shulman, "Acknowledgment and Disavowal as an Idiom for Theorizing Politics," 2011.

9. Toni Morrison, cited in Lawrie Balfour, *Democracy's Reconstruction*, 2011, 115.

10. Arendt, "Revolution and Freedom," 582.

11. Arendt, "What Is Freedom?" 146; Arendt, *The Promise of Politics*, 2005, 108.

12. Hannah Arendt, *On Revolution*, 1965, 319, n. 1. On Arendt's distinction, see Dana Villa, *Socratic Citizenship*, 2001, 249–78. For broader examination of the relationship between philosophy and politics, see Jacques Rancière's *Dis-agreement*, 1999.

13. Hannah Arendt, *Lectures on Kant's Political Philosophy*, 1982; Ronald Beiner and Jennifer Nedelsky, eds., *Judgment, Imagination, and Politics*, 2001; Jennifer Culbert, "Judging the Events of Our Times," in *Thinking in Dark Times*, 2010, ed. R. Berkowitz, T. Keenan, and J. Katz, 145–50.

14. Arendt, *Between Past and Future*, 144–45.

15. Ibid., 145, 151.

16. Hannah Arendt, *The Human Condition*, 1998, 7. Orig. pub. in 1958.

17. Ibid., 192–99.

18. Arendt, *On Revolution*, 281.

19. Ibid., 223. Arendt published this book in the same year as the controversial *Eichmann in Jerusalem* and second edition of C. L. R. James's *The Black Jacobins*. The 2012 popular movie *Hannah Arendt*, starring Barbara Sukowa and directed by Margarethe von Trotta, while engrossing, reinforces the disproportionate coverage of Arendt's judgments on Adolph Eichmann and the banality of evil. The writings on revolution from the early 1960s offer us deeper insights into disavowal and the experience of freedom.

20. Arendt, *On Revolution*, 11.

21. Ibid., 42–45.

22. Ibid., 47–48, 179–214. John Markoff details these asymmetrical feudal relationships around the time of the French Revolution's outbreak by narrating the grievances (*cahiers de doléances*) catalogued by insurrectionary peasants and members of the

Third Estate who sought to overthrow the absolutist *ancien régime*. See Markoff, *The Abolition of Feudalism*, 1996.

23. Arendt, *On Revolution*, 55.

24. Ibid., 211; Arendt, *The Human Condition*, 9. Arendt locates the idea of natality in Augustine's conceptions of the will and freedom. Not until the 1950s, however, does Arendt revisit her early work on Augustine, including the doctoral dissertation and subsequent 1929 book, *Augustine's Concept of Love*. The result of this return is Arendt's insertion of the term *natality* into newer writings such as *On Revolution* and *The Human Condition*, the final incomplete trilogy *The Life of the Mind*, and previously published texts from *Augustine's Concept of Love* to *The Origins of Totalitarianism*. See Roy Tsao, "Arendt's Augustine," in *Politics in Dark Times*, 2010, ed. Seyla Benhabib, 39–57.

25. Patchen Markell, "The Experience of Action," in Berkowitz, Keenan, and Katz, *Thinking in Dark Times*, 98, 279, n. 21.

26. Arendt, *On Revolution*, 32.

27. Ibid., 18, 19.

28. Hannah Arendt, *On Violence*, 1970, 44, 52, 56. Arendt goes so far as to conclude, with bravado or hyperbole: "No government exclusively based on the means of violence has ever existed" (50). In "Thoughts on Politics and Revolution," Arendt states further, "The revolutionaries are those who know when power is lying in the street and when they can pick it up. Armed uprising by itself has never yet led to a revolution"; see Hannah Arendt, *Crises of the Republic*, 1972, 206.

29. Alan Keenan, *Democracy in Question*, 2003, 76–101; Jason Frank, *Constituent Moments*, 2010.

30. Carl Schmitt, *Constitutional Theory*, 2008, 125–35.

31. Arendt, *On Revolution*, 33, 141–78, 218.

32. The character Morpheus in the movie *The Matrix* demonstrates an example of Arendt's interpretation of liberation during the moment in which Morpheus shatters the chains that hold his arms in bondage. The entities that capture and put Morpheus in chains are called "Agents," a term that points to the range of agencies interacting in the social world. The polity named Zion exemplifies in Arendtian political language the state of freedom. Whereas Arendt would separate the project of Morpheus from those trapped in the Matrix seeking to reach and build Zion, I argue later against disaggregating projects of liberation and freedom.

33. Arendt, *The Human Condition*, 234.

34. Arendt, *Between Past and Future*, 164.

35. Arendt, *On Revolution*, 76–88, 153. Other perspectives on Arendt and non-sovereignty include Dana Villa, "Beyond Good and Evil," 1992, 274–77; Andrew Arato and Jean Cohen, "Banishing the Sovereign?" in Benhabib, *Politics in Dark Times*, 137–71. As an alternative to generality, Arendt proposes the unrealized council system outlined by Jefferson in private letters that never made it into his public policy. The council system is "an entirely new form of government, with a new public space for freedom." The councils are "spaces of freedom" consisting of numerous wards, or small republics, within the larger republic that foster the active participation of citizens in decision-making (249, 264). The bureaucratic structure and architecture of sovereignty in modern nation-states habitually obliterates the preservation of councils. It is the description of the lost revolutionary council tradition that Arendt's freedom aims to recover and that marks the crescendo of *On Revolution*.

36. Arendt, *The Human Condition*, 177.

37. Pitkin, *The Attack of the Blob*, 1–18. Norma Moruzzi has another reading of the social question and Arendt's notion of the social that emphasizes the abject. See her *Speaking Through the Mask*, 2000.
38. Arendt, *On Revolution*, 61, 111–12.
39. Ibid., 68.
40. Hannah Arendt, *The Jewish Writings*, 2007. "Antisemitism" is a lengthy essay predating and separate from the first part of *The Origins of Totalitarianism*, which has the same title.
41. Arendt, *On Revolution*, 70.
42. Ibid., 71–72.
43. Saidiya Hartman, *Scenes of Subjection*, 1997.
44. The lecture, if cited at all, usually garners scholarly reference as a selection from Arendt's then forthcoming *On Revolution*. Arendt's biographer, Elisabeth Young-Bruehl (2004), joins the long list of scholars who do not discuss the talk.
45. Arendt, "Revolution and Freedom," 578–79.
46. Ibid., 599.
47. On Cuba, racial equality, and freedom, see Alejandro de la Fuente, *A Nation for All*, 2001.
48. Arendt, "Revolution and Freedom," 597; W. E. B. Du Bois, *The Souls of Black Folk*, 1997 [1903], 45. Arendt accurately portrays elements of this contradiction in a terse comment on slavery in *The Origins of Totalitarianism*:

> Slavery's fundamental offense against human rights was not that it took liberty away (which can happen in many other situations), but that it excluded a certain category of people even from the possibility of fighting for freedom. . . . Slavery's crime against humanity did not begin when one people defeated and enslaved its enemies (though of course this was bad enough), but when slavery became an institution in which some men were "born" free and others slaves, when it was forgotten that it was man who had deprived his fellow-men of freedom, and when the sanction for the crime was attributed to nature. . . . To be a slave was after all to have a distinctive character, a place in society—more than the abstract nakedness of being human and nothing but human. Not the loss of specific rights, then, but the loss of a community willing and able to guarantee any rights whatsoever, has been the calamity which has befallen ever-increasing numbers of people. Man, it turns out, can lose all so-called Rights of Man without losing his essential quality as man, his human dignity. Only the loss of a polity itself expels him from humanity (1973, 297).

It is *racial slavery* wherein Arendt's disavowal of slavery occurs, and this is instructive, beyond Arendt, for discourses of republicanism.
49. Arendt, *Crises of the Republic*, 90, 91,n. 67.
50. Ibid., 91, 92–94; original emphasis.
51. Charles Mills, *The Racial Contract*, 1997, 16, 28, 53–57, 127.
52. Arendt, "Revolution and Freedom," 595. Arendt's antipathy to the social does not justify disavowing slavery and the agents therein, especially given her interest in an agent's capacity to participate in republican government. For critical readings of Arendt on race-thinking and the phenomenology of race, consult Karuna Mantena's "Genealogies of Catastrophe" and Richard King's "On Race and Culture," in Benhabib, *Politics in Dark Times*, 83–112, 113-34. Even Alexis de Tocqueville, a figure Arendt cites minimally in the lecture and in *On Revolution*, devotes greater attention to noting the problems raised by America's racial state, notwithstanding his own

contradictory stances on French colonialism and the political ramifications of black slavery. See Mark Reinhardt, *The Art of Being Free*, 1997; Alexis de Tocqueville, *Writings on Empire and Slavery*, 2001. The longest chapter in volume 1 of Tocqueville's *Democracy in America*, "The Three Races that Inhabit the United States," interrogates the contours of the black slave population. Reinhardt does note an effacement surrounding Tocqueville on slave agency. Tocqueville's discussion of US black slavery "is oddly free of agents or struggles, as if there were not *politics* involved" (65).

53. Danielle Allen, *Talking to Strangers*, 2004, 29. Ralph Ellison routinely used the phrase "social-political." Ellison elaborates on his critique of the division between the social and political spheres in two venues: an interview with Robert Penn Warren published in Warren's *Who Speaks for the Negro?* and a *New Leader* essay, "The World and the Jug."

54. Maurizio Viroli, *Republicanism*, 2002, 35.

55. J. G. A. Pocock, *The Machiavellian Moment*, 1975; Quentin Skinner, *Liberty before Liberalism*, 1998; Viroli, *Republicanism*; Pocock, *Political Thought and History*, 2008; Skinner, *Hobbes and Republican Liberty*, 2008. For debates on neo-Roman republicanism, see Joyce Appleby, *Liberalism and Republicanism in the Historical Imagination*, 1992; Cécile Laborde and John Maynor, eds., *Republicanism and Political Theory*, 2008; Eric MacGilvray, *The Invention of Market Freedom*, 2011; John McCormick, *Machiavellian Democracy*, 2011.

56. Pettit, *Republicanism*, 283–305. The postscript is intended to clarify differences, first between Pettit's thought and Quentin Skinner's, and second between liberalism and republicanism more broadly. Other works on freedom by Pettit include *A Theory of Freedom*, 2001; "Keeping Republican Freedom Simple," 2002; "Free Persons and Free Choices" 2007; "Republican Freedom," in Laborde and Maynor, *Republicanism and Political Theory*, 102–30; *On the People's Terms*, 2012; *Just Freedom*, 2014.

57. Pettit, *Republicanism*, 17–50.

58. Berlin, "Two Concepts of Liberty," 191–242; Pettit, *Republicanism*, 18.

59. Pettit, *Republicanism*, 50, 80.

60. Ibid., 5–6, 19–20, 283–86.

61. Ibid., 52, 55; Pettit, "Republican Freedom," 106–10.

62. Pettit, "Free Persons and Free Choices," 709–18.

63. Pettit, *Republicanism*, 35–41.

64. Ibid., 55–56.

65. Ibid., 13, 112, 171.

66. Ibid., 31.

67. Ibid., 63–64, 284. On the term *dominus*, see William Smith, William Wayte, and G. E. Marindin, eds., *A Dictionary of Greek and Roman Antiquities*, 1890 (Perseus Digital Library, online at http://www.perseus.tufts.edu/hopper). In *Slavery and Social Death*, Orlando Patterson notes that when *dominus* first appeared in the third century BCE, it meant "slave master." The term was later used to mean "owner." *Dominium* came to refer to "absolute ownership" near the end of Republican Rome, transforming slavery in law and social practice from a relationship between persons to one between persons *and* things (31–32). In classical Roman jurisprudence, the condition of the slave was antithetical to the situation of individuals possessing citizenship (*civitas*).

68. C. Wirszubski, *Libertas as a Political Idea*, 1960, 3; Pitkin, "Are Freedom and Liberty Twins?" 534–35; Pettit, *Republicanism*, 27–31. See also W. W. Buckland, *The Roman Law of Slavery*, 1970; Keith Bradley, *Slavery and Society at Rome*, 1994; Richard Alston, Edith Hall, and Laura Proffitt, eds., *Reading Ancient Slavery*, 2011.

69. With attunement to philology, Patchen Markell argues in "The Insufficiency of Non-Domination" (2005) that Pettit's notion of non-domination remains insufficient and misrepresents the Roman tradition. Domination alone cannot explain the unfreedom of slavery because, for Markell, slavery concurrently comprises domination *as well as* "usurpation" (7, 34–38). Classical Roman writers from Cicero to Livy regularly invoked the political language of usurpation in written texts and public speeches. The "object of usurpation is not merely a state of security from arbitrary interference, but something actively done or carried out: the usurpation of liberty, for example, is not identical to its erosion or violation" (34). Whereas domination narrates agency's relationship to control and its loss, usurpation captures the perspective that an enslaved agent harbors when the agent's active involvement in various daily activities is interrupted or displaced altogether. Usurpation stifles the agency of the oppressed. Markell's spirited criticism, however, avoids pointing out the fundamental disavowal of slave agency that Pettit engages in.

70. Pettit, *Republicanism*, viii, 5, 64.

71. Ibid., 26, n. 1, 56, n. 3, 76; Pettit, "Keeping Republican Freedom Simple," 347.

72. Pettit, *Republicanism*, 65.

73. Ibid., 76. Pettit earlier notes, "Notice that this means, under a conception of freedom as non-domination, that neither a tax levy, nor even a term of imprisonment, need take away from someone's freedom. But while such burdens do not compromise someone's freedom, still, as I put it later in this chapter, they do condition it. And so, while they do not compromise someone's freedom as non-domination, they do allow us to say that the person is not free to spend or travel as they wish" (56, n. 3).

74. Pettit, "Keeping Republican Freedom Simple," 347.

75. The administration of Spain's Prime Minister José Luis Rodríguez Zapatero illuminates the paradox. Zapatero was elected in 2004 and reelected in 2008. He became the first major world leader openly to base his administration's goals on Pettit's philosophy of republicanism, or *civicism* (*civismo*), as it is known in Spain. Zapatero had ambivalent results implementing Pettit's system over two terms. Pettit and coauthor José Luis Martí detail in *A Political Philosophy in Pubic Life* (2010) Zapatero's successes and challenges during the first term. Zapatero's second tenure also experienced notable problems. Zapatero amended his leadership policies to offset critique of civicist rhetoric in times of fiscal austerity, unemployment, and domestic terrorism. This still was not enough. As noted in *The Economist* ("Spain's Election: Mañana Is Too Late," November 19, 2011, 54), Spain had in 2011 the highest overall unemployment rate in the European Union. The Basque organization ETA, whose very name is a plea for a homeland and freedom, was resolute in voicing intrastate ethno-national concerns. Zapatero's legacy is forever questionable.

76. James, *Every Cook Can Govern*, 15. See a similar position in his *Mariners, Renegades and Castaways*, 2001; James, *You Don't Play with Revolution*, 2009.

77. James C. Scott, *Domination and the Arts of Resistance*, 1990, 183. Scott (2009, 2012) has since moved away from the language of domination to describe unfreedom, notably focusing even closer on the actions of peasants and subaltern groups.

78. Arendt, *On Revolution*, 34.

79. Eugene Genovese, *Roll, Jordan, Roll*, 1969; Finley, *Ancient Slavery and Modern Ideology*, 1980; Herbert Aptheker, "Maroons within the Present Limits of the United States" [1939], in Price, *Maroon Societies*, 1996, 151–67; Angela Davis, "Reflections on the Black Woman's Role in the Community of Slaves" [1971], in James, *Angela Y. Davis Reader*, 1998, 111–28; Stephanie McCurry, *Confederate Reckoning*, 2010.

80. Du Bois, *Souls of Black Folk*, 45–61.

81. Ibid., 37–44.

82. Ibid., 46, 60, 73–81. Du Bois conceives of slavery and freedom in terms of a politicized "social condition," or what Ellison, as noted earlier, calls the social-political.

83. Alexis de Tocqueville, *Democracy in America*, cited in Reinhardt, *Art of Being Free*, vi.

84. W. E. B. Du Bois, "Jefferson Davis as a Representative of Civilization" [1890], in *Writings*, 1986, 811. Du Bois asserts in "The Study of the Negro Problems" (1898), "So far as the Negro race is concerned, the Civil War simply left us face to face with the same sort of problems of social condition and caste which were beginning to face the nation a century ago. It is these problems that we are to-day somewhat helplessly— not to say carelessly—facing, forgetful that they are living, growing social questions whose progeny will survive to curse the nation, unless we grapple with them manfully and intelligently" (6).

85. For a sample of other interpretations of Du Bois's thought, see Shamoon Zamir, *Dark Voices*, 1995; Cedric Robinson, *Black Marxism*, 2000; Anthony Bogues, *Black Heretics, Black Prophets*, 2003; Joel Olson, *The Abolition of White Democracy*, 2004; Robert Gooding-Williams, *In the Shadow of Du Bois*, 2009; Balfour, *Democracy's Reconstruction*.

86. W. E. B. Du Bois, *Black Reconstruction in America*, 1992 [1935]. The full title is *Black Reconstruction in America: An Essay Toward a History of the Part Which Black Folk Played in the Attempt to Reconstruct Democracy in America, 1860–1880*.

87. Judith Shklar, *American Citizenship*, 1991, 1, 21; Shklar, *Redeeming American Political Thought*, 1998.

88. Du Bois, *Black Reconstruction*, 722. See David Levering Lewis's introduction for context on the composition of the text (vii–xvii). As Balfour notes, Du Bois's "righting" of Reconstruction history occurs through writing (*Democracy's Reconstruction*, 27). Balfour explores the idea of fugitivity documented in Du Bois's acts of righting/ writing.

89. Du Bois, *Black Reconstruction*, xix.

90. Ibid., 13. Soon thereafter Du Bois states that the slaves' relation to democracy is slavery's true significance to American social development.

91. Ibid., 55–83.

92. Walter Benjamin, "The Critique of Violence," in *Reflections*, 1978, 291.

93. Steven Hahn, *The Political Worlds of Slavery and Freedom*, 2009, 57. See as well David Blight, *Race and Reunion*, 2001.

94. Du Bois, *Black Reconstruction*, 82–83.

95. Ibid., 121.

96. Ibid., 182–85, 219. Du Bois coins a phrase for the second vision: *abolition-democracy*. Angela Davis draws upon this, in conjunction with Frederick Douglass's fugitive thought, to rethink the status of prisons, mass incarceration, and punishment in late modern America.

97. Ibid., 182–83.

98. Ibid., 706.

99. Frantz Fanon refers to this in *Black Skin, White Masks* (2008) as the black body being "overdetermined from the outside" (95).

100. Du Bois, *Black Reconstruction*, 325, 708. Chapter 9's title is "The Price of Disaster."

101. James Baldwin, "The Price of the Ticket" [1985], in *Collected Essays*, 1998, 830–42.

102. Du Bois, *Black Reconstruction*, 708.

103. Steven Hahn uses this phrase in *A Nation Under Our Feet*, 2003, 1–10.

CHAPTER TWO

1. Frederick Douglass, *My Bondage and My Freedom*, edited with an introduction by John D. Smith, 2003 [1855], 180–81. All citations of *Bondage* henceforth are from this Penguin edition unless indicated otherwise.
2. Samuel Taylor Coleridge, epigraph to Douglass's *Bondage*, 3.
3. Angela Davis, *Lectures on Liberation*, c. 1971, 3.
4. Angela Davis, ed., *If They Come in the Morning*, 1971, 264–88. In "An Open Letter to My Sister Angela Y. Davis," James Baldwin writes, "If we know, then we must fight for your life as though it were our own—which it is—and render impassable with our bodies the corridor to the gas chamber. For, if they take you in the morning, they will be coming for us that night" (published in the *New York Review of Books*; reprinted in Davis, *If They Come*, 23). On the circumstances of the imprisonment and trial of Davis, see Göran Hugo Olsson's *The Black Power Mixtape 1967–1975* (2011) and Shola Lynch's *Free Angela Davis and All Political Prisoners* (2012). These documentaries include previously unreleased footage and interviews, and they are apt illustrations of the global scale of Davis's case.
5. W. E. B. Du Bois, *Souls of Black Folk*, 1997, 66; Booker T. Washington, *Frederick Douglass*, 2003, 15. In other writings, including *Black Reconstruction in America*, Du Bois underscores the centrality of Douglass as a political leader and the critical role of fugitive slaves in the actualization of freedom and implementation of "abolition-democracy" (1992, 13–14, 184).
6. Douglass continues to inform the thought of Davis. See Angela Davis, "From the Prison of Slavery to the Slavery of Prison," 1998, 74–95; Davis, interview with Amy Goodman, "Angela Davis on the Prison Abolitionist Movement, Frederick Douglass, the 40th Anniversary of Her Arrest and President Obama's First Two Years," online at http://www.democracynow.org/2010/10/19/angela_davis_on_the_prison_abolishment.
7. Douglass's thought distinguishes itself from late modern discourse centered on the relationship of the fugitive to important, albeit distinct, concepts, such as democracy and justice, that do not examine the implications of fugitivity for freedom. Two prominent formulations addressing the role of the fugitive are notable. For Sheldon Wolin, the evanescent character of the fugitive captures the paradoxical manifestation of democracy in the late modern United States via the establishment of an inverted totalitarian regime. Stephen Best and Saidiya Hartman, in contrast, invoke the fugitive to explain the prospects for justice in slavery's aftermath. See Best and Hartman, "Fugitive Justice," 2005; Wolin, "Fugitive Democracy," 1996; Hartman, *Lose Your Mother*, 2007. While Wolin, Best, and Hartman theorize democracy and justice, they fail to devote proper attention to the fugitive's relation to the idea of freedom. Hartman devotes the last chapter of her memoir to "fugitive dreams" of contemporary West Africans who flee across nation-state borders to escape slave raiders. "Flight," Hartman notes, "was the language of freedom" (*Lose Your Mother*, 222). The book, however, does not examine the conceptual relevance of this point. Douglass's political thought offers an answer. I focus on Douglass to highlight the stakes of considering the fugitive's place in theories of freedom and to outline the tenets of his theory.
8. Davis, *Lectures on Liberation*, 4, 5.
9. Shklar, *American Citizenship*, 23. Shklar offers a complementary assessment of American slavery in *Redeeming American Political Thought*, 111–26.
10. Joy James, *Shadowboxing*, 1999, 93–122. Davis's key prison writings include "Political Prisoners, Prisons, and Black Liberation," "Lessons: From Attica to Soledad," "Trials

of Political Prisoners Today," and "Notes for Arguments in Court on the Issue of Self-Representation," in *If They Come*, 27–47, 77–105, 246–55. In *Angela Davis*, Davis—like autobiographical slave narrative authors—classifies her text as a *"political auto-biography"* (1988 [1974], xvi, orig. emphasis).

11. Davis, "Unfinished Lecture on Liberation—II" [1983], in James, *Angela Y. Davis Reader*, 53–60. Davis, in conjunction with City Lights Press, published in 2010 a critical edition of the *Narrative of the Life of Frederick Douglass*. The updated text includes a reprint of Davis's *Lectures on Liberation*. I cite throughout from the original lectures pamphlet.

12. Lewis R. Gordon, *Existentia Africana*, 2000, 41–61.

13. Davis, *Lectures on Liberation*, 1.

14. Ibid.

15. Douglass delivered the lecture, "'It Moves'; or The Philosophy of Reform," to the Bethel Literary Society, Washington, DC, November 20, 1883. On the principle of *movement*, Douglass observes: "It is just as natural for man to seek and discover improved conditions of existence, as it is for birds to fly in the air or to fill the morning with melody or to build their nests in the spring. The very conditions of helplessness in which men are born suggest reform and progress as the necessity of their nature . . . I do not know that I am an evolutionist, but to this extent I am one. I certainly have more patience with those who trace mankind upward from a low condition, even from the lower animals, then with those that start him at a high point of perfection and conduct him to a level with the brutes. I have no sympathy with a theory that starts man in heaven and stops him in hell. To this complexion it must come at last, if no progress is made, and the only movement of mankind is a downward or retrograde movement. Happily for us the world does move, and better still, its movement is an upward movement. Kingdoms, empires, powers, principalities and dominions, may appear and disappear; may flourish and decay; but mankind as a whole must ever move onward, and increase in the perfection of character and in the grandeur of achievement." See Douglass, "It Moves," in *The Frederick Douglass Papers: Series 1 (Vol. 5: 1881–95)*, 1992, ed. J. Blassingame and J. McKivigan, eds., 129–30.

16. Davis, *Lectures on Liberation*, 4–8.

17. *The Meaning of Freedom* (2012) is a compilation of twelve previously unpublished lectures by Davis spanning 1994 to 2009. They complement the 1969 *Lectures*, provide greater philosophical precision, and contain expanded probing into the idea of freedom beyond emancipation. Among the lecture topics are the prison-industrial complex; race, crime, and punishment; neoliberalism and black politics; prisons since 9/11; black history month; lesbian, gay, bisexual, and transgendered communities; difficult dialogues; and a lecture with the same title as the book. Although none of the lectures is on Douglass or *My Bondage and My Freedom*, *The Meaning of Freedom* has relevance to interpreting Douglass's idea of freedom. I thank Stacey Lewis and Greg Ruggiero of City Lights Press for sharing with me Davis's unpublished book MS.

18. William Andrews, *To Tell a Free Story*, 1986; Henry Louis Gates Jr., *The Signifying Monkey*, 1988; Eric Sundquist, ed., *Frederick Douglass*, 1990; Valerie Smith, *Self-Discovery and Authority in Afro-American Narrative*, 1991; Robert Levine, *Martin Delany, Frederick Douglass, and the Politics of Representative Identity*, 1997.

19. Howard McGary and Bill Lawson, *Between Slavery and Freedom*, 1992, xxi; Paul Gilroy, *The Black Atlantic*, 1993, 41–71; Michael Dawson, *Black Visions*, 2001, 2.

20. Robert Gooding-Williams, *Look, A Negro!*, 2006, 109–120. Recent works by philosophers and political theorists addressing Douglass's slave narratives and overall

thought include Cynthia Willett, *Maternal Ethics and Other Slave Moralities*, 1995; Charles Mills, *Blackness Visible*, 1998; Bill Lawson and Frank Kirkland, eds., *Frederick Douglass*, 1999; Peter Myers, *Frederick Douglass*, 2008; Gooding-Williams, *In the Shadow of Du Bois*, 2009; Jason Frank, *Constituent Moments*, 2010; Stephen Marshall, *The City on the Hill from Below*, 2011; Nicholas Buccola, *The Political Thought of Frederick Douglass*, 2012; Jack Turner, *Awakening to Race*, 2012; Nick Bromell, *The Time Is Always Now*, 2013.

21. Bernard Boxill, "Douglass, Frederick," 2005.

22. Douglass biographer William McFeely concurs with this assessment in *Frederick Douglass*, 1991, 180–82.

23. Previous scholarship primarily focuses on Douglass's relationship to American, rather than British, Romanticism. The work of William Andrews is a notable example of this narrow tendency that I argue we must shift away from. See Andrews, "Introduction" to the 1987 edition of *My Bondage and My Freedom*, xi–xxviii; Andrews, "The 1850s," in *Literary Romanticism in America*, 1981, ed. W. Andrews, 38–60. Bill Lawson notes the philosophical Romanticism of Douglass and Douglass's convergence with the intellectual movement of Transcendentalism. Lawson, too, neglects inquiry into Douglass and British Romanticism, for reasons other than those of Andrews. Lawson contends that American Romanticism draws upon elements of British and German Romanticism, but he provides no specifics on principles of British Romanticism that could be considered part of an American Romanticist tradition and central to *Bondage*. The most egregious oversight is an entire volume on Douglass's thought and activism in Great Britain that has no entry on any forms of Romanticism. See Alan Rice and Martin Crawford, eds., *Liberating Sojourn*, 1999; Lawson, "Douglass among the Romantics," in *The Cambridge Companion to Frederick Douglass*, 2009, ed. Maurice Lee, 118–31.

24. Douglass, *Bondage*, 30. Michael Hanchard's characterization of *racial time* in Afromodern politics presents a political vocabulary with which to interpret the temporal bondage and flux in Douglass's reflections on his age. See Hanchard, "Afro-Modernity," 1999, 253.

25. Douglass, *Bondage*, 49.

26. Bernard Boxill, "Two Traditions in African-American Political Philosophy," 1992–93: 125–31.

27. Waldo Martin Jr., *The Mind of Frederick Douglass*, 1984, 18–54; William Rogers, "We Are All Together Now," 1995; George Shulman, *American Prophecy*, 2008.

28. Frank Kirkland, "Enslavement, Moral Suasion, and Struggles for Recognition," in Lawson and Kirkland, *Frederick Douglass*, 244.

29. Bernard Boxill, "Douglass Against the Emigrationists," in Lawson and Kirkland, *Frederick Douglass*, 21–49; Douglass, "A Trip to Haiti" [1861], in *Frederick Douglass*, 1999, ed. Philip Foner and Yuval Taylor, 439–42.

30. Douglass, *Bondage*, 116–17.

31. Ibid., 120–21; orig. emphasis.

32. Ibid., 265–66; orig. emphasis. Henceforth, all italicized citations from the works of Douglass including *Bondage* are Douglass's own emphasis.

33. Ibid., 266.

34. For further inquiries into the importance of structure in *Bondage*, see John Sekora, "'Mr. Editor, If You Please,'" 1994, 608–26; Peter Dorsey, "Becoming the Other," 1996, 435–50. In *Talking to Strangers*, Danielle Allen highlights the importance of a text's structure and the frontispiece chosen by an author. Allen describes the frontispiece to Thomas Hobbes's *Leviathan*, noting how the shifting pictorial depiction of "the

people" from the draft version to the final frontispiece reconfigured Hobbes's understanding of the people's relation to the Leviathan (80–84). Here, I highlight the importance of Douglass's structural devices and frontispiece for framing his argument about freedom following the Garrisonian break.

35. The image of "The Fugitive's Song" (1845) is available online at: http://www.loc.gov/pictures/item/2008661459/. On the music cover sheet, Douglass is shown as a fugitive on the run from dogs and two slave catchers across the river. Douglass is dressed, yet visibly barefoot, and he is listed as a "Graduate from the 'PECULIAR INSTITUTION.'" Slavery, however, was a legal fixture of the antebellum American South, and Douglass at the time could still be sent back into slavery if caught in the North. The phantasmagoric representation of Douglass among Garrisonian sympathizers is distinct from Douglass's own conception of himself, his experiences, and political thought in *Bondage* following the Garrisonian break.

36. James McCune Smith wrote *A Lecture on the Haytien Revolutions; With a Sketch of the Character of Toussaint L'Ouverture. Delivered at the Stuyvesant Institute* (1841).

37. Frederick Douglass, *Narrative of the Life of Frederick Douglass* [1845] (Signet edition, 1987), 376.

38. Nancy Rosenblum, *Another Liberalism*, 1987.

39. Helen Thomas "endeavors to disclose a hitherto obscured dialogue of exchange and negotiation: that is, between the discourse of Romanticism as it emerged out of eighteenth-century dissent and enthusiasm, and the narratives of displaced subjects, the slaves from the African diaspora." See Thomas, *Romanticism and Slave Narratives*, 2000, 5. I extend Thomas's imperative to the study of Douglass and British Romanticism. Additional studies analyzing the relationships among Romanticism, colonialism, and slave narratives include Alan Richardson and Sonia Hofkosh, eds., *Romanticism, Race, and Imperial Culture, 1780–1834*, 1996; Debbie Lee, *Slavery and the Romantic Imagination*, 2002; Deirdre Coleman, *Romantic Colonization and British Anti-Slavery*, 2005.

40. Douglass, *Bondage*, 275.

41. Ibid., 273, 280.

42. Douglass, *The Heroic Slave* [1853], in Foner and Taylor, *Frederick Douglass*, 241. *The Heroic Slave* originally appeared in a serialized version in the newspaper the *North Star* as well as in Julia Griffith's edited collection, *Autographs for Freedom*.

43. Douglass, *Bondage*, 182.

44. Du Bois, *The Souls of Black Folk*, 62.

45. On Byron and Douglass, see Bernard Boxill's insightful essay, "The Fight with Covey," 1997.

46. The point here is not to construct Douglass as a theorist derivative of British thought since several British Romanticists formulated their ideas after reading black slave narratives. Analyzing Douglass via Coleridge is essential to explaining Douglass's ideas of slavery, property, and agency developed in light of the Britain sojourn. Surprisingly, negligible commentary on Douglass and Coleridge exists. The introduction by John Wright to another critical edition of *Bondage* published by Simon and Schuster (2003) notably accentuates this oversight. Although concentrating on myriad texts that situate the milieu to which Douglass gains interest in Coleridge, Wright does not locate the specific work of Coleridge underlying Douglass's political imagination in *Bondage*. I address this generations-old omission.

47. Malcolm Ware, "Coleridge's 'Spectre Bark,'" 1961; John Morrow, *Coleridge's Political Thought*, 1990; Thomas, *Romanticism and Slave Narratives*, 89–104; Tim Fulford,

"Slavery and Superstition in the Supernatural Poems"; Pamela Edwards, *The Statesman's Science*, 2004.

48. Coleridge, "On the Slave Trade" [1796], 130–40; Coleridge, "Lecture on the Slave-Trade" [1795], 231–51.
49. Coleridge's *Lecture* took place in the same year that the Second Maroon War erupted in Britain's colony of Jamaica, a sign that the question of slavery loomed large in the British Romanticist political imaginary.
50. Coleridge, "Lecture on the Slave-Trade," 235; Coleridge, "On the Slave Trade," 130; orig. emphasis. All italics in citations from Coleridge are his own emphasis.
51. Coleridge, "On the Slave Trade," 131.
52. Coleridge, "Lecture on the Slave-Trade," 236.
53. Ibid., 247.
54. Ibid., 240.
55. Coleridge, "On the Slave Trade," 135–36.
56. Coleridge, "Lecture on the Slave-Trade," 250, 251; Coleridge, "On the Slave Trade," 140.
57. Douglass, *Bondage*, 330.
58. Coleridge, "On the Slave Trade," xxvii.
59. Thomas, *Romanticism and Slave Narratives*, 175.
60. Walter Johnson, "On Agency," 2003, 115. According to the *Oxford English Dictionary*, the reference to Coleridge on agency that Johnson cites falls under the *OED*'s primary definition of agency as the "faculty of an agent or of acting; active working or operation; action, activity" (www.oed.com, *s.v.* "agency"). Coleridge defines "personal free agency" in *On the Constitution of the Church and State* (1830), and he proposes the following: "The State shall leave the largest portion of personal free agency to each of its citizens, that is compatible with the free agency of all."
61. Coleridge, epigraph to *Bondage*, 3.
62. Douglass cites as the epigraph to *Bondage* only a portion of a sentence from Coleridge's *Dissertation*. The full sentence of Coleridge's treatise reads as follows: "We allude to the gradual abolition of domestic slavery, in virtue of a Principle essential to Christianity, by which a *person* is eternally differenced from a *thing*; so that the *Idea* of a Human Being necessarily excludes the Idea of property in that Being." See Coleridge, *A Dissertation on the Science of Method*, 1854 [1818], 56–57 (orig. emphasis).
63. Coleridge, *A Dissertation on the Science of Method*, 21–22.
64. Douglass, *Bondage*, 61–62, 233.
65. Ibid., 140.
66. Patterson, *Slavery and Social Death*, 31–32.
67. Douglass, *Bondage*, 41, 162.
68. Ibid., 302.
69. Ibid., 108.
70. Arendt, *Origins of Totalitarianism*, 297.
71. Douglass, *Bondage*, 252.
72. Ibid., 159.
73. Ibid., 128–29.
74. Stephen Best, *The Fugitive's Properties*, 2004.
75. Douglass, *Bondage*, 155, 157, 171, 326, 328.
76. Shklar, *American Citizenship*, 1.
77. Douglass, *Bondage*, 29, 34–35, 90, 101, 181, 251, 252.

78. For alternative appreciations of Douglass's famous abolitionist speech, consult Mills, *Blackness Visible*, 167–200; James Colaiaco, *Frederick Douglass and the Fourth of July*, 2006; Frank, *Constituent Moments*, 209–36. *Bondage* includes only an excerpt of the speech. The full text also is in print under the title, "The Meaning of July Fourth for the Negro."
79. Douglass, *Bondage*, 341.
80. Ibid., 340–41, 344.
81. Ibid., 289, 292–93. Douglass expands on comparative constitutionalism in "The Constitution and Slavery" [1849], in Foner and Taylor, *Frederick Douglass*, 129–33.
82. Amartya Sen's *Development as Freedom* (1999) exemplifies this approach.
83. Douglass, *Bondage*, 279. For interpretations of Douglass as a liberal thinker, see Sharon Krause, *Liberalism with Honor*, 2002; Nick Bromell, "The Liberal Imagination of Frederick Douglass," 2008; Myers, *Frederick Douglass*; Buccola, *Political Thought of Frederick Douglass*.
84. Scholars such as Paul Gilroy, Cynthia Willet, Margaret Kohn, and the early Angela Davis have compared intricately Douglass's thought to that of G. W. F. Hegel, particularly Hegel's theory of recognition put forth in the *Phenomenology of Spirit*. See Davis, *Lectures on Liberation*, 7–8; Gilroy, *Black Atlantic*, 58–71; Willett, *Maternal Ethics*, 129–75; Margaret Kohn, "Frederick Douglass's Master-Slave Dialectic," 2005. I, however, do not read Douglass through the Hegelian master-slave dialectic for two reasons. First, unlike what we know about W. E. B. Du Bois's interaction with German thought, no evidence supports the contention that Douglass had interacted with German idealism by the time of *Bondage*. Douglass did not engage with German thought until *after Bondage*'s publication, mainly due to his association with the text's German translator, Ottelia Assing. Second, I wish to create a dialogue between scholars of freedom, slave narratives, and Romanticism in a way that the literature on struggles for recognition rarely addresses.
85. Douglass, "West India Emancipation" [1857], 367.
86. Douglass, *Bondage*, 298.
87. I only recount select aspects of the Douglass-Covey fight in order to illustrate Douglass's idea of struggle.
88. On the role of slave resistance in freedom struggles, see Howard McGary, "Resistance and Slavery," in McGary and Lawson, *Between Slavery and Freedom*, 35–54.
89. Douglass, *Bondage*, 171, 177, 178.
90. Davis, *Lectures on Liberation*, 3.
91. Douglass, *Bondage*, 180.
92. Ibid., 180–81.
93. Douglass, *Narrative*, 395 (Signet edition). There are other notable revisions in *Bondage*, such as Douglass's markedly different discussions of the slave woman, Caroline, in the first two autobiographies (Andrews, *To Tell a Free Story*, 285–86). These accounts take place when Douglass is describing Covey. In *Narrative*, Caroline does not appear in the crux of the fight with Covey scene, and Douglass mentions her in a single, brief section. Douglass refers to her simply as a "miserable woman" and a "wretched woman" whose sole purpose was as a "breeder" (orig. emphasis, 387). By contrast, in *Bondage*, Caroline becomes integral to the Douglass-Covey fight. Douglass describes Caroline this time in "The Last Flogging" chapter as a "powerful woman" who "could have mastered me very easily, exhausted as I now was." Caroline was Covey's personal slave, and when Covey demanded that she take hold of Douglass to strengthen his standing during the altercation, Caroline refused. Covey

later "gave her several sharp blows" as a result. "We were all in open rebellion, that morning" (2003, 179, 180). Careful examination of Douglass's use of words across the autobiographies, even when reading historical scenes in his oeuvre considered by readers the most familiar, is essential to discerning the conceptual breakthrough on freedom in *Bondage*.

94. Davis, *Lectures on Liberation*, 2. Robert Gooding-Williams, in a deft study of Du Bois and Douglass, responds to an earlier paper on Douglass in which I first mention the fact-form distinction. Gooding-Williams argues that *fact* in *Bondage* means a *deed* instead of a moral, psychological, or metaphysical valence. He challenges my reading by referring to Douglass's discussion of form and fact in *Life and Times*. Three points serve to question the validity of this critique. First, my argument focuses on Douglass's formulations in *Bondage*, not the third autobiography. In spite of this disclaimer, though, it is noteworthy that the passages cited from *Bondage* by Gooding-Williams actually support my position rather than deny it. Second, Gooding-Williams fails to address the crucial shift in Douglass's political language between the *Narrative* and *Bondage* in the catalytic fight with Covey scene, which is arguably the most well-known section in Douglass's three autobiographies. Third, Gooding-Williams's entire reading of Douglass on freedom is through the framework of Philip Pettit's theory of freedom as non-domination. I have detailed already in chapter 1 the insufficiencies in Pettit's theory, but beyond this, Douglass's conception of freedom is avowedly one that moves outside of a solely negative freedom model. See Gooding-Williams, *In the Shadow of Du Bois*, 170–71, 178–82, 308, n. 60–61, 309, n. 64, 301, n. 65.

95. Abraham Lincoln, "A House Divided," June 16, 1858; online at http://quod.lib .umich.edu/l/lincoln. Lincoln's speech in Springfield, Illinois, was delivered three years after *Bondage*. Douglass at the time did not yet fully support Lincoln because he believed Lincoln's position regarding radical antislavery politics was ambiguous. However, Douglass commented approvingly on Lincoln's speech. On Douglass and Lincoln, see James Oakes, *The Radical and the Republican*, 2007; John Stauffer, *Giants*, 2008. Douglass's approval of Lincoln's address must be understood in relation to the theory of comparative freedom and the fact-form distinction.

96. Douglass, "We Are Not Yet Quite Free" [1869], in *The Frederick Douglass Papers: Series 1 (Vol. 4: 1864–80)*, ed. J. Blassingame and J. McKivigan, 231.

97. Douglass, *Bondage*, 200.

98. Du Bois, *Souls of Black Folk*, 66–67; orig. emphasis.

99. Douglass, *Bondage*, 193–197.

100. Ibid., 200.

101. Ibid., 292.

102. On the difference between emancipation and freedom, see Ernesto Laclau, *Emancipation(s)*, 1996; Rebecca Scott, *Degrees of Freedom*, 2005; Richard Follett, Eric Foner, and Walter Johnson, *Slavery's Ghost*, 2011; Dussel, *Ethics of Liberation in the Age of Globalization and Exclusion*, 2013, David Brion Davis, *The Problem of Slavery in the Age of Emancipation*, 2014.

103. Shklar, *American Citizenship*, 54.

104. Davis, *Lectures on Liberation*, 2–8.

105. Saidiya Hartman, *Scenes of Subjection*, 1997, 3–4.

106. Douglass, *Bondage*, 185–87.

107. For a more detailed plot summary, see McFeely, *Frederick Douglass*, 174–75.

108. Douglass, *The Heroic Slave*, 221–22.

109. Ibid., 245.
110. Ibid., 247; orig. emphasis.
111. David Blight, *Frederick Douglass' Civil War*, 1989, 98. Douglass's conflicting statements on violence are addressed also in Goldstein, "Violence as an Instrument for Social Change," 1976; Richard Yarborough, "Race, Violence, and Manhood," in Sundquist, *Frederick Douglass*, 166–88; Boxill, "Fight with Covey"; Maurice Wallace, "Violence, Manhood, and War in Douglass," in Lee, *Cambridge Companion to Frederick Douglass*, 73–88.
112. David Scott, *Conscripts of Modernity*, 2004, 58–97.
113. Levine, *Martin Delany, Frederick Douglass, and the Politics of Representative Identity*, 101.
114. The discourse on physical violence, rhetorical violence, and revolution concerns an agent's existence in the commodity market of slavery. Comparative freedom does not address another level of violence that I do not consider because of space: the violence of the market as a market. This critique applies to fugitive dilemmas on violence and to problems regarding Douglass's discussion of property. The critique also raises post–Civil War issues about the violence of the "free" wage labor market and how black bodies remain constantly nonaligned in fact and form via Jim Crow policies designed to normalize inegalitarian commodity market forces.
115. In *John Brown*, W. E. B. Du Bois declares in his critique of Douglass that "John Brown was right" (202). Leonard Harris also interrogates this conclusion in "Honor and Insurrection or A Short Story about Why John Brown (with David Walker's Spirit) was Right and Frederick Douglass (with Benjamin Banneker's Spirit) was Wrong," in Lawson and Kirkland, *Frederick Douglass*, 227–42.
116. Douglass, *Bondage*, 180, 181.
117. On the archetype of the race man, see Hazel Carby, *Race Men*, 1998. Angela Davis notes her own failure to examine in *Lectures on Liberation* Douglass's gendered conception of freedom. In *Women, Race and Class* (1981), Davis attributes to Douglass an "admirably anti-sexist posture" (30). Yet this accurately describes Douglass's widespread involvement with white women suffragettes and not black women activists and organizations, a critique leveled against Douglass in his time and more expansively by twentieth and twenty-first century feminists of color. Davis submits in the introduction to Douglass's *Narrative* (City Lights edition) that "today I find it simultaneously somewhat embarrassing to realize that my UCLA lectures on Douglass rely on an implicitly masculinist notion of freedom" (28). It is only after the *Lectures* that Davis utilizes an intersectional framework in her thought and activism. The later Davis maintains, "One of the implications of the definition of 'freedom' in terms of 'manhood' is that the closest black women can come to freedom is to achieve the status not of a free man, but rather the unliberated status of white woman" (25).
118. Patricia Hill Collins, *Black Feminist Thought*, 2000; Carole Pateman and Charles Mills, *Contract and Domination*, 2007; Ange-Marie Hancock, *Solidarity Politics for Millennials*, 2011. Mills refers to the intersections of race and gender structuring modern world systems as the *racia-sexual contract* (Pateman and Mills 2007, 165–99). Feminist thinkers rebuke Douglass for the elision of intersectionality, representation of enslaved black women within his autobiographies, and failure over a long career to systematically criticize violence against female slaves and black women's bodies after Emancipation. See Jenny Franchot, "The Punishment of Esther," in Sundquist, *Frederick Douglass*, 141–65; Deborah McDowell's introduction to the 1999 Oxford edition of Douglass's *Narrative* (cited in Douglass 2010).

119. Joy James clarifies the distinctions among masculinism, patriarchy, and misogyny in *Transcending the Talented Tenth*, 1997, 36. Consult as well Katherine McKittrick, *Demonic Grounds*, 2006; Melissa Harris-Perry, *Sister Citizen*, 2011.
120. Patterson, *Slavery and Social Death*, 21.
121. Gordon, *Existentia Africana*, 54–60.
122. Thomas, *Romanticism and Slave Narratives*, 97.
123. Nathan Huggins, *Slave and Citizen*, 1980, 21–43.
124. Rayford Logan, *The Diplomatic Relations of the United States with Haiti, 1776–1891*, 1941; Ifeoma Nwankwo, *Black Cosmopolitanism*, 2005; Robert Levine, *Dislocating Race and Nation*, 2008; Millery Polyné, *From Douglass to Duvalier*, 2010.
125. Anténor Firmin's *The Equality of the Human Races* (2002 [1885]) critically responds to Gobineau's multivolume *Essay on the Inequality of the Human Races* (1853–55). A picture of Toussaint L'Ouverture adorns the frontispiece of Firmin's book.
126. Giorgio Agamben, *State of Exception*, 2005. Agamben bases the notion of a sovereign state of exception on Carl Schmitt's 1922 treatise, *Political Theology*.
127. Angela Davis more recently explores the oversights of Douglass on the nineteenth-century convict lease system, forerunner to the late-modern panoptical American prison apparatus. Douglass privileges acquisition of the right to vote over questioning the structures of punishment that adversely affected black bodies during and after Reconstruction. For Davis, the "duly convicted" clause of the Thirteenth Amendment paves the way for legalized penal servitude, the equating of blacks with crime, and the emergence of the neo-slave prison industry. See Davis, "Race and Criminalization," "From the Prison of Slavery to the Slavery of Prison," and "Racialized Punishment and Prison Abolition," all in James, *Angela Y. Davis Reader*, 61–107; Davis, *Abolition Democracy*, 2005; Davis, *The Meaning of Freedom*. Davis's criticisms justifiably apply to Douglass's political practice, but not to his theory of freedom. Comparative freedom is a theory compatible with discourse on abolition-democracy and the contemporary prison-industrial complex.
128. Frederick Douglass, *Life and Times of Frederick Douglass* [1892], in *Autobiographies*, 1994, 1045.
129. Frederick Douglass, *Lecture on Haiti* [1893], in Blassingame and McKivigan, *Frederick Douglass Papers: Series 1 (Vol. 5: 1881–95)*, 528.

CHAPTER THREE

1. C. L. R. James, *The Black Jacobins*, 1963 [1938], 95.
2. Carolyn Fick, *The Making of Haiti*, 1990, 49.
3. Toussaint L'Ouverture, "Letter to the Directory, 5 November 1797," in *Toussaint L'Ouverture*, 1973, ed. George Tyson Jr., 45; orig. emphasis.
4. James, *Black Jacobins*, 391. For contending views on race and the political economy of Caribbean slavery, see Sidney Mintz, *Sweetness and Power*, 1985; Eric Williams, *Capitalism and Slavery*, 1994; Gordon K. Lewis, *Main Currents in Caribbean Thought*, 2004; Scott, *Degrees of Freedom*, 2005; Philippe Girard, *Haiti*, 2010; Stephan Palmié and Francisco Scarano, eds., *The Caribbean*, 2011.
5. Fick, *Making of Haiti*, 22.
6. It is also notable that in world history there were only three recorded rebellions with a hundred thousand or more slaves: two were in Sicily during the second century BCE, and the third was in colonial Haiti. The third resulted in revolution. The Haitian Revolution, unlike the uprisings in other islands—including Jamaica, which

had several quelled rebellions—occurred in a territory with fewer previous revolts. See Fick, *Making of Haiti*, 22; Thomas Holt, *The Problem of Freedom*, 1992; David Geggus, *Haitian Revolutionary Studies*, 2002, 55; Laurent Dubois, *Avengers of the New World*, 2004, 19, 30; United States Census Bureau: http://www.census.gov/.

7. Judith Butler, Ernesto Laclau, and Slavoj Žižek, *Contingency, Hegemony, Universality*, 2000; Max Horkheimer and Theodor Adorno, *Dialectic of Enlightenment*, 2002; Yves Benot, *Les lumière, l'esclavage, la colonisation*, 2005; Laurent Dubois, "An Enslaved Enlightenment," 2006. Scholars such as Jonathan Israel insist that there was not *the* Enlightenment, but rather multiple Enlightenments. Whether the French Enlightenment overlapped with principles of Enlightenment movements across the modern world during the Age of Revolution does not negate contradictions in the discourse of the era.

8. Thomas Ott, *The Haitian Revolution, 1789–1804*, 1973; Thomas Madiou, *Histoire d'Haïti*, 8 vols., 1987; Gérard Barthélemy, *Créoles-Bossales*, 2000; Franklin Knight, "The Haitian Revolution," 2000; Geggus, *Haitian Revolutionary Studies*; Claude Moïse, ed., *Dictionnaire historique de la Révolution haïtienne (1789–1804)*, 2003; Dubois, *Avengers of the New World*; Cécile Accilien, Jessica Adams, and Elmide Méléance, eds., *Revolutionary Freedoms*, 2006; David Geggus and Norman Fiering, eds., *The World of the Haitian Revolution*, 2009; Jeremy Popkin, *You Are All Free*, 2010; Philippe Girard, *The Slaves Who Defeated Napoleon*, 2011; Alyssa Sepinwall, ed., *Haitian History*, 2013.

9. Michel-Rolph Trouillot, *Silencing the Past*, 1995, 73.

10. Joan Dayan, *Haiti, History, and the Gods*, 1995; Susan Buck-Morss, "Hegel and Haiti," 2000; Sibylle Fischer, *Modernity Disavowed*, 2004; David Scott, *Conscripts of Modernity*, 2004; Clinton Hutton, *The Logic and Historical Significance of the Haitian Revolution and the Cosmological Roots of Haitian Freedom*, 2005; Louis Sala-Molins, *Dark Side of the Light*, 2006; Nick Nesbitt, *Universal Emancipation*, 2008; Buck-Morss, *Hegel, Haiti, and Universal History*, 2009; Deborah Jenson, *Beyond the Slave Narrative*, 2011; Nesbitt, *Caribbean Critique*, 2013. Jean Fouchard's *Les marrons de la liberté* (1988 [1972]), translated into English as *The Haitian Maroons* (1981), is among the few substantive works during this period on Haitian maroons and freedom. The text, however, focuses only on pre-revolutionary marronage, privileging historical documentation over conceptual examination.

11. Alexis de Tocqueville, *The Old Regime and the Revolution*, 1998, 88–89.

12. Colin Dayan, *The Story of Cruel and Unusual*, 2007, 10; Malick Ghachem, *The Old Regime and the Haitian Revolution*, 2012, 30. Sala-Molins (in *Le Code Noir* and *Dark Side of the Light*) also offers an arresting interpretation of the *Code Noir*. While I share many of Sala-Molins's critiques of Enlightenment philosophies, my concern is not simply to expose those contradictions. My interest is the relevance of the juridical paradox for movement and flight.

13. I base my translation of the *Code Noir* on the following texts: Louis Sala-Molins, *Le Code Noir ou le calvaire de Canaan*, 1987; Dayan, *Haiti, History, and the Gods*, 199–212; "The Code Noir," in Laurent Dubois and John Garrigus, eds., *Slave Revolution in the Caribbean, 1789–1804*, 2006, 49–54; "Le Code Noir," in *The Louverture Project*, online at http://thelouvertureproject.org/index.php?title=Le_Code_Noir.

14. Jean-Paul Sartre, Frantz Fanon, and Sylvia Wynter probe the logics of white supremacy and bad faith in, respectively, *Anti-Semite and Jew*, *Black Skin, White Masks*, and "Unsettling the Coloniality of Being/Power/Truth/Freedom." Additionally, as Charles Mills notes in *The Racial Contract*, anti-Semitism and antiblack racism are premised upon an "epistemology of ignorance" that buttresses the basic structure of modern racial states (18).

15. *Declaration of the Rights of Man and of the Citizen* [1789], in *The Old Regime and the French Revolution*, 1987, ed. Keith Baker, 237–39. All subsequent *Declaration* citations are from this source.
16. Jean-Jacques Rousseau, *The Social Contract and Other Later Political Writings*, 1997.
17. Marie Olympe de Gouges, "Declaration of the Rights of Woman," in Baker, *Old Regime*, 261–68; Shanti Singham, "Betwixt Cattle and Men," 1994.
18. The Free Citizens of Color, "Address to the National Assembly, October 22, 1789," in Dubois and Garrigus, *Slave Revolution*, 68.
19. "Letters from the Uprising of Vincent Ogé," in Dubois and Garrigus, *Slave Revolution*, 75–78.
20. On petit marronage, see Gabriel Debien, "Le marronage aux Antilles Francaises au XVIIIe siècle,"1966; Gabriel Debien and Jean Fouchard, "Le petit marronage autour du Cap,"1969; Debien, "Marronage in the French Caribbean," 1996; Bernard Delpêche, ed., *Marronnage in the Caribbean*, 2002. Geggus questions the causal roles of petit marronage and vodou in the revolution's outbreak, and assumes that petit marronage is entirely distinct from activities of revolution (*Haitian Revolutionary Studies*, 55–80). While the judgments on vodou are feasible, Geggus's analysis of marronage is unsustainable. Fick provides empirically informed historical counterarguments in *The Making of Haiti*, as does Alvin Thompson in the *Flight to Freedom*. Beyond the historical debate in Haitian revolutionary studies, my disagreement with the Geggus camp is on philosophical grounds, both as pertains to the Haitian Revolution and to thinking about freedom and the interrelationships among modalities of marronage throughout space and time. Note that Thompson has one of the most extensive accounts of marronage comparatively across the Caribbean and the Americas. However, in describing differences between petit and grand marronage and arguing for a change in our political language with regard to "individual marronage" versus "collective marronage," Thompson remains locked in a conceptual knot plaguing other scholars that fails to acknowledge what I call sovereign and sociogenic marronage. Thompson does not change marronage's philosophical landscape; only the phrasing is altered. He also reifies a language begun by John Hope Franklin that situates flight as the "flight to freedom" instead of freedom *as* flight.
21. Debien, "Marronage in the French Caribbean," 118–19.
22. For discourse on grand marronage, see Yvan Debbasch, "Le marronnage," 1961; Leslie Manigat, "The Relationship between Marronage and Slave Revolts and Revolution in St. Domingue-Haiti," 1977; Eugene Genovese, *From Rebellion to Revolution*, 1979; Fouchard, *The Haitian Maroons*; Carlos Esteban Deive, *Los Cimarrones del Maniel de Neiba*, 1985; Gad Heuman, ed., *Out of the House of Bondage*, 1986; E. Kofi Agorsah, ed., *Maroon Heritage*, 1994; Price, *Maroon Societies*; Kenneth Bilby, *True-Born Maroons*, 2006; Timothy Lockley, ed., *Maroon Communities in South Carolina*, 2009; Werner Zips, *Nanny's Asafo Warriors*, 2012.
23. Fouchard, *Haitian Maroons*, 106, 123–43. James observes, "Many of these rebel leaders struck terror into the hearts of the colonists by their raids on plantations and the strength and determination of the resistance they organized against attempts to exterminate them. The greatest of these chiefs was Mackandal" (1963, 20). Alejo Carpentier writes in the magical realist novel, *The Kingdom of This World*: "Macandal, the one-armed, now a *houngan* of the Rada rite, invested with superhuman powers as a result of his possession by the major gods on several occasions, was the Lord of Poison. Endowed with supreme authority by the Rulers of the Other Shore, he proclaimed the crusade of extermination, chosen as he was to wipe out the whites and

create a great empire of free Negroes in Santo Domingo" (1989, 36). For the political biography of Makandal, see Fick's *Making of Haiti* and Dubois's *Avengers of the New World*.

24. Fick, *Making of Haiti*, 51; Bernard Moitt, *Women and Slavery in the French Antilles, 1635–1848*, 2001, xv, 133–39, 174–75.

25. M. L. E. Moreau de Saint-Méry, *Description topographique, physique, civile, politique et historique de la partie française de l'isle Saint-Domingue*, 1796; Debbasch, and Moreau de Saint-Méry, "The Border Maroons of Saint-Domingue," in Price, *Maroon Societies*.

26. Negotiations between Le Maniel maroons and the French took place from 1782 to 1786. Debbasch emphasizes the processes of recognition operating there ("Le Maniel," 146–47).

27. Fick, *Making of Haiti*, 137–56, 313, n. 79, citation at 150. The isolationism of maroon communities should not be mistaken for a "restorationist" impulse to adopt premodern, reactionary, counter-revolutionary African retentions in the New World as Genovese contends (*From Rebellion to Revolution*, xiii–xxiv, 82–85). We must not disaggregate the Caribbean integration of traditional African ways of life from proto-revolutionary strivings. Grand marronage in Saint-Domingue involves the concerted flight of *modern* slaves.

28. Accounts of Toussaint's life and thought include John Beard, *Toussaint L'Ouverture*, 1863; Victor Schoelcher, *Vie de Toussaint Louverture*, 1889; Aimé Césaire, *Toussaint Louverture*, 1961; James, *Black Jacobins*; Mats Lundahl, "Toussaint L'Ouverture and the War Economy of Saint-Domingue, 1796–1802," 1985; Pierre Pluchon, *Toussaint Louverture*, 1989; Jacques Cauna, ed., *Toussaint Louverture et l'indépendance d'Haïti*, 2004; Madison Smartt Bell, *Toussaint Louverture*, 2007; Matthew Calvin, *Toussaint Louverture and the American Civil War*, 2009.

29. Toussaint L'Ouverture, "Proclamation of 29 August 1793," in Tyson, *Toussaint L'Ouverture*, 28.

30. Césaire, *Toussaint Louverture*, 180.

31. Abbé Guillaume-Thomas Raynal, *Histoire philosophique et politique des établissements et du commerce des Européens dans les deux Indes*, 10 vols., 1780. The English translation is *The Philosophical and Political History of the Establishments and Commerce of the Europeans in Two Indies*. *Histoire* was one of the most popular underground works of the eighteenth century to attack the evils of empire, and the contributions to it were anonymous. Raynal's name was listed as the only author of the volumes. In *Enlightenment against Empire*, Sankar Muthu reveals that the passages from *Histoire* read by Toussaint and attributed to Raynal were written by Diderot (72–121). The iconography of Raynal in the aesthetics of abolitionism is apparent in Anne-Louis Girodet's celebrated "Portrait of Jean-Baptiste Belley," c. 1798. Girodet paints an image of the bossale turned affranchis, Belley, leaning against a bust of Raynal in between his speeches to the French National Convention in support of Saint-Domingue emancipation.

32. Raynal, cited in James, *Black Jacobins*, 25; Toussaint L'Ouverture, "Self-Portrait" [1801], in *The Haitian Revolution*, 41. On autobiography as political thought, see Toussaint's memoires, first published in Joseph Saint-Rémy, ed., *Mémoires du général Toussaint-Louverture, écrits par lui-même, pouvant servir à l'histoire de sa vie*, 1853.

33. L'Ouverture, "Letter to the Directory, October 28, 1797," in Tyson, *Toussaint L'Ouverture*, 43.

34. I base my translation of the Haitian 1801 Constitution on Dubois and Garrigus, *Slave Revolution*, 167–70 and *The Louverture Project*, online at: http://thelouverture

project.org/index.php?title=Haitian_Constitution_of_1801_(English). For poignant constitutional commentaries, see Louis-Joseph Janvier, *Les constitutions d-Haïti (1801–1885)*, 1886; Claude Moïse, *Le Projet nationale de Toussaint Louverture et la Constitution de 1801*, 2001. Although Toussaint's constitution is not a primary focus, Fischer stresses in *Modernity Disavowed* the significance of Haitian constitutionalism for political philosophy.

35. L'Ouverture, "Address to Soldiers for the Universal Destruction of Slavery" [18 May, 1797], in *Haitian Revolution*, 28.

36. L'Ouverture, "A Refutation of Some Assertions in a Speech Pronounced in the Corp Législatif . . . by Viénot Vaublanc" [1797], in Dubois and Garrigus, *Slave Revolution*, 151. For a useful comparison, see the letters of Toussaint in Gérard Laurent, ed., *Toussaint L'Ouverture à travers sa correspondance, 1794–1798*, 1953.

37. Nesbitt, *Universal Emancipation*, 153–77. Nesbitt surmises that the Haitian Revolution is a "Spinozist" event without temporal or textual evidentiary support. While disagreeing with this conclusion and other claims of Nesbitt in both *Universal Emancipation* and *Caribbean Critique* (2013), my argument that competing conceptions of freedom irreducible to Toussaint's are operative during the insurrection is not contingent upon disproving them.

38. In *Free and French in the Caribbean* (2013), John Walsh charts a direct line in thought from what I call the cosmopolitan nationalism of Toussaint to Césaire's advocacy of Martinican departmentalization instead of independence. Césaire knows well Toussaint's political biography and Haitian revolutionary political philosophy. There are problems, however, in juxtaposing Toussaint and Césaire as political leaders, for Césaire neither functions in the role of a lawgiver nor espouses sovereign marronage. Also unlike Toussaint, Césaire comes to regret his longtime support of a gradualist approach to independence. Césaire conceives of departmentalization as a stage toward independence and freedom, yet he ends up in a double bind similar to Toussaint through a mistaken collapsing of "free" and "French" as coterminous in constitutionalism. The crucial point is not the leaders' modes of rule, but the overlap in logic of cosmopolitan nationalism and the departmentalization of Guadeloupe and Martinique.

39. James, *Black Jacobins*, 242.

40. Robert Fatton Jr., *The Roots of Haitian Despotism*, 2007; Dubois, *Haiti*, 31.

41. L'Ouverture, "Forced Labor Decree, 12 October 1800," in Tyson, *Toussaint L'Ouverture*, 52, 56. Article 14 of the 1801 Constitution states: "Since the colony is essentially agricultural, it cannot be allowed to suffer even the slightest interruption in the work of cultivation." The fifteenth article renders every plantation a "factory" and "peaceful refuge" that requires "the union of cultivators and workers." The plantation economy is referred to in terms of patriarchal right, with fathers "of necessity" being the property owners.

42. Archie Singham, *The Hero and the Crowd in a Colonial Polity*, 1968; Michel-Rolph Trouillot, *Haiti: State Against Nation*, 1990. Like the philosophical poetics of Edwidge Danticat, Madison Smartt Bell, Ntozake Shange, Jean-Claude Fignolé, Jacques Roumain, Édouard Glissant, and Derek Walcott in its wake, Aimé Césaire's epic poem encapsulates Toussaint's double bind and late realization. See Césaire, *Notebook of a Return to the Native Land* [1939], 47, 51.

43. C. L. R. James, "Lectures on *The Black Jacobins*," 2000, 99. On the relationship between the lectures and first two editions of James's text, see Anthony Bogues, "Afterword," 2000; Scott, *Conscripts of Modernity*. James gestures toward this retrospective deduc-

tion in the longest chapter of *Black Jacobins*, "The War of Independence": "Once more the masses had shown greater political understanding than their leaders" (339). Georges Lefebvre argued in several works such as *The Coming of the French Revolution* and *The Great Fear of 1789* that 1789 would never be interpreted properly if popular leaders were the sole objects of study. Although Lefebvre unfortunately did not explore the Haitian Revolution, the point about decentering the study of sovereigns alone in revolutions is prescient.

44. C. L. R. James, *You Don't Play with Revolution*, 2009, 51–70. James gave this lecture at the Montréal Congress of Black Writers.

45. L'Ouverture, cited in Dubois, *Avengers of the New World*, 278.

46. Aristide wrote in exile a lengthy introduction to an updated compilation of Toussaint's writings. Note also Robert Fatton Jr.'s "The Rise, Fall, and Second Coming of Jean-Bertrand Aristide," in Sepinwall, *Haitian History*, 294–311.

CHAPTER FOUR

1. Jean-Jacques Dessalines in consultation with Louis Boisrond-Tonnerre, "The Haitian Declaration of Independence" [1804], in *Slave Revolution in the Caribbean, 1789–1804*, 2006, ed. Laurent Dubois and John Garrigus, 188, 189, 190.

2. Laurent Dubois, *Haiti*, 2012, 16–17.

3. Frantz Fanon, *Black Skin, White Masks*, 2008 [1952], xii.

4. Edwidge Danticat, *Create Dangerously*, 2011.

5. Gordon Wood, *Empire of Liberty*, 2009; Anthony Bogues, *Empire of Liberty*, 2010. For discussion of the performative and constative elements of the American Declaration of Independence that question reading Jefferson narrowly in terms of natural law, consult Bonnie Honig, "Declarations of Independence," 1991.

6. United States Declaration of Independence [1776], online at: http://www.archives. gov/exhibits/charters/declaration_transcript.html.

7. Thomas Jefferson, draft of the US Declaration of Independence, cited in David Brion Davis, *The Problem of Slavery in the Age of Revolution, 1770–1823*, 1999, 9.

8. The United States approved legislation to arm Saint-Domingue insurrectionists, mindful of the war between France and Britain that had implications for early US strategic interests. When Jefferson became president, he feared the effects of the Haitian Revolution on the activities of slaves and the status of slavery in America. Jefferson, with the support of Congress, reversed US support of the revolutionaries. The change in foreign policy ended the exportation of arms to the island and began a period of isolationism that would continue into the Haitian postrevolutionary period. See Gordon Brown, *Toussaint's Clause*, 2005; Ashli White, *Encountering Revolution*, 2010.

9. James C. Scott, *Two Cheers for Anarchism*, 2012, 1–29.

10. In *Haiti: State Against Nation*, Michel-Rolph Trouillot states: "The long overdue reconciliation of state and nation requires the fundamental understanding that, in Haiti, the peasantry *is* the nation" (230). Trouillot's contention that the Haitian peasantry is equal to the nation and the nation-qua-people are essential to understanding Haitian private, political, and social activities is insightful. Whereas Trouillot's prime focus is the actions of the peasantry vis-à-vis the state in postrevolutionary Haiti, I suggest we return to analysis of peasants' activities during the Saint Domingue revolution, as it proves useful in the interpretation of freedom both within the upheaval and in the initial set of postrevolutionary documents. According to Orlando Figes, the failure to systematize the actions of rural peasants has been a reason for misin-

terpretations of the causes and course of the Russian Revolution. See Figes, *Peasant Russia, Civil War*, 1989. Frantz Fanon, Thomas Holt, Robin Kelley, Barrington Moore Jr., Theda Skocpol, and James Scott also demonstrate the centrality of peasants to revolution and flight. With regard to the Caribbean, Sidney Mintz has maintained in *Caribbean Transformations* (1974) and other works that slaves were at most a "proto-peasantry," reconstituted in phases from pre-emancipation squatters and yeoman to postslavery peasants. I refer to the peasantry throughout as persons located primarily in rural spaces across time who imagine their daily worldview and subsistence either in relation to land not possessed or owned by them or who have possession and ownership over the land intimately connected to that quotidian existence.

11. Orlando Patterson, "Slavery and Slave Revolts" [1970]; Patterson, *Slavery and Social Death*, 1982. See the introduction for limitations on Patterson's idea of social death.

12. In *Nietzsche, Psychology, and First Philosophy* (2010), Robert Pippin explores Nietzsche's reference to psychology as the "queen of the sciences" in *Beyond Good and Evil*. Another point on Nietzsche, underappreciated in Pippin's account, is found in *On the Genealogy of Morals*. In *Genealogy* Nietzsche describes "master morality" and "slave morality," with *ressentiment* as the driving catalyst causing struggle between the two. While Fanon was fond of Nietzsche on the question of maturity, Nietzsche could have learned from Fanon the significance of lived experience for mastery, slavery, and the psychology of freedom. Along with the revolt in morality, experiences affect our struggles, revolutionary actions, and flight.

13. Fanon, *Black Skin, White Masks*, xii.

14. Ibid., 93. *Nègre* translates as both "negro" and "nigger."

15. Ibid., 197.

16. Fanon extends the description of the zone's revolutionary potential in *Toward the African Revolution* (1967), particularly "First Truths on the Colonial Problem," "Racism and Culture," "West Indians and Africans," "Decolonization and Independence," and "This Africa to Come."

17. Fanon writes, "Reacting against the constitutionalizing trend at the end of the nineteenth century, Freud demanded that the individual factor be taken into account in psychoanalysis. He replaced the phylogenetic theory by an ontogenetic approach. We shall see that the alienation of the black man is not an individual question. Alongside phylogeny and ontogeny, there is sociogeny. . . . Society, unlike biochemical processes, does not escape human influence. Man is what brings society into being" (*Black Skin, White Masks*, xv). For other appreciations of Fanon on sociogenesis, consult Sylvia Wynter, "Unsettling the Coloniality of Being/Power/Truth/Freedom," 2003; Paul Gilroy, "Fanon and the Value of the Human," 2011.

18. Fanon, *Black Skin, White Masks*, 205.

19. Frantz Fanon, *The Wretched of the Earth*, 2004 [1961], 138, 239, translation modified. Fanon's *Year Five of the Algerian Revolution* (1959) ends with a similar declaration: a revolution *"changes man (l'homme) and renews society."* See *Oeuvres*, 2011, 410; orig. emphasis.

20. Fanon, *Wretched of the Earth*, 239.

21. "The Haitian Declaration of Independence," in Dubois and Garrigus, *Slave Revolution*, 189.

22. George Lamming, "The Negro Writer and His World," 1956; Ludwig Wittgenstein, *Philosophical Investigations*, 2001, 38, 16. Whereas Wittgenstein and Lamming consider the cognitive benefits and promise of names and naming, Scott discusses the instrumental utilization of naming by rational state planners for purposes of legibility,

rule making, homogenization, the obliteration and replacement of vernacular orders with hierarchical official orders of knowledge, and the construction of "landscapes of control and appropriation." See Scott, *Two Cheers for Anarchism*, 30–56. The three observations are consistent with the complexity of definitions offered for names and naming.

23. Cuban discourses on the turn of the twentieth century, for example, recount stories of a national "Cuban War of Independence," a war that was unsuccessful and would be resumed with the onset of the Cuban Revolution. "The Spanish-American War" is the phrase used in national narratives of the United States and Spain for the final stages of conflict between the states. To view the end of war as the maintenance of a colony or the failure to achieve independence is reliant on language and one's interpretation. Ernesto Ché Guevara's "Socialism and Man in Cuba" (1965), heir to José Martí's "Our America" (1891), "The Cuban Revolutionary Party in Cuba" (1895) by Martí and Máximo Gómez, and impending discourses on the Cuban War of Independence and Cuban Revolution, portrays facets of contending political languages.

24. Mahmood Mamdani, "The Politics of Naming," 2007. See also J. G. A. Pocock, *Politics, Language and Time*, 1971.

25. Dessalines was illiterate and had the assistance of secretaries, including Boisrond-Tonnerre, who transcribed dictations for use as official documents and letters. Dessalines would sign the transcribed texts.

26. Marcus Rainsford's magisterial *An Historical Account of the Black Empire of Hayti* (2013 [1805]) was the first published account of the Haitian Revolution in the English language. A British army officer, eyewitness to insurrection, and author who met with Toussaint L'Ouverture, among other revolutionary and counter-revolutionary figures, Rainsford reprinted the contested proclamation in his narrative (260–61).

27. On the naming of Haiti and indigenism in Haitian thought, see Jean Price-Mars, *So Spoke the Uncle*, 1983; David Geggus, *Haitian Revolutionary Studies*, 2002, 207–20; Matthew Smith, *Red and Black in Haiti*, 2009.

28. "The Haitian Declaration of Independence," 188.

29. Ibid., 189, 190.

30. Ibid., 188.

31. Ibid., 191.

32. Jean-Jacques Dessalines in consultation with Juste Chanlatte, "Liberty or Death! A Proclamation" [April 28, 1804], cited in Rainsford, *An Historical Account*, 265.

33. "The Haitian Declaration of Independence," 188, 189.

34. Leslie Desmangles, *The Faces of the Gods*, 1992; Joan Dayan, *Haiti, History, and the Gods*, 1995; Kate Ramsey, *The Spirits and the Law*, 2011. The ethnographies of vodou metaphysics and philosophy by Zora Neale Hurston and Katherine Dunham are still useful. In the influential study *Divine Horsemen* (1953), Maya Deren says that "virtuoso is the province of divinity. Only the loa are virtuosi" (cited in Danticat's *Create Dangerously*, 131). While not a primary deity, Dessalines is the only Haitian revolutionary leader to become a lwa. Dayan depicts a sign of virtuosity: "Neither the radical rationality of Toussaint nor the sovereign pomp of Christophe led to apotheosis. Yet Dessalines, so resistant to enlightened heroics, gradually acquired unequaled power in the Haitian imagination" (*Haiti, History, and the Gods*, 17).

35. The consequences of competing conceptions of freedom in tension with one another during the Haitian Revolution prefigure the collapse of forced Soviet collectivization, Tanzania's *ujamaa* villagization experiment, and other projects of what James Scott

calls "authoritarian high-modernism" (though the philosophical rationale demonstrated by the revolution's events precedes its emergence). The imposition on inhabitants by state bureaucrats of modes of legibility and rationalism intended to augment human well-being have backfired. Top-down models of freedom distort freedom itself. In *Seeing Like a State* (1998), James Scott proposes as an alternative the use of *metis* (local knowledge) in social and political formations. While *metis* is integral, there is neither a separation of *metis* from intuitions of statecraft, nor the erection of walls between the state, non-state actors, and the people in sociogenesis, as Scott's more recent philosophical anarchism explores. Sociogenic marronage indicates that flight, interpreted through the prism of peasants and everyday people, uncovers a logic of freedom pertaining to individuals and masses, civil society and political society.

36. John Thornton, "African Soldiers in the Haitian Revolution," 1991; Thornton, "'I Am the Subject of the King of Congo,'" 1993, 185.

37. Thornton, "'I Am the Subject of the King of Congo,'" 210–14. Although Carolyn Fick, C. L. R. James, Jean Fouchard, David Geggus, Thornton, and commentators in French, English, and Kreyòl, among other languages, disagree on translation, there is general consensus on the following Bois-Caïman chant transliteration:

> Eh! Eh! Bomba, hen! hen!
> Canga bafio té
> Canga moune dé lé
> Canga doki la
> Cango li.

38. Boukman Dutty, cited in Dubois, *Haiti*, 91–92.

39. Fanon, *Wretched of the Earth*, 3–5.

40. Achille Mbembe, *On the Postcolony*, 2001, 236–37.

41. The Haitian colonial state has a family resemblance to the bifurcated state structure that Mahmood Mamdani attributes to African colonial states. Among the areas differentiating the anticolonial movement and the vision of the postcolonial state in Saint-Domingue from movements in those African polities is its conception of state architecture. Saint-Domingue's peasants sought deracialization only of civil society, not the state. Their vèvè architectonics and formal state constitutionalism after the Toussaint moment portray this. Toussaint's proposed political order is closer to what Mamdani describes as the pitfalls of "decentralized despotism," the two-tiered statecraft of direct and indirect rule. See Mamdani, *Citizen and Subject*, 1996.

42. Carolyn Fick, *The Making of Haiti*, 1990, 168–69, 180; Anthony Bogues, "Investigating the Radical Caribbean Intellectual Tradition," 1998; Fick, "The Saint-Domingue Slave Revolution and the Unfolding of Independence, 1791–1804," 2009.

43. Fick, *Making of Haiti*, 170.

44. *Intersectionality*, a term coined by legal scholar Kimberlé Crenshaw to highlight how intersecting elements such as gender, race, class, sexual orientation, and disability affect a person's condition, has been used beyond the original area of jurisprudence (Hancock, *Solidarity Politics for Millennials*, 2011). Anna Julia Cooper, a figure whose 1892 treatise *A Voice from the South* is considered by late modern black feminists the founding text of intersectional thought, later composed *Slavery and the French Revolutionists, 1788–1805* (1988). Cooper's investigations into vectors of gender and race echoed the debates begun by enslaved black women in the proto-constituent assemblies of the Haitian Revolution.

45. The reconstructed Arendtian distinction between liberation and the foundation of freedom has been discussed earlier in the book. On violence as an intrinsic facet of decolonization and postcolonial statecraft, see Fanon, *Wretched of the Earth*, 1–62; Neil Roberts, "Fanon, Sartre, Violence, and Freedom," 2004. Fanon states in a famous passage, "National liberation, national reawakening, restoration of the nation to the people or Commonwealth, whatever the name used, whatever the latest expression, decolonization is always a violent event" (1).

46. Examinations of the 1805 Constitution include Claude Moïse, *Constitutions et luttes de pouvoir en Haïti*, 2 vols., 1988; Sibylle Fischer, *Modernity Disavowed*, 2004; Anthony Bogues, "The 1805 Haitian Constitution," 2009. What remains to be discussed is the significance of the document to marronage. In what follows, I base my translation of the constitution on Louis Joseph Janvier, *Les constitutions d'Haïti (1801–1885)*, 1886, 30–41; Dubois and Garrigus, *Slave Revolution*, 191–96; and *The Louverture Project*, online at: http://thelouvertureproject.org/index.php?title=Haitian_Constitution _of_1805.

47. Vicki Hseuh, *Hybrid Constitutions*, 2010.

48. C. L. R. James, *The Black Jacobins*, 1963, 86. James's incisive observation is an anomaly in that *Black Jacobins* otherwise disregards the relationship between vodou and freedom in revolutionary Saint-Domingue because of its orientation as a study of Toussaint and elite leadership rather than slaves. Anthony Bogues attributes this to James's membership in Caribbean and black radical "heretical" traditions that shun prophecy and metaphysics in their political thought (*Black Heretics, Black Prophets*, 69–93). Determining whether heretics and prophets belong to distinct intellectual traditions does not alter this accurate assessment of *Black Jacobins*.

49. James, *Black Jacobins*, 11–12, 13.

50. Lewis R. Gordon, *Bad Faith and Antiblack Racism*, 1995, 146; orig. emphasis. David Brion Davis charts the development of antiblack racism and its impact on the revolutionary age before the Haitian categorical inversion of blackness in *Inhuman Bondage*, 2006, 48–76. In "Racism and Culture" (1956), Fanon contends that "the racist in a culture with racism is therefore normal" and "racism is therefore not a constant of the human spirit" (*Toward the African Revolution*, 40–41). Colonialism normalized the biopolitics of antiblack racism and treated the negation of the black as an affirmation of a universal. Haitian constitutionalism was attentive to the cultural relativism of colonialism that presented itself as an unalterable universal order. The 1805 Constitution developed in response to the stated biocentric order.

51. On the reactions of white observers to Dessalines's massacre decree and the bloody last days of revolution, consult the letters of Leonora Sansay (pseudonym Mary Hassel) to Aaron Burr in *Secret History; or, the Horrors of St. Domingo* (1808); Mlle de Palaiseau's *Histoire des Mesdemoiselles de Saint-Janvier* (1812); and Peter Chazotte's *Historical Sketches of the Revolution and the Foreign and Civil Wars in the Island of St. Domingo* (1840), reprinted in Jeremy Popkin, *Facing Racial Revolution*, 2007. In *From Dessalines to Duvalier* (1979), David Nicholls chronicles Dessalines's thought in the context of contemporaneous Haitian geopolitics. For Susan Buck-Morss, the massacre order of Dessalines amounts to political jihad. "Osama bin Laden meets Jean-Jacques Dessalines" when the logic of the September 11, 2001 al-Qaeda terrorist architect is paired with "Dessalines's justification of racial slaughter." See Buck-Morss, *Hegel, Haiti, and Universal History*, 2009, 142, 143. The idea of jihad reduces to a narrow fundamentalist political theology the greater complexity of Dessalines's

sovereign decisionism. What Buck-Morss, Nicholls, and the white observers in Saint-Domingue expose are the effects of the unsuccessful attempt by Dessalines to balance competing macropolitical visions of flight.

52. Jean-Luc Nancy, in *The Inoperative Community* (1991), probes inoperative modes of communal organization. For Nancy, communities are to be understood in relation to their resistance to imminent state power and agents of those states.

53. Article 9 states: "No one is worthy of being a Haitian if he is not a good father, a good husband, and above all, a good soldier." Hilary Beckles contests the situatedness of enslaved black women in the revolution and construction of the new Haitian state. For Beckles, contemporary feminist thinkers are as complicit as other observers in the selective treatment of Haitian revolutionary details: "Despite the abundance of evidence which shows the active involvement of women in the revolutionary process, the independent nation of Haiti was constructed, in both its constitutional and administrative scaffolds, as an expression and representation of masculinist authority that systematically sidelined and repressed women into second-class citizenship. Indeed, successive constitutions, within the first two decades of independence, denied women rights that men took for granted as expressions of their citizenship." See Beckles, *Centering Woman*, 1999, 188. Beckles's deft indictment is more germane to post-revolutionary rollbacks in constitutionalism than the 1805 text. On feminist thought dispelling select accounts of the past, see Patricia Mohammed, ed., *Gendered Realities*, 2002; Rhoda Reddock, ed., *Interrogating Caribbean Masculinities*, 2004; Pamela Scully and Diana Paton, eds., *Gender and Slave Emancipation in the Atlantic World*, 2005; Verene Shepherd, ed., *Engendering Caribbean History*, 2011.

54. Edwidge Danticat, "Children of the Sea," in *Krik? Krak!* 1995, 1–29.

55. Danticat employs the term *dew breaker* in another work of the same title.

56. Derek Walcott and Edward Kamau Brathwaite, cited as epigraphs to Édouard Glissant, *Poetics of Relation*, 1997; Stephanie Smallwood, *Saltwater Slavery*, 2007.

57. Danticat, *Krik? Krak!* 27, 28.

58. Mimi Sheller, *Democracy After Slavery*, 2000; Smith, *Red and Black in Haiti*, 71–148; Alyssa Sepinwall, ed., *Haitian History*, 2013.

59. Trouillot, *Haiti: State Against Nation*; Peter Hallward, *Damning the Flood*, 2010; Millery Polyné, ed., *The Idea of Haiti*, 2013; Alex Dupuy, *Haiti*, 2014.

CHAPTER FIVE

1. Édouard Glissant, *The Fourth Century*, 2001 [1964], 141.

2. Édouard Glissant, *Caribbean Discourse*, 1989, 255–56.

3. Sylvia Wynter, "Beyond the Word of Man," 1989, 638.

4. On the 1998 debates, see Catherine Reinhardt, *Claims to Memory*, 2006, 1–21. The passage of the French decree to annually commemorate slavery occurred after the publication of Reinhardt's text. Also pertinent is Françoise Vergès, *Mémoire enchaînée*, 2006.

5. Glissant's commentary on the committee tasks includes *Mémoires des esclavages* (2007).

6. Ernest Breleur, Édouard Glissant, et al., *Manifeste pour les 'produits' de haute nécessité*, 2009; Yarimar Bonilla, "Guadeloupe Is Ours," 2010.

7. For overviews of Glissant's life and work, consult Beverley Ormerod, "Beyond *Négritude*," 1974; J. Michael Dash, *Édouard Glissant*, 1995; Celia Britton, *Édouard Glissant and Postcolonial Theory*, 1999; Jeannie Suk, *Postcolonial Paradoxes in French Caribbean Writing*, 2001; Georges Desportes, *La paraphilosophie d'Edouard Glissant*, 2008; Lorna Burns, "Becoming-Postcolonial, Becoming-Caribbean," 2009; Charles Forsdick, "Late

Glissant," 2010; Alain Ménil, *Les voies de la créolisation*, 2011; Marisa Parham and John Drabinski, eds., *The Work of Édouard Glissant*, 2012; Britton, ed., *Édouard Glissant*, 2013.

8. Édouard Glissant and Patrick Chamoiseau, *Quand les murs tombent*, 2007.

9. For other studies on the maroon figure and marronage in Glissant's oeuvre, see Suzanne Crosta, *Le marronnage créateur*, 1991; Peter Hitchcock, "Antillanité and the Art of Resistance," 1996; Richard Burton, *Le roman marron*, 1997; Michèle Praeger, *The Imaginary Caribbean and Caribbean Imaginary*, 2003; Celia Britton, *The Sense of Community in French Caribbean Fiction*, 2008.

10. Criticisms of Glissant on this point, to which I offer a rebuttal, include Peter Hallward's *Absolutely Postcolonial* (2001).

11. Kathleen Balutansky and Marie-Agnès Sourieau, eds., *Caribbean Creolization*, 1998; Okwui Enwezor et. al., eds., *Créolité and Creolization*, 2003; Michaeline Crichlow, *Globalization and the Post-Creole Imagination*, 2009; Robin Cohen and Paola Toninato, eds., *The Creolization Reader*, 2010; Françoise Lionnet and Shu-mei Shih, eds., *The Creolization of Theory*, 2011; Michael Monahan, *The Creolizing Subject*, 2011; Jane Anna Gordon, *Creolizing Political Theory*, 2014.

12. Paget Henry, *Caliban's Reason*, 2000, 88.

13. Antonio Benítez-Rojo, "Three Words towards Creolization," in Balutansky and Sourieau, *Caribbean Creolization*, 53–61.

14. Wilson Harris, "Creoleness," in Balutansky and Sourieau, *Caribbean Creolization*, 31.

15. Jean Bernabé, Patrick Chamoiseau, and Raphaël Confiant, "In Praise of Creoleness," 1990, 886.

16. Maryse Condé, "*Créolité* without Creole Language?" in Balutansky and Sourieau, *Caribbean Creolization*, 101–9. It is noteworthy that the *Créolité* movement manifesto cites Glissant as the founding theoritician. Glissant has subsequently rejected this role numerous times due to some of the same concerns listed by Condé. In one response, Glissant remarks: "I told them [Bernabé, Chamoiseau, and Confiant] that I did not agree with the theory of créolité. Because for me, *creolization* is a process which diffracts. . . . We are in a process of *creolization*. We are no definition of being Creole. That makes a big difference." See Kamau Brathwaite and Édouard Glissant, "A Dialogue," in *Presencia criolla en el Caribe y América Latina*, 1996, ed. I. Phaf, 24.

17. Kamau Brathwaite, *Roots*, 1993.

18. Stuart Hall, "Negotiating Caribbean Identities," 1995; Hall, "Creolization, Diaspora, and Hybridity in the Context of Globalization," in Enwezor, *Créolité and Creolization*, 185–98; Hall, "*Créolité* and the Process of Creolization," in Cohen and Toninato, *Creolization Reader*, 26–38.

19. I draw upon here a position advanced previously in Jane Anna Gordon and Neil Roberts, "Introduction: The Project of Creolizing Rousseau," 2009.

20. Édouard Glissant, *Poetics of Relation*, 1997, 34. Henceforth cited as *Poetics*.

21. Édouard Glissant, "Identity and Diversity," 1997; Glissant, *Faulkner, Mississippi*, 1999, 114–15; Glissant, *Introduction à une poétique du divers*, 2006, 11–32.

22. Édouard Glissant, "Europe and the Antilles" [1998].

23. Édouard Glissant, "Creolization and the Making of the Americas" [1995].

24. Carol Gluck and Anne Tsing, eds., *Words in Motion*, 2009.

25. My use of *poeticism* and *historicism* follows that of Paget Henry. Jürgen Habermas develops a communicative model of critical thinking and an antimythic mode of rational discourse in *The Theory of Communicative Action*, vol. 1 (1984), *The Theory of Communicative Action*, vol. 2 (1987), and *Between Facts and Norms* (1996). For Henry's critique of Jürgen Habermas on mythic discourse and reason, see *Caliban's*

Reason, 167–94. Glissant shares Henry's view that the notions of reason and freedom are a confluence of the rational/non-rational and mythic/non-mythic.

26. Wilson Harris, "Tradition and the West Indian Novel" and "History, Fable and Myth in the Caribbean and Guianas," in *The Selected Essays of Wilson Harris*, 1999, ed. Andrew Bundy, 140–51, 152–54.

27. Édouard Glissant, *Poetic Intention*, 2010 [1969], 183. William Connolly's *A World of Becoming* (2011) supports Glissant's contention that relational dynamism is intrinsic to states of becoming: "No system in a world of becoming composed of multiple, interacting systems of different types, with different capacities of self-organization, is closed. It is both more vulnerable to the outside than the carriers of hubris imagine and periodically susceptible to creative movement from within and without simultaneously" (147).

28. Glissant, *Poetics*, 21.

29. Glissant, *Poetic Intention*, 19.

30. Michael Hanchard, *Party/Politics*, 2006, 154–55.

31. Jacques Rancière, "The Politics of Literature," 2004, 10.

32. Glissant, *Fourth Century*, 29, 38.

33. Ibid., 127.

34. In *Le discours antillais*, Glissant argues that the maroon "is the only true popular hero of the Antilles" and "an incontestable example of systematic opposition, of total refusal" (1997, 180; my translation).

35. Glissant, *Fourth Century*, 63.

36. Ibid., 29, 30.

37. For an expanded, albeit different, interpretation of Ariel in Caribbean thought, see Holger Henke, "Ariel's Ethos," 2004.

38. Glissant, *Fourth Century*, 95.

39. Ibid., 94.

40. Ibid., 9.

41. Glissant, *The Overseer's Cabin*, 2011 [1981], 99.

42. Priska Degras, "Name of the Fathers, History of the Name," 1989, 615.

43. Glissant, *Fourth Century*, 154.

44. Ibid., 177–78.

45. James C. Scott, *The Art of Not Being Governed*, 2009, 40–63, 85–97, 127–77; Neil Roberts, "State, Power, Anarchism," 2011.

46. My utilization of Frantz Fanon's idea of the *zone of nonbeing* in *Black Skin, White Masks* has been explored in previous chapters. However, the relationships among Glissant's thought, Scott's, and Fanon's are discussed here for the first time.

47. Glissant, *Fourth Century*, 273–74.

48. Ibid., 290.

49. Ibid., 286.

50. Patrick Chamoiseau's *Texaco* (1998) is a more recent poeticist account of the trials and tribulations facing maroon communities and the ecology of being a maroon.

51. Wynter, "Beyond the Word of Man," 646.

52. Imprecise and incomplete translations of Glissant's writings have accounted for significant misreadings by critics and a general neglect of various Glissant writings by Anglophone scholars, of which *Le discours antillais* perhaps is the archetypal example. For instance, Glissant's *Caribbean Discourse* (1989) is the English translation of the 1981 *Le discours antillais*. *Caribbean Discourse* is 270 pages, a fraction of the more than 500-page original French text and 839-page 1997 Gallimard French edition.

Additionally, the English translation of *Le discours antillais* does not include several
of Glissant's numerous theoretical discussions of maroons and marronage. Due to
the plot of Glissant's novels and play, the excising of maroons and marronage has
not taken place to a comparable degree. Therefore, I cite henceforth from Glissant's
Caribbean Discourse when ideas are included in both language versions. When referring to passages deleted from the translation, I refer to the 1997 French edition.

53. For one of Glissant's last examinations of Césaire's thought, see *Philosophie de la relation*, 2009, 128–37.
54. Frantz Fanon, "West Indians and Africans" [1955], in *Toward the African Revolution*,
1967, 21–22; orig. emphasis.
55. Glissant, *Caribbean Discourse*, 88.
56. Aspects of my biographical account of Glissant draw from Daniel Radford, *Edouard
Glissant*, 1982; Dash, *Édouard Glissant*, 1995, 4–25.
57. Cited from the second epigraph to *Caribbean Discourse*.
58. Glissant, *Caribbean Discourse*, 25; orig. emphasis.
59. Ibid., 62.
60. Walter Benjamin, *Illuminations*, 2007, 257. Benjamin states in proposition eight of
"Theses on the Philosophy of History," "The tradition of the oppressed teaches us
that the 'state of emergency' in which we live is not the exception but the rule. We
must attain to a conception of history that is in keeping with this insight."
61. Glissant, *Caribbean Discourse*, 66–67, 138–39.
62. Ibid., 62–63, orig. emphasis.
63. Ibid., 33, 37–42.
64. Ibid., 31–32, 34–35; orig. emphasis.
65. Ibid., 50, n. 6.
66. Ibid., 13–18.
67. Ibid., 121–34.
68. Ibid., 19–26
69. Ibid., 11.
70. Frantz Fanon, *Wretched of the Earth*, 2004, 9.
71. Glissant, *Caribbean Discourse*, 10–11, 105, 159–61. Alternative appreciations of land
and landscape in Glissant include Alain Baudot, "Edouard Glissant," 1989; Katherine McKittrick, *Demonic Grounds*, 2006.
72. Glissant, *Caribbean Discourse*, 69–87.
73. Wynter, "Beyond the Word of Man," 638.
74. Sylvia Wynter, "Unsettling the Coloniality of Being/Power/Truth/Freedom," 2003.
75. Sylvia Wynter, "The Ceremony Must be Found," 1984, 19–70.
76. Glissant, *Caribbean Discourse*, 26.
77. Jorge Luis Borges, "Las versions homéricas," cited in Edith Grossman, *Why Translation Matters*, 2010, 1.
78. Benjamin, *Illuminations*, 70.
79. Glissant, *Le discours antillais*, 113, 115.
80. Ibid., 123–24. The lyrical thought of the Wailers on *Survival* (1979) aptly captures
this principle, given Glissant's acknowledgment of the originality of Rastafari reggae,
the phenomenology of music, and poeticism as an aesthetic form to convey attitudes
on the landscape expressed insufficiently in historicist prose alone. While not refer-
encing the album, Glissant remarks on reggae and musical thought: "Reggae in the
realm of the 'audio-visual' corresponds to 'poetry' . . . A Caribbean discourse finds
its expression as much in the explosion of the original cry, as in the patience of the

landscape when it is recognized, as in the imposition of lived rhythms" (*Caribbean Discourse*, 108–9).

81. Sylvia Wynter, *Black Metamorphosis*, unpublished MS., 71–75.
82. Glissant, *Caribbean Discourse*, 221.
83. Ibid., 222.
84. Ibid., 196–97.
85. Ibid., 209–10, n. 3.
86. Ibid., 195–220.
87. Hitchcock, "Antillanité and the Art of Resistance," 48.
88. Glissant, *Caribbean Discourse*, 255.
89. Ibid., 258–59.
90. Ibid., 256.
91. Édouard Glissant, *Monsieur Toussaint*, 2005 [1961]. The four acts are "The Gods," "The Dead," "The People," and "The Heroes." Glissant's theatrical account of Toussaint is foremost in the twentieth century along with C. L. R. James's *Toussaint L'Ouverture*, a three-act play written in 1934, staged at London's Westminster Theater in 1936, with Paul Robeson as Toussaint, and published before *The Black Jacobins*.
92. The temporality of *Monsieur Toussaint* is decipherable after we recognize that the play's original preface is where Glissant first coins the phrase "a prophetic vision of the past." *Le discours antillais* offers an elaboration of this concept two decades later. Glissant observes that the play "is linked to what I would call, paradoxically, *a prophetic vision of the past*. For those whose history has been reduced by others to darkness and despair, the recovery of the near or distant past is imperative. To renew acquaintance with one's history, obscured or obliterated by others, is to relish fully the present, for the experience of the past, stripped of its roots in time, yields only hollow delights" (15–16; orig. emphasis).
93. Glissant, *Monsieur Toussaint*, 14. Glissant associates inclusion of the dead in the play with traditions in the Antilles of "casual communication with the dead" (16). This corresponds to Glissant's notion of landscape integral to political systems.
94. Glissant, *Poetics*, 185–86.
95. Scott, *Art of Not Being Governed*, 32.
96. Glissant, *Poetics*, 199–201.
97. Ibid., 11–14. The body of scholarship labeling Glissant a "Deleuzian" with the publication of *Poetics* is erroneous. First, such a claim positions Glissant's thought as a version of derivative discourse from another thinker. Second, Glissant develops the notion of Relation from his early writings in the late 1950s–1960s. Relevant is the importance Glissant finds in integrating the concepts of rhizome and lines of flight with his theorizations of marronage.
98. Gilles Deleuze and Félix Guattari, *A Thousand Plateaus*, 1987, 6–7.
99. Deleuze and Guattari, *A Thousand Plateaus*, 25.
100. Deleuze and Guattari, *A Thousand Plateaus*, 9, 502–8.
101. Glissant, *Poetics*, 6–8.
102. Ibid., xii; Maryse Condé, *Crossing the Mangrove*, 1995; Suk, *Postcolonial Paradoxes in French Caribbean Writing*, 178–80; Manthia Diawara (director), *Edouard Glissant*, 2010.
103. Glissant's first epigraph in *Poetics* is from Derek Walcott's celebrated poem, "The Sea Is History," published in the Walcott collection, *The Star-Apple-Kingdom* (1979). The volume contains as well "The Schooner *Flight*," "The Saddhu of Couva," and "Forest of Europe."

104. Derek Walcott, "The Schooner *Flight*," in *Selected Poems*, 2007, 127–36.

105. Glissant, *Poetics*, 103–9.

106. Ibid., 217, n. 1.

107. Édouard Glissant, *Une nouvelle région du monde*, 2006.

108. Glissant, *Poetics*, 144.

109. Ibid., 201.

110. Ibid., 207–9.

111. Glissant and Chamoiseau, *Quand les murs tombent*, 8, 11, 16–17.

112. Glissant "Europe and the Antilles," 258.

113. Ibid., 256, 257.

114. Glissant and Chamoiseau, *Quand les murs tombent*, 21–25.

115. Thomas McCarthy, *Race, Empire, and the Idea of Human Development*, 2009.

116. Scott, *Art of Not Being Governed*, 324.

117. Glissant and Chamoiseau, *Quand les murs tombent*, 23, 25–26.

118. Sheldon Wolin, "Political Theory as a Vocation," 1969, 1062–82.

119. Glissant, *Fourth Century*, 141.

AFTERWORD

1. Peter Tosh, "400 Years," on Bob Marley and the Wailers, *Catch a Fire* (1973).

2. Tosh, "400 Years." The two previous tracks of *Catch a Fire* are the opening "Concrete Jungle" and "Slave Driver," with Bob Marley as lead singer. While Marley has received wider popular reception than Tosh, Tosh is the Wailer who understood earliest the principles of marronage. He was also the first Wailer member to convert to Rastafari.

3. Édouard Glissant, *Caribbean Discourse*, 1989, 64.

4. On the origins and genesis of Rastafari, see Barry Chevannes, *Rastafari*, 1994; Ennis Edmonds, *Rastafari*, 2003; Yasus Afari, *Overstanding Rastafari*, 2007; Oliver Hill (director), *Coping with Babylon*, 2007; Jahlani Niaah and Erin MacLeod, eds., *Let Us Start with Africa*, 2013.

5. Michael Barnett, "Rastafari in the New Millennium: Rastafari at the Dawn of the Fifth Epoch," in *Rastafari in the New Millennium*, 2012, ed. M. Barnett, 1–10.

6. Barry Chevannes, "Rastafari and the Coming of Age," in Barnett, *Rastafari*, 13–32.

7. Ludwig Wittgenstein, *Philosophical Investigations*, 2001, 43, 18.

8. Rupert Lewis, "Marcus Garvey and the Early Rastafarians," in *Rastafari*, 2006, ed. Werner Zips, 42–58.

9. Neil Roberts, "Violence, Livity, Freedom," *Small Axe* 43 (March 2014): 181–92.

10. On Rastafari and Bad Friday, see Deborah Thomas's *Exceptional Violence* (2011) and the documentary *Bad Friday: Rastafari after Coral Gardens* (2011), directed by Deborah Thomas and John Jackson Jr.

11. Joseph Owens, *Dread*, 1976, 3.

12. Velma Pollard, "Dread Talk," in *Rastafari*, 2008, ed. Rex Nettleford and Veronica Salter, 205–17.

13. For the Bobo Shanti use of international law to support repatriation, see Werner Zips, "'Repatriation is a Must!': The Rastafari Struggle to Utterly *Downstroy* Slavery," in Zips, *Rastafari*, 129–68.

14 United Nations, *The Universal Declaration of Human Rights*, online at: https://www.un.org/en/documents/udhr/.

15. Jahlani Niaah, "The Rastafari Presence in Ethiopia," and Erin MacLeod, "Water Development Projects and Cultural Citizenship," in Barnett, *Rastafari*, 66–103; Erin MacLeod, *Visions of Zion*, 2014.

16. See, for instance, Haile Selassie's speeches in *The Third Testament*, 2010.
17. Chevannes, "Rastafari and the Coming of Age," 25–32.
18. Katrin Hansing, *Rasta, Race and Revolution*, 2006; Samuel Furé Davis, "Rastafari and Popular Culture in Contemporary Cuba," in Nettleford and Salter, *Rastafari*, 297–309.
19. The widespread conversations on Rastafari, repatriation, and the state during and after the formation of the Ethio-Africa Diaspora Union Millennium Council (EADUMC), the 2012 Jamaican 50th Anniversary of Independence celebrations, and the 2010 and 2013 Rastafari Studies conferences at the University of the West Indies, Mona, Jamaica, reflect this shift.

BIBLIOGRAPHY

Accilien, Cécile, Jessica Adams, and Elmide Méléance, eds., *Revolutionary Freedoms: A History of Survival, Strength, and Imagination in Haiti*. Coconut Creek, FL: Caribbean Studies Press, 2006.

Afari, Yasus. *Overstanding Rastafari: "Jamaica's Gift to the World."* Kingston: Senya-Cum, 2007.

Agamben, Giorgio. *State of Exception*. Chicago: University of Chicago Press, 2005.

Agorsah, E. Kofi., ed. *Maroon Heritage: Archaeological, Ethnographic and Historical Perspectives*. Kingston: Canoe Press, 1994.

Allen, Danielle. *Talking to Strangers: Anxieties of Citizenship since* Brown v. Board of Education. Chicago: University of Chicago Press, 2004.

Alpers, Edward. "The Idea of *Marronage*: Reflections on Literature and Politics in *Réunion*." *Slavery and Abolition* 25, no. 2 (2004): 18–29.

Alston, Richard, Edith Hall, and Laura Proffitt, eds. *Reading Ancient Slavery*. London: Bristol Classical, 2011.

Andrews, William L. "The 1850s: The First Afro-American Literary Renaissance." In *Literary Romanticism in America*, edited by W. Andrews, 38–60. Baton Rouge: LSU Press, 1981.

———. *To Tell a Free Story: The First Century of Afro-American Autobiography, 1760–1865*. Urbana: University of Illinois Press, 1986.

Appleby, Joyce. *Liberalism and Republicanism in the Historical Imagination*. Cambridge, MA: Harvard University Press, 1992.

Arendt, Hannah. *Between Past and Future: Eight Exercises in Political Thought*. New York: Penguin, 1993.

———. *Crises of the Republic*. New York: Harcourt Brace, 1972.

———. *The Human Condition*. Chicago: University of Chicago Press, 1998.

———. *The Jewish Writings*. New York: Schocken, 2007.

———. *Lectures on Kant's Political Philosophy*. Chicago: University of Chicago Press, 1982.

———. *The Origins of Totalitarianism*. New York: Harcourt Brace, 1973.

———. *The Promise of Politics*. New York: Schocken, 2005.

———. *On Revolution*. New York: Penguin, 1965.

———. "Revolution and Freedom: A Lecture." In *In Zwei Welten: Siegfried Moses zum fünfundsiebzigsten Geburtstag*, edited by H. Tramer, 578–600. Tel Aviv: Bitaon, 1962.

———. *On Violence*. New York: Harcourt Brace, 1970.

Arrom, José J., and Manuel A. Arévalo. *Cimarrón*. Santo Domingo: Fundación García Arévalo, 1986.

Baker, Keith, ed. *The Old Regime and the French Revolution*. Chicago: University of Chicago Press, 1987.

Baldwin, James. *Collected Essays*. New York: Library of America, 1998.

Balfour, Lawrie. *Democracy's Reconstruction: Thinking Politically with W. E. B. Du Bois*. Oxford: Oxford University Press, 2011.

Balutansky, Kathleen, and Marie-Agnès Sourieau, eds. *Caribbean Creolization: Reflections on the Cultural Dynamics of Language, Literature, and Identity*. Gainsville: University Press of Florida, 1998.

Barnett, Michael, ed. *Rastafari in the New Millennium*. Syracuse, NY: Syracuse University Press, 2012.

Barthélemy, Gérard. *Créoles-Bossales: Conflit in Haïti*. Petit-Bourg: Ibis Rouge, 2000.

Baudot, Alain. "Edouard Glissant: A Poet in Search of His Landscape." *World Literature Today* 63, no. 1 (1989): 583–88.

Beard, John. *Toussaint L'Ouverture: A Biography and Autobiography*. Boston: James Redpath, 1863.

Beckles, Hilary. *Centering Woman: Gender Discourses in Caribbean Slave Society*. Kingston: Ian Randle, 1999.

Beiner, Ronald, and Jennifer Nedelsky, eds. *Judgment, Imagination, and Politics: Themes from Kant and Arendt*. Lanham, MD: Rowman & Littlefield, 2001.

Bell, Madison Smartt. *Toussaint Louverture: A Biography*. New York: Pantheon, 2007.

Beltrán, Cristina. *The Trouble with Unity: Latino Politics and the Creation of Identity*. Oxford: Oxford University Press, 2010.

Benhabib, Seyla, ed. *Politics in Dark Times: Encounters with Hannah Arendt*. Cambridge: Cambridge University Press, 2010.

———. *The Reluctant Modernism of Hannah Arendt*. Lanham, MD: Rowman & Littlefield, 2003.

Benjamin, Walter. *Illuminations*. New York: Schocken, 2007.

———. *Reflections*. New York: Harcourt Brace, 1978.

Benot, Yves. *Les lumière, l'esclavage, la colonization*. Paris: Éditions La Découverte, 2005.

Berkowitz, Roger, Thomas Keenan, and Jeffrey Katz, eds. *Thinking in Dark Times: Hannah Arendt on Ethics and Politics*. Bronx, NY: Fordham University Press, 2010.

Berlin, Isaiah. *The Proper Study of Mankind*. New York: Farrar, Straus and Giroux, 1997.

Bernabé, Jean Patrick Chamoiseau, and Raphaël Confiant. "In Praise of Creoleness." *Callaloo* 13, no. 4 (1990): 886–909.

Best, Stephen. *The Fugitive's Properties: Law and the Poetics of Possession*. Chicago: University of Chicago Press, 2004.

———, and Saidiya Hartman. "Fugitive Justice." *Representations* 92, no. 1 (2005): 1–15.

Bewell, Alan. *Romanticism and Colonial Disease*. Baltimore, MD: Johns Hopkins University Press, 1999.

Bhabha, Homi. *The Location of Culture*. New York: Routledge, 1994.

Bilby, Kenneth. *True-Born Maroons*. Kingston: Ian Randle, 2006.

Blackburn, Robin. *The Overthrow of Colonial Slavery, 1776–1848*. London: Verso, 1988.

Blassingame, John, gen. ed. *The Frederick Douglass Papers*. 5 vols. New Haven, CT: Yale University Press, 1979–92.

Blight, David. *Frederick Douglass' Civil War: Keeping Faith in Jubilee*. Baton Rouge: Louisiana State University Press, 1989.

———. *Race and Reunion: The Civil War in American Memory*. Cambridge, MA: Harvard University Press, 2001.

Bogues, Anthony. *Black Heretics, Black Prophets: Radical Political Intellectuals*. New York: Routledge, 2003.

———. *Empire of Liberty: Power, Desire, and Freedom.* Hanover, NH: University Press of New England, 2010.

———. "The 1805 Haitian Constitution: The Making of Slave Freedom in the Atlantic World." In *Freedom: Retrospective and Prospective*, edited by S. Wilmot, 144–71. Kingston: Ian Randle, 2009.

———. "Afterword." *Small Axe* 8 (September 2000): 113–17.

———. "Investigating the Radical Caribbean Intellectual Tradition." *Small Axe* 4 (September 1998): 38–43.

Bonilla, Yarimar. "Guadeloupe Is Ours: The Prefigurative Politics of the Mass Strike in the French Antilles." *Interventions* 12, no. 1 (2010): 125–37.

Boxill, Bernard. "The Fight with Covey." In *Existence in Black: An Anthology of Black Existential Philosophy*, edited by L. Gordon, 273–90. New York: Routledge, 1997.

———. "Two Traditions in African-American Political Philosophy." *Philosophical Forum* 24, nos. 1–3 (1992–93): 125–31.

———. "Frederick Douglass." In *Routledge Encyclopedia of Philosophy*, edited by E. Craig. London: Routledge, 2005. Online at http://www.rep.routledge.com.

Bradley, Keith. *Slavery and Society at Rome.* Cambridge: Cambridge University Press, 1994.

Brathwaite, Kamau. *Roots.* Ann Arbor: University of Michigan Press, 1993.

———. *Wars of Respect: Nanny, Sam Sharpe, and the Struggle for People's Liberation.* Kingston: Agency for Public Information, 1977.

Breleur, Ernest, Patrick Chamoiseau, Serge Domi, Gérard Delver, Édouard Glissant, Guillame P. de Gurbert, et. al. *Manifeste pour les 'produits' de haute nécessité.* Paris: Institute du Tout-Monde, 2009.

Britton, Celia, ed. *Édouard Glissant.* Special issue of *Callaloo* 36, no. 4 (2013).

———. *Édouard Glissant and Postcolonial Theory: Strategies of Language and Resistance.* Charlottesville: University Press of Virginia, 1999.

———. *The Sense of Community in French Caribbean Fiction.* Liverpool: University of Liverpool Press, 2008.

Bromell, Nick. "The Liberal Imagination of Frederick Douglass." *American Scholar* 77, no. 2 (2008): 34–45.

———. *The Time Is Always Now: Black Thought and the Transformation of US Democracy.* Oxford: Oxford University Press, 2013.

Brown, Gordon. *Toussaint's Clause: The Founding Fathers and the Haitian Revolution.* Jackson: University of Mississippi Press, 2005.

Brown, Vincent. "Social Death and Political Life in the Study of Slavery." *American Historical Review* 114, no. 5 (2009): 1231–49.

Brunt, P. A. *The Fall of the Roman Republic and Related Essays.* Oxford: Oxford University Press, 1988.

Buccola, Nicholas. *The Political Thought of Frederick Douglass: In Pursuit of American Liberty.* New York: New York University Press, 2012.

Buck-Morss, Susan. "Hegel and Haiti." *Critical Inquiry* 26, no. 4 (2000): 821–65.

———. *Hegel, Haiti, and Universal History.* Pittsburgh: University of Pittsburgh Press, 2009.

Buckland, W. W. *The Roman Law of Slavery: The Condition of the Slave in Private Law from Augustus to Justinian.* Cambridge: Cambridge University Press, 1970.

Bundy, Andrew, ed. *The Selected Essays of Wilson Harris.* New York: Routledge, 1999.

Burke, Edmund. *Reflections on the Revolution in France.* New York: Penguin, 1969.

Burns, Lorna. "Becoming-Postcolonial, Becoming-Caribbean: Édouard Glissant and the Poetics of Creolization." *Textual Practice* 23, no. 1 (2009): 99–117.

Burton, Richard. *Le roman marron: Études sur la littérature martiniquaise contemporaine*. Paris: L'Harmattan, 1997.

Bush, Barbara. *Slave Women in Caribbean Society, 1650–1838*. London: James Curry, 1990.

Butler, Judith, Ernesto Laclau, and Slavoj Žižek. *Contingency, Hegemony, Universality: Contemporary Dialogues on the Left*. London: Verso, 2000.

Calhoun, Craig, and John McGowan, eds. *Hannah Arendt and the Meaning of Politics*. Minneapolis: University of Minnesota Press, 1997.

Calvin, Matthew. *Toussaint Louverture and the American Civil War: The Promise and Peril of a Second Haitian Revolution*. Philadelphia: University of Pennsylvania Press, 2009.

Carby, Hazel. *Race Men*. Cambridge, MA: Harvard University Press, 1998.

Carpentier, Alejo. *The Kingdom of This World*. New York: Farrar, Straus and Giroux, 1989.

Cauna, Jacques de, ed. *Toussaint Louverture et l'indépendance d'Haïti: Témoignages Pour un bicentenaire*. Paris: Karthala, 2004.

Césaire, Aimé. *Discourse on Colonialism*. New York: Monthly Review, 1972.

———. "Le verbe marronner/à René Depestre, poète haïtien." In Eshleman and Smith, *Aimé Césaire*, 368–71.

———. *Notebook of a Return to the Native Land*. In Eshleman and Smith, *Aimé Césaire*, 32–85.

———. *A Tempest*. New York: Three Communications Groups, 2002.

———. *Toussaint Louverture: La révolution française et le problème colonial*. Paris: Présence Africaine, 1961.

Chakrabarty, Dipesh. *Provincializing Europe: Postcolonial Thought and Historical Difference*. Princeton, NJ: Princeton University Press, 2000.

Chamoiseau, Patrick. *Texaco*. New York: Vintage, 1998.

Chevannes, Barry. *Rastafari: Roots and Ideology*. Syracuse, NY: Syracuse University Press, 1994.

Clavin, Matthew. *Toussaint Louverture and the American Civil War*. Philadelphia: University of Pennsylvania Press, 2010.

Clifford, James. *The Predicament of Culture: Twentieth-Century Ethnography, Literature, and Art*. Cambridge, MA: Harvard University Press, 1988.

Cohen, Robin, and Paola Toninato, eds. *The Creolization Reader: Studies in Mixed Identities and Cultures*. New York: Routledge, 2010.

Colaiaco, James. *Frederick Douglass and the Fourth of July*. New York: Palgrave Macmillan, 2006.

Coleman, Deirdre. *Romantic Colonization and British Anti-Slavery*. Cambridge: Cambridge University Press, 2005.

Coleridge, Samuel T. "Lecture on the Slave-Trade." In *The Collected Works of Samuel Taylor Coleridge*. Vol. 1. *Lectures, 1795: On Politics and Religion*, 231–51. Princeton, NJ: Princeton University Press, 1971.

———. "On the Slave Trade." In *The Collected Works of Samuel Taylor Coleridge*. Vol. 2. *The Watchman*, 130–40. Princeton, NJ: Princeton University Press, 1970.

———. *A Dissertation on the Science of Method; or, The Laws and Regulative Principles of Education*. Glasgow: Richard Griffin, 1854.

———. *The Rime of the Ancient Mariner and Other Poems*. Mineola, NY: Dover, 1992.

Coles, Romand, Mark Reinhardt, and George Shulman, eds. *Radical Future Pasts: Untimely Political Theory*. Lexington: University Press of Kentucky, 2014.

Collins, Patricia Hill. *Black Feminist Thought: Knowledge, Consciousness, and the Politics of Empowerment*. New York: Routledge, 2000.

Condé, Maryse. *Crossing the Mangrove*. New York: Anchor, 1995.

———. "'Fous-t-en, laisse dire Aragon': Pour une poèsie nationale: Césaire, Depestre, Aragon." Paper delivered at Columbia University, October 14, 2000.

Connolly, William. *Identity\Difference: Democratic Negotiations of Political Paradox*. Ithaca, NY: Cornell University Press, 1991.

———. *A World of Becoming*. Durham, NC: Duke University Press, 2011.

Cooper, Anna Julia. *Slavery and the French Revolutionists, 1788–1805*. Lewiston, NY: Edward Millen, 1988.

Crichlow, Michaeline. *Globalization and the Post-Creole Imagination: Notes on Fleeing the Plantation*. Durham, NC: Duke University Press, 2009.

Crosta, Suzanne. *Le marronnage créateur: Dynamique textuelle chez Edouard Glissant*. Laval: GLELCA, 1991.

Dallmayr, Fred. "Beyond Monologue: For a Comparative Political Theory." *Perspectives on Politics* 2, no. 2 (2004): 249–57.

Danticat, Edwidge. *Create Dangerously: The Immigrant Artist at Work*. Princeton, NJ: Princeton University Press, 2011.

———. *Krik? Krak!*. New York: Vintage, 1995.

Dash, J. Michael. *Édouard Glissant*. Cambridge: Cambridge University Press, 1995.

Davis, Angela. *Abolition Democracy: Beyond Empire, Prisons, and Torture; Interviews with Angela Davis*. New York: Seven Stories Press, 2005.

———. *Angela Davis: An Autobiography*. New York: Random House, 1988.

———, ed. *If They Come in the Morning: Voices of Resistance*. New York: Signet, 1971.

———. "From the Prison of Slavery to the Slavery of Prison: Frederick Douglass and the Convict Lease System." In James, *Angela Y. Davis Reader*, 74–95.

———. *Lectures on Liberation*. Los Angeles: National United Committee to Free Angela Davis, c. 1971.

———. *The Meaning of Freedom*. San Francisco: City Lights, 2012 (MS version).

———. *Women, Race and Class*. New York: Vintage, 1981.

Davis, David Brion. *Inhuman Bondage: The Rise and Fall of Slavery in the New World*. Oxford: Oxford University Press, 2006.

———. *The Problem of Slavery in the Age of Emancipation*. New York: Alfred Knopf, 2014.

———. *The Problem of Slavery in the Age of Revolution, 1770–1823*. Oxford: Oxford University Press, 1999.

———. *The Problem of Slavery in Western Culture*. Oxford: Oxford University Press, 1966.

Dawson, Michael C. *Black Visions: The Roots of Contemporary African-American Political Ideologies*. Chicago: University of Chicago Press, 2001.

Dayan, Colin. *The Story of Cruel and Unusual*. Boston: MIT Press, 2007.

Dayan, Joan. *Haiti, History, and the Gods*. Berkeley and Los Angeles: University of California Press, 1995.

Dean, Jodi, ed. *Cultural Studies and Political Theory*. Ithaca, NY: Cornell University Press, 2000.

Debbasch, Yvan. "Le Maniel: Further Notes." In Price, *Maroon Societies*, 143–48

———. "Le marronnage: Essai sur la désertion de l'esclave antillais." *Année Sociologique* 3 (1961): 1–112.

———. "Le marronnage: Essai sur la désertion de l'esclave antillais." *Année Sociologique* 3 (1962): 117–95.

Debien, Gabriel. "Le marronage aux Antilles Francaises au XVIIIe siècle." *Caribbean Studies* 6, no. 3 (1966): 3–44.

———. "Marronage in the French Caribbean." In Price, *Maroon Societies*, 107–34.

———, and Jean Fouchard. "Le petit marronage autour du Cap." *Cahiers des Amériques Latines* 3 (January–June 1969): 31–67.

———, Jean Fouchard, and Marie-Antoinette Menier. "Toussaint Louverture avant 1789: Légendes et réalités." *Conjonction: Revue Franco-Haïtienne* 134 (June/July 1977): 67–80.

Degras, Priska. "Name of the Fathers, History of the Name: Odono as Memory." *World Literature Today* 63, no.4 (1989): 613–19.

Deive, Carlos Esteban. *Los Cimarrones del Maniel de Neiba*. Santo Domingo: Banco Central de la República Dominicana, 1985.

Deleuze, Gilles, and Félix Guattari. *A Thousand Plateaus: Capitalism and Schizophrenia*. Minneapolis: University of Minnesota Press, 1987.

Delpêche, Bernard, ed. *Marronnage in the Caribbean: Myth and Reality*. Montreal: Centre International de Documentation et d'Information Haïtienne Caraïbéenne et Afro-Canadienne, 2002.

Desmangles, Leslie. *The Faces of the Gods: Vodou and Roman Catholicism*. Chapel Hill: University of North Carolina Press, 1992.

Desportes, Georges. *La paraphilosophie d'Edouard Glissant*. Paris: L'Harmattan, 2008.

Diawara, Manthia, director. *Édouard Glissant: One World in Relation*. New York: Third World Newsreel, 2010.

Diedrich, Maria. *Love Across Color Lines: Ottilie Assing and Frederick Douglass*. New York: Hill and Wang, 1999.

Diouf, Sylviane. *Slavery's Exiles: The Story of the American Maroons*. New York: New York University Press, 2014.

Dorsey, Peter. *Common Bondage: Slavery as Metaphor in Revolutionary America*. Knoxville: University of Tennessee Press, 2009.

———. "Becoming the Other: The Mimesis of Metaphor in Douglass's *My Bondage and My Freedom*." *PMLA* 111, no. 3 (1996): 435–50.

Douglass, Frederick. "An Appeal to the British People." In Foner and Taylor, *Frederick Douglass*, 30–40.

———. *Autobiographies*. New York: The Library of America, 1994.

———. "The Heroic Slave." In Foner and Taylor, *Frederick Douglass*, 220–47.

———. "The Meaning of July Fourth for the Negro." In Foner and Taylor, *Frederick Douglass*, 188–206.

———. *My Bondage and My Freedom*. Urbana: University of Illinois Press, 1987.

———. *My Bondage and My Freedom*. New York: Penguin, 2003.

———. *My Bondage and My Freedom*. New York: Simon and Schuster, 2003.

———. *Narrative of the Life of Frederick Douglass, an American Slave, Written by Himself* (1845). In *The Classic Slave Narratives*, edited by H. Gates Jr. New York: Signet Classic, 1987.

———. *Narrative of the Life of Frederick Douglass, an American Slave, Written by Himself*. San Francisco: City Lights, 2010.

———. "West India Emancipation." In Foner and Taylor, *Frederick Douglass*, 358–69.

Dryzek, John, Bonnie Honig, and Anne Phillips, eds. *The Oxford Handbook of Political Theory*. Oxford: Oxford University Press, 2006.

Dubois, Laurent. *Avengers of the New World: The Story of the Haitian Revolution*. Cambridge, MA: Harvard University Press, 2004.

———. *A Colony of Citizens: Revolution and Slave Emancipation in the French Caribbean, 1787–1804*. Durham, NC: University of North Carolina Press, 2004.

———. "An Enslaved Enlightenment: Rethinking the Intellectual History of the French Antilles." *Social History* 31, no. 1 (2006): 1–14.

———. *Haiti: The Aftershocks of History*. New York: Metropolitan Books, 2012.

Dubois, Laurent, and John Garrigus, eds. *Slave Revolution in the Caribbean, 1789–1804*. New York: Palgrave Macmillan, 2006.

duBois, Page. *Slaves and Other Objects*. Chicago: University of Chicago Press, 2003.

Du Bois, W. E. B. *Black Reconstruction in America, 1860–1880*. New York: Free Press, 1992.

———. *John Brown*. New York: The Modern Library, 2001.

———. *The Souls of Black Folk*. Boston: Beacon, 1997. Orig. pub. 1903.

———. "The Study of the Negro Problems." *Annals of the American Academy of Political and Social Science* 11 (1898): 1–23.

———. *Writings*. New York: Library of America, 1986.

Dupuy, Alex. *Haiti: From Revolutionary Slaves to Powerless Citizens*. New York: Routledge, 2014.

Dussel, Enrique. *Ethics of Liberation in the Age of Globalization and Exclusion*. Durham, NC: Duke University Press, 2013.

———. "Origen de la filosofía política moderna: Las Casas, Vitoria y Suárez (1514–1617)." *Caribbean Studies* 33, no. 2 (2005): 35–80.

———. *The Underside of Modernity: Apel, Ricoeur, Rorty, Taylor, and the Philosophy of Liberation*. Atlantic Highlands, NJ: Humanities Press, 1996.

Edmonds, Ennis. *Rastafari: From Outcasts to Culture Bearers*. Oxford: Oxford University Press, 2003.

Edwards, Pamela. *The Statesman's Science: History, Nature, and Law in the Political Thought of Samuel Taylor Coleridge*. New York: Columbia University Press, 2004.

Enwezor, Okwui, Carlos Basualdo, Ute Meta Bauer, Susanne Ghez, Sarat Maharaj, Mark Nash, and Octavio Zaya, eds. *Créolité and Creolization: Document 11_Platform 3*. Ostfildern: Hatje Cantz, 2003.

Eshleman, Clayton, and Annette Smith, eds. *Aimé Césaire: The Collected Poetry*. Berkeley and Los Angeles: University of California Press, 1983.

Euben, Roxanne. *Enemy in the Mirror: Islamic Fundamentalism and the Limits of Modern Rationalism*. Princeton, NJ: Princeton University Press, 1999.

Fanon, Frantz. *Black Skin, White Masks*. New York: Grove Press, 2008.

———. *Oeuvres*. Paris: La Découverte, 2012.

———. *Toward the African Revolution*. New York: Grove Press, 1967.

———. *The Wretched of the Earth*. New York: Grove Press, 2004.

Fatton, Robert, Jr. *The Roots of Haitian Despotism*. Boulder: Lynne Rienner, 2007.

Fick, Carolyn. *The Making of Haiti: The Saint Domingue Revolution from Below*. Knoxville: University of Tennessee Press, 1990.

———. "The Saint-Domingue Slave Revolution and the Unfolding of Independence, 1791–1804." In Geggus and Fiering, *The World of the Haitian Revolution*, 177–95.

Figes, Orlando. *Peasant Russia, Civil War: The Volga Countryside in Revolution (1917–1921)*. Oxford: Clarendon Press, 1989.

Finley, Moses. *Ancient Slavery and Modern Ideology*. New York: Viking, 1980.

Firmin, Anténor. *The Equality of the Human Races: Positivist Anthropology*. Urbana: University of Illinois Press, 2002. Orig. pub. 1885.

Fischer, David Hackett. *Liberty and Freedom: A Visual History of America's Founding Ideas*. Oxford: Oxford University Press, 2004.

Fischer, Sibylle. *Modernity Disavowed: Haiti and the Cultures of Slavery in the Age of Revolution*. Durham, NC: Duke University Press, 2004.

Follett, Richard, Eric Foner, and Walter Johnson. *Slavery's Ghost: The Problem of Freedom in an Age of Emancipation*. Baltimore, MD: Johns Hopkins University Press, 2011.

Foner, Eric. *The Story of American Freedom*. New York: W. W. Norton, 1998.

Foner, Philip, ed. *The Life and Writings of Frederick Douglass*. 5 vols. New York: International Publishers, 1950–1975.

Foner, Philip, and Yuval Taylor, eds. *Frederick Douglass: Selected Speeches and Writings*. Chicago: Lawrence Hill Books, 1999.

Forsdick, Charles. "Late Glissant: History, 'World Literature,' and the Persistence of the Political." *Small Axe* 14, no. 3 (2010): 121–34.

Fouchard, Jean. *The Haitian Maroons: Liberty or Death*. New York: Edward Blyden, 1981.

———. *Les marrons de la liberté*. Port-au-Prince: Henri Deschamps, 1988.

Frank, Jason. *Constituent Moments: Enacting the People in Postrevolutionary America*. Durham, NC: Duke University Press, 2010.

Franklin, John Hope. *From Slavery to Freedom: A History of American Negroes*. New York: Knopf, 1947.

Franklin, John Hope, and Loren Schweninger. *Runaway Slaves: Rebels on the Plantation*. Oxford: Oxford University Press, 1999.

Fuente, Alejandro de la. *A Nation for All: Race, Inequality, and Politics in Twentieth-Century Cuba*. Chapel Hill: University of North Carolina Press, 2001.

Fulford, Tim. "Slavery and Superstition in the Supernatural Poems." In *The Cambridge Companion to Coleridge*, edited by L. Newlyn, 45–58. Cambridge: Cambridge University Press, 2002.

Garnsey, Peter. *Ideas of Slavery from Aristotle to Augustine*. Cambridge: Cambridge University Press, 1996.

Gates, Henry Louis, Jr. *The Signifying Monkey: A Theory of African-American Literary Criticism*. Oxford: Oxford University Press, 1988.

Geggus, David. *Haitian Revolutionary Studies*. Bloomington: Indiana University Press, 2002.

———, ed. *The Impact of the Haitian Revolution in the Atlantic World*. Columbia: University of South Carolina Press, 2001.

———. "On the Eve of the Haitian Revolution: Slave Runaways in Saint Domingue in the Year 1790." *Slavery and Abolition* 6, no. 3 (1985): 112–28.

Geggus, David, and Norman Fiering, eds. *The World of the Haitian Revolution*. Bloomington: Indiana University Press, 2009.

Genovese, Eugene. *From Rebellion to Revolution: Afro-American Slave Revolts in the Making of the Modern World*. New York: Vintage Books, 1979.

———. *Roll, Jordan, Roll: The World the Slaves Made*. New York: Vintage, 1969.

Ghachem, Malick. *The Old Regime and the Haitian Revolution*. Cambridge: Cambridge University Press, 2012.

Gilroy, Paul. *The Black Atlantic: Modernity and Double Consciousness*. Cambridge, MA: Harvard University Press, 1993.

———. "Fanon and the Value of the Human." *Salon* 4 (2011): 7–14.

Girard, Philippe. *Haiti: The Tumultuous History—From Pearl of the Caribbean to Broken Nation*. New York: Palgrave Macmillan, 2010.

———. *The Slaves Who Defeated Napoleon: Toussaint Louverture and the Haitian War of Independence, 1801–1804*. Tuscaloosa: University of Alabama Press, 2011.

Glissant, Édouard. *Caribbean Discourse: Selected Essays*. Charlottesville: University Press of Virginia, 1989.

———. *The Collected Poems of Édouard Glissant*. Minneapolis: University of Minnesota Press, 2005.

———. "Creolization and the Making of the Americas." *Caribbean Quarterly* 54, nos. 1–2 (2008): 82–83.

——— *Le discours antillais*. Paris: Éditions Gallimard, 1997.

———. "Europe and the Antilles: An Interview with Édouard Glissant." In Lionnet and Shih, *The Creolization of Theory*, 255–61.

———. *Faulkner, Mississippi*. Chicago: University of Chicago Press, 1999.

———. *The Fourth Century*. Lincoln: University of Nebraska Press, 2001.

———. "Identity and Diversity." Paper presented at Brown University, October 8, 1997.

———. *Introduction à une poétique du divers*. Paris: Éditions Gallimard, 2006.

———. *Mémoires des esclavages: la fondation d'un centre national pour la mémoire des esclavages et de leurs abolitions*. Paris: Éditions Gallimard, 2007.

———. *Monsieur Toussaint: A Play*. Boulder, CO: Lynne Riener, 2005.

———. *Une nouvelle région du monde*. Paris: Éditions Gallimard, 2006.

———. *The Overseer's Cabin*. Lincoln: University of Nebraska Press, 2011.

———. *Philosophie de la relation: poésie en éntendue*. Paris: Éditions Gallimard, 2009.

———. *Poetic Intention*. Callicoon, NY: Nightboat, 2010.

———. *Poetics of Relation*. Ann Arbor: University of Michigan Press, 1997.

———. *Le Quatrième Siècle*. Paris: Éditions Gallimard, 1997.

Glissant, Édouard, and Patrick Chamoiseau. *Quand les murs tombent: L'identité nationale hors-la-loi?* Paris: Institute du Tout-Monde, 2007.

Gluck, Carol, and Anne Tsing, eds. *Words in Motion: Toward a Global Lexicon*. Durham, NC: Duke University Press, 2009.

Godrej, Farah. *Cosmopolitan Political Thought: Method, Practice, Discipline*. Oxford: Oxford University Press, 2011.

Goldstein, Leslie F. "Violence as an Instrument for Social Change: The Views of Frederick Douglass (1817–1895)." *Journal of Negro History* 41, no. 1 (1976): 61–72.

Gooding-Williams, Robert. *In the Shadow of Du Bois: Afro-Modern Political Thought*. Cambridge, MA: Harvard University Press, 2009.

———. *Look, A Negro! Philosophical Essays on Race, Culture and Politics*. New York: Routledge, 2006.

Gordon, Jane Anna. *Creolizing Political Theory: Reading Rousseau through Fanon*. Bronx, NY: Fordham University Press, 2014.

———, and Neil Roberts. "Introduction: The Project of Creolizing Rousseau." *C.L.R. James Journal* 15, no. 1 (2009): 3–16.

Gordon, Lewis R. *Bad Faith and Antiblack Racism*. Atlantic Highlands, NJ: Humanities Press, 1995.

———. *Existentia Africana: Understanding Africana Existential Thought*. New York: Routledge, 2000.

Greenblatt, Stephen. *Learning to Curse: Essays in Early Modern Culture*. New York: Routledge, 1990.

Grossman, Edith. *Why Translation Matters*. New Haven, CT: Yale University Press, 2010.

Hahn, Steven. *A Nation under Our Feet: Black Political Struggles in the Rural South from Slavery to the Great Migration*. Cambridge, MA: Harvard University Press, 2003.

———. *The Political Worlds of Slavery and Freedom*. Cambridge, MA: Harvard University Press, 2009.

Hall, Stuart. "Negotiating Caribbean Identities." *New Left Review* 209 (January/February 1995): 3–14.

Hallward, Peter. *Absolutely Postcolonial: Writing Between the Singular and the Specific*. Manchester: Manchester University Press, 2001.

———. *Damning the Flood: Haiti and the Politics of Containment*. London: Verso, 2010.

Hanchard, Michael. "Afro-Modernity: Temporality, Politics, and the African Diaspora." *Public Culture* 11, no. 1 (1999): 245–68.

———. "Contours of Black Political Thought: An Introduction and Perspective." *Political Theory* 38, no. 4 (2010): 510–36.

———. *Party/Politics: Horizons in Black Political Thought*. Oxford: Oxford University Press, 2006.

Hancock, Ange-Marie. *Solidarity Politics for Millennials: A Guide to Ending the Oppression Olympics*. New York: Palgrave Macmillan, 2011.

Hansing, Katrin. *Rasta, Race and Revolution: The Emergence and Development of the Rastafari Movement in Socialist Cuba*. Berlin: Lit Verlag, 2006.

Harris-Perry, Melissa. *Sister Citizen: Shame, Stereotypes, and Black Women in America*. New Haven, CT: Yale University Press, 2011.

Harris, Wilson. "Creoleness: The Crossroads of a Civilization?" In Balutansky and Sourieau, *Caribbean Creolization*, 23–35.

Hartman, Saidiya. *Lose Your Mother: A Journey Along the Atlantic Slave Route*. New York: Farrar, Straus and Giroux, 2007.

———. *Scenes of Subjection: Terror, Slavery, and Self-Making in Nineteenth-Century America*. Oxford: Oxford University Press, 1997.

Henke, Holger. "Ariel's Ethos: On the Moral Economy of Caribbean Experience." *Cultural Critique* 56 (Winter 2004): 33–63.

Henry, Paget. *Caliban's Reason: Introducing Afro-Caribbean Philosophy*. New York: Routledge, 2000.

Heuman, Gad, ed. *Out of the House of Bondage: Runaways, Resistance and Marronage in Africa and the New World*. London: Frank Cass, 1986.

Hill, Oliver, director. *Coping with Babylon: The Proper Rastology*. Oaks, PA: Sonerito Productions, 2007.

Hitchcock Peter. "Antillanité and the Art of Resistance." *Research in African Literatures* 27, no. 2 (1996): 33–50.

Hobbes, Thomas. *Leviathan*. Cambridge: Cambridge University Press, 1991.

Holt, Thomas. *The Problem of Freedom: Race, Labor, and Politics in Jamaica and Britain, 1832–1938*. Baltimore, MD: Johns Hopkins University Press, 1992.

Honig, Bonnie. "Declarations of Independence: Arendt and Derrida on the Problem of Founding a Republic." *American Political Science Review* 85, no. 1 (1991): 97–113.

Horkheimer, Max, and Theodor Adorno. *Dialectic of Enlightenment*. Stanford, CA: Stanford University Press, 2002.

Hseuh, Vicki. *Hybrid Constitutions: Challenging Legacies of Law, Privilege, and Culture in Colonial America*. Durham, NC: Duke University Press, 2010.

Huggins, Nathan. *Slave and Citizen: The Life of Frederick Douglass*. Boston: Little, Brown, 1980.

Hutton, Clinton. *The Logic and Historical Significance of the Haitian Revolution and the Cosmological Roots of Haitian Freedom*. Kingston: Arawak Monographs, 2005.

James, C. L. R. *Beyond a Boundary*. Durham, NC: Duke University Press, 1993.

———. *The Black Jacobins: Toussaint L'Ouverture and the San Domingo Revolution*. New York: Vintage Books, 1963. Orig. pub. 1938.

———. *Every Cook Can Govern: A Study of Democracy in Ancient Greece, Its Meaning for Today*. Detroit, MI: Correspondence, 1992.

———. "Lectures on *The Black Jacobins*." *Small Axe* 8 (September 2000): 65–112.

———. *Mariners, Renegades and Castaways: The Story of Herman Melville and the World We Live In*. Hanover, NH: University Press of New England, 2001.

———. "Preface." In Fouchard, *The Haitian Maroons* .

———. *You Don't Play with Revolution: The Montréal Lectures of C. L. R. James*. Oakland, CA: AK Press, 2009.

James, Joy, ed. *The Angela Y. Davis Reader*. Oxford: Blackwell, 1998.

———. *Shadowboxing: Representations of Black Feminist Politics*. New York: St. Martin's Press, 1999.

———. *Transcending the Talented Tenth: Black Leaders and American Intellectuals*. New York: Routledge, 1997.

Janvier, Louis-Joseph. *Les constitutions d'Haïti (1801–1885)*. Paris: Flammarion, 1886.

Jenson, Deborah. *Beyond the Slave Narrative: Politics, Sex, and Manuscripts in the Haitian Revolution*. Liverpool: Liverpool University Press, 2011.

Johnson, Walter. "On Agency." *Journal of Social History* 37, no. 1 (2003): 113–24.

Keenan, Alan. *Democracy in Question: Democratic Openness in a Time of Political Closure*. Stanford, CA: Stanford University Press, 2003.

Kelley, Robin D. G. *Freedom Dreams: The Black Radical Imagination*. Boston: Beacon, 2002.

Kirkland, Frank. "Enslavement, Moral Suasion, and Struggles for Recognition." In Lawson and Kirkland, *Frederick Douglass*, 243–310.

Klausen, Jimmy. *Fugitive Rousseau: Slavery, Primitivism, and Political Freedom*. Bronx, NY: Fordham University Press, 2014.

Kley, Dale Van, ed. *The French Idea of Freedom: The Old Regime and the Declaration of Rights of 1789*. Stanford, CA: Stanford University Press, 1994.

Knight, Franklin. "The Haitian Revolution." *American Historical Review* 105, no. 1 (2000): 103–15.

Kohn, Margaret. "Frederick Douglass's Master-Slave Dialectic." *Journal of Politics* 6, no. 2 (2005): 497–514.

Krause, Sharon. *Liberalism with Honor*. Cambridge, MA: Harvard University Press, 2002.

Laborde, Cécile, and John Maynor, eds. *Republicanism and Political Theory*. Oxford: Wiley-Blackwell, 2008.

Laclau, Ernesto. *Emancipation(s)*. London: Verso, 1996.

Lamming, George. *The Pleasures of Exile*. Ann Arbor: University of Michigan Press, 1991.

———. "The Negro Writer and His World." Special issue of *Présence Africaine* 1, nos. 8–10 (1956): 324–32.

Las Casas, Bartolomé de. *A Short Account of the Destruction of the Indies*. New York: Penguin, 1992.

Laurent, Gérard, ed. *Toussaint L'Ouverture à travers sa correspondance, 1794–1798*. Madrid: 1953.

Lawson, Bill, and Frank Kirkland, eds. *Frederick Douglass: A Critical Reader*. Oxford: Blackwell, 1999.

Lee, Debbie. *Slavery and the Romantic Imagination*. Philadelphia: University of Pennsylvania Press, 2002.

Lee, Maurice, ed. *The Cambridge Companion to Frederick Douglass*. Cambridge: Cambridge University Press, 2009.

Levine, Robert. *Dislocating Race and Nation: Episodes in Nineteenth-Century American Literary Nationalism*. Chapel Hill: University of North Carolina Press, 2008.

———. *Martin Delany, Frederick Douglass, and the Politics of Representative Identity*. Chapel Hill: University of North Carolina Press, 1997.

Lewis, Gordon K. *Main Currents in Caribbean Thought: The Historical Evolution of Caribbean Society in Its Ideological Aspects, 1492–1900*. Lincoln: University of Nebraska Press, 2004.

Lionnet, Françoise, and Shu-mei Shih, eds. *The Creolization of Theory*. Durham, NC: Duke University Press, 2011.

Lockley, Timothy, ed., *Maroon Communities in South Carolina*. Columbia: University of South Carolina Press, 2009.

Logan, Rayford. *The Diplomatic Relations of the United States with Haiti, 1776–1891*. Chapel Hill: University of North Carolina Press, 1941.

L'Ouverture, Toussaint. *The Haitian Revolution*. London: Verso, 2008.

Lundahl, Mats. "Toussaint L'Ouverture and the War Economy of Saint-Domingue, 1796–1802." *Slavery and Abolition* 6, no. 2 (1985): 122–38.

Lynch, Shola, director. *Free Angela Davis and All Political Prisoners.* Santa Monica, CA: Lions Gate Entertainment, 2013.

Mackey, Nathaniel. "Other: From Noun to Verb." *Representations* 39 (Summer 1992): 51–70.

MacGilvray, Eric. *The Invention of Market Freedom.* Cambridge: Cambridge University Press, 2011.

MacLeod, Erin. *Visions of Zion: Ethiopians and Rastafari in Search for the Promised Land.* New York: New York University Press, 2014.

Madiou, Thomas. *Histoire d'Haïti.* 8 vols. Port-au-Prince: Henri Deschamps, 1987.

Mamdani, Mahmood. *Citizen and Subject: Contemporary Africa and the Legacy of Late Colonialism.* Princeton, NJ: Princeton University Press, 1996.

———. "The Politics of Naming: Genocide, Civil War, Insurgency." *London Review of Books* 29, no. 5 (2007). Online at http://www.lrb.co.uk/v29/n05/mahmood-mamdani/the-politics-of-naming-genocide-civil-war-insurgency.

Manigat, Leslie. "The Relationship between Marronage and Slave Revolts and Revolution in St. Domingue-Haiti." In *Comparative Perspectives on Slavery in New World Plantation Societies,* edited by V. Rubin and A. Tuden, 420–73. New York: New York Academy of Sciences, 1977.

Markell, Patchen. *Bound by Recognition.* Princeton, NJ: Princeton University Press, 2003.

———. "The Insufficiency of Non-Domination." Paper presented at the APSA Annual Meeting, Washington, DC, September 2005.

Markoff, John. *The Abolition of Feudalism: Peasants, Lords, and Legislators in the French Revolution.* University Park: Pennsylvania State University Press, 1996.

Marley, Bob, and The Wailers. *Catch a Fire.* Tuff Gong: Island Records, 1973.

Marshall, Stephen. *The City on the Hill from Below: The Crisis of Prophetic Black Politics.* Philadelphia, PA: Temple University Press, 2011.

Martí, José Luis, and Philip Pettit. *A Political Philosophy in Public Life: Civic Republicanism in Zapatero's Spain.* Princeton, NJ: Princeton University Press, 2010.

Martin, Dale. *Slavery as Salvation: The Metaphor of Slavery in Pauline Christianity.* New Haven, CT: Yale University Press, 1990.

Martin, Waldo, Jr. *The Mind of Frederick Douglass.* Chapel Hill: University of North Carolina Press, 1984.

Maynor, John. *Republicanism in the Modern World.* Cambridge: Polity Press, 2003.

Mbembe, Achille. *On the Postcolony.* Berkeley and Los Angeles: University of California Press, 2001.

McCarthy, Thomas. *Race, Empire, and the Idea of Human Development.* Cambridge: Cambridge University Press, 2009.

McCormick, John. *Machiavellian Democracy.* Cambridge: Cambridge University Press, 2011.

McCurry, Stephanie. *Confederate Reckoning: Power and Politics in the Civil War South.* Cambridge, MA: Harvard University Press, 2010.

McFeely, William S. *Frederick Douglass.* New York: W. W. Norton, 1991.

McGary, Howard, and Bill Lawson. *Between Slavery and Freedom: Philosophy and American Slavery.* Bloomington: Indiana University Press, 1992.

McKittrick, Katherine. *Demonic Grounds: Black Women and the Cartographies of Struggle.* Minneapolis: University of Minnesota Press, 2006

Ménil, Alain. *Les voies de la créolisation: Essai sur Édouard Glissant.* Grenoble: De l'incidence, 2011.

Mignolo, Walter. *The Idea of Latin America.* Oxford: Blackwell, 2005.

Mills, Charles W. *Blackness Visible: Essays on Philosophy and Race.* Ithaca, NY: Cornell University Press, 1998.

———. "'Ideal Theory' as Ideology." *Hypatia* 20, no. 3 (2005): 165–84.

———. *The Racial Contract.* Ithaca, NY: Cornell University Press, 1997.

Mintz, Sidney. *Caribbean Transformations.* New York: Columbia University Press, 1974.

———. *Sweetness and Power: The Place of Sugar in Modern History.* New York: Penguin, 1985.

Mohammed, Patricia, ed. *Gendered Realities: Essays in Caribbean Feminist Thought.* Kingston: University of the West Indies Press, 2002.

Monahan, Michael. *The Creolizing Subject: Race, Reason, and the Politics of Purity.* Bronx, NY: Fordham University Press, 2011.

Moïse, Claude. *Constitutions et luttes de pouvoir en Haïti.* 2 vols. Montréal: Éditions du CIDIHCA, 1988.

———, ed. *Dictionnaire historique de la Révolution haïtienne (1789–1804).* Montréal: Éditions du CIDIHCA, 2003.

———. *Le Projet nationale de Toussaint Louverture et la Constitution de 1801.* Port-au-Prince: Éditions Mémoire, 2001.

Moitt, Bernard. *Women and Slavery in the French Antilles, 1635–1848.* Bloomington: Indiana University Press, 2001.

Moreau de Saint-Méry, M. L. E. "The Border Maroons of Saint-Domingue: Le Maniel." In Price, *Maroon Societies,* 135–42.

———. *Description topographique, physique, civile, politique et historique de la partie française de l'isle Saint-Domingue.* Philadelphia, PA: Chez l'auteur, 1796.

Morrow, John. *Coleridge's Political Thought: Property, Morality and the Limits of Traditional Discourse.* Basingstoke: Macmillan, 1990.

Moruzzi, Norma. *Speaking Through the Mask: Hannah Arendt and the Politics of Social Identity.* Ithaca, NY: Cornell University Press, 2000.

Murphy, Liam. *Moral Demands in Nonideal Theory.* Oxford: Oxford University Press, 2000.

Muthu, Sankar. *Enlightenment against Empire.* Princeton, NJ: Princeton University Press, 2003.

Myers, Peter. *Frederick Douglass: Race and the Rebirth of Liberalism.* Lawrence: University Press of Kansas, 2008.

Nancy, Jean-Luc. *The Inoperative Community.* Minneapolis: University of Minnesota Press, 1991.

Nesbitt, Nick. *Caribbean Critique: Antillean Critical Theory from Toussaint to Glissant.* Liverpool: Liverpool University Press, 2013.

———. *Universal Emancipation: The Haitian Revolution and the Radical Enlightenment.* Charlottesville: University of Virginia Press, 2008.

Nettleford, Rex, and Veronica Salter, eds. *Rastafari.* Kingston: Caribbean Quarterly, 2008.

Newlyn, Lucy, ed. *The Cambridge Companion to Coleridge.* Cambridge: Cambridge University Press, 2002.

Niaah, Jahlani, and Erin MacLeod, eds. *Let Us Start with Africa: Foundations of Rastafari Scholarship.* Kingston: University of the West Indies Press, 2013.

Nicholls, David. *From Dessalines to Duvalier: Race, Colour, and National Independence in Haiti.* Cambridge: Cambridge University Press, 1979.

Nwankwo, Ifeoma. *Black Cosmopolitanism: Racial Consciousness and Transnational Identity in the Nineteenth-Century Americas.* Philadelphia: University of Pennsylvania Press, 2005.

Oakes, James. *The Radical and the Republican: Frederick Douglass, Abraham Lincoln, and the Triumph of Antislavery Politics.* New York: W. W. Norton, 2007.

Olson, Joel. *The Abolition of White Democracy.* Minneapolis: University of Minnesota Press, 2004.

Olsson, Göran Hugo, director. *The Black Power Mixtape, 1967–1975.* New York: Sundance Selects, 2011.

Ormerod Beverley. "Beyond *Négritude*: Some Aspects of the Work of Édouard Glissant." *Contemporary Literature* 15, no. 3 (1974): 360–69.

Ott, Thomas. *The Haitian Revolution, 1789–1804.* Knoxville: University of Tennessee Press, 1973.

Owens, Joseph. *Dread: The Rastafarians of Jamaica.* London: Heinemann, 1976.

Pagden, Anthony. *The Fall of Natural Man: The American Indian and the Origins of Comparative Ethnology.* Cambridge: Cambridge University Press, 1982.

Palmié, Stephan, and Francisco Scarano, eds. *The Caribbean: A History of the Region and Its Peoples.* Chicago: University of Chicago Press, 2011.

Parham, Marisa, and John Drabinski, eds. *The Work of Édouard Glissant.* Special issue of *The C. L. R. James Journal* 18 , no. 1 (2012): 1–225.

Pateman, Carole, and Charles Mills. *Contract and Domination.* Malden: Polity, 2007.

Paton, Diana, and Pamela Scully, eds. *Gender and Slave Emancipation in the Atlantic World.* Kingston: University of the West Indies Press, 2005.

Patterson, Orlando. *The Children of Sisyphus.* Essex: Longman, 1964.

———. "Emancipation, Independence and the Way Forward." Kingston: Ministry of Local Government, Community Development and Sport, 2002.

———. *Freedom.* Vol. 1. *Freedom in the Making of Western Culture.* New York: Basic Books, 1991.

———. "Freedom and 9/11." *Democracy* 22 (Fall 2011): 9–13.

———. "God's Gift?" *New York Times,* December 19, 2006, A33.

———. *The Ordeal of Integration: Progress and Resentment in America's "Racial" Crisis.* Washington, DC: Civitas Counterpoint, 1997.

———. *Rituals of Blood: Consequences of Slavery in Two American Centuries.* New York: Basic Civitas, 1998.

———. "Slavery and Slave Revolts: A Sociohistorical Analysis of the First Maroon War, 1665–1740" [1970]. In Price, *Maroon Societies,* 246–92.

———. *Slavery and Social Death: A Comparative Study.* Cambridge, MA: Harvard University Press, 1982.

———. *The Sociology of Slavery: An Analysis of the Origins, Development and Structure of Negro Slave Society in Jamaica.* London: Macgibbon and Kee, 1967.

Pettit, Philip. "Free Persons and Free Choices." *History of Political Thought* 28, no. 4 (2007): 709–18.

———. *Just Freedom: A Moral Compass for a Complex World.* New York: W. W. Norton, 2014.

———. *On the People's Terms: A Republican Theory and Model of Democracy.* Oxford: Oxford University Press, 2012.

———. "Keeping Republican Freedom Simple: On a Difference with Quentin Skinner." *Political Theory* 30, no. 3 (2002): 339–56.

———. *Republicanism: A Theory of Freedom and Government.* Oxford: Oxford University Press, 1999.

———. *A Theory of Freedom: From the Psychology to the Politics of Agency.* Oxford: Oxford University Press, 2001.

Phaf, Ineke, ed. *Presencia criolla en el Caribe y América Latina.* Frankfurt am Main: Vervuert, 1996.

Pippin, Robert. *Nietzsche, Psychology, and First Philosophy.* Chicago: University of Chicago Press, 2010.

Pitkin, Hanna. *The Attack of the Blob: Hannah Arendt's Concept of the Social.* Chicago: University of Chicago Press, 1998.

———. *The Concept of Representation*. Berkeley and Los Angeles: University of California Press, 1967.

———. "Are Freedom and Liberty Twins?" *Political Theory* 16, no. 4 (1988): 523–52.

———. *Wittgenstein and Justice: On the Significance of Ludwig Wittgenstein for Social and Political Thought*. Berkeley and Los Angeles: University of California Press, 1972.

Pluchon, Pierre. *Toussaint Louverture: un révolutionnaire noir d'Ancien régime*. Paris: Fayard, 1989.

Pocock, J. G. A. *The Machiavellian Moment: Florentine Political Thought and the Atlantic Republican Tradition*. Princeton, NJ: Princeton University Press, 1975.

———. *Political Thought and History: Essays on Theory and Method*. Cambridge: Cambridge University Press, 2008.

———. *Politics, Language and Time: Essays on Political Thought and History*. New York: Atheneum, 1971.

Polyné, Millery. *From Douglass to Duvalier: U. S. African Americans, Haiti and Pan Americanism, 1870–1964*. Gainesville: University Press of Florida, 2010.

———. *The Idea of Haiti: Rethinking Crisis and Development*. Minneapolis: University of Minnesota Press, 2013.

Popkin, Jeremy. *Facing Racial Revolution: Eyewitness Accounts of the Haitian Insurrection*. Chicago: University of Chicago Press, 2007.

———. *You Are All Free: The Haitian Revolution and the Abolition of Slavery*. Cambridge: Cambridge University Press, 2010.

Praeger, Michèle. *The Imaginary Caribbean and Caribbean Imaginary*. Lincoln: University of Nebraska Press, 2003.

Price, Richard, ed. *Maroon Societies: Rebel Slave Communities in the Americas*. 2nd ed. Baltimore, MD: Johns Hopkins University Press, 1996.

Price-Mars, Jean. *So Spoke the Uncle*. Washington, DC: Three Continents, 1983.

Radford, Daniel. *Edouard Glissant*. Paris: Seghers, 1982.

Rainsford, Marcus. *An Historical Account of the Black Empire of Hayti*. Durham, NC: Duke University Press, 2013.

Ramsey, Kate. *The Spirits and the Law: Vodou and Power in Haiti*. Chicago: University of Chicago Press, 2011.

Rana, Aziz. *The Two Faces of American Freedom*. Cambridge, MA: Harvard University Press, 2010.

Rancière, Jacques. *Dis-agreement: Politics and Philosophy*. Minneapolis: University of Minnesota Press, 2004.

———. "The Politics of Literature." *SubStance* 33, no. 1 (2004): 10–24.

Rawls, John. *A Theory of Justice*. Cambridge, MA: Harvard University Press, 1971.

Reddock, Rhoda, ed. *Interrogating Caribbean Masculinities: Theoretical and Empirical Analyses*. Kingston: University of the West Indies Press, 2004.

Reinhardt, Catherine. *Claims to Memory: Beyond Slavery and Emancipation in the French Caribbean*. New York: Berghahn Books, 2006.

Reinhardt, Mark. *The Art of Being Free: Taking Liberties with Tocqueville, Marx, and Arendt*. Ithaca, NY: Cornell University Press, 1997.

Rice, Alan, and Martin Crawford, eds. *Liberating Sojourn: Frederick Douglass and Transatlantic Reform*. Athens: University of Georgia Press, 1999.

Richardson, Alan, and Sonia Hofkosh, eds. *Romanticism, Race, and Imperial Culture, 1780–1834*. Bloomington: Indiana University Press, 1996.

Richardson, Michael, and Krzysztof Fijałkowski, eds. *Refusal of the Shadow: Surrealism and the Caribbean*. London: Verso, 1996.

Roberts, Neil. "State, Power, Anarchism." *Perspectives on Politics* 9, no. 1 (2011): 84–88.

———. "Fanon, Sartre, Violence, and Freedom." *Sartre Studies International* 10, no. 2 (2004): 139–60.

———. "Violence, Livity, Freedom." *Small Axe* 43 (March 2014): 181–92.

Robinson, Cedric. *Black Marxism: The Making of the Black Radical Tradition*. Chapel Hill: University of North Carolina Press, 2000.

Rogers, William. *"We Are All Together Now": Frederick Douglass, William Lloyd Garrison, and the Prophetic Tradition*. New York: Garland Press, 1995.

Rosenblum, Nancy. *Another Liberalism: Romanticism and the Reconstruction of Liberal Thought*. Cambridge, MA: Harvard University Press, 1987.

Rousseau, Jean-Jacques. *The Social Contract and Other Later Political Writings*. Cambridge: Cambridge University Press, 1997.

Saint-Rémy, Joseph, ed. *Mémoires du général Toussaint-Louverture, écrits par lui-même, pouvant servir à l'histoire de sa vie*. Paris: Pagnerre, 1853.

Sala-Molins, Louis. *Le Code Noir, ou le calvaire de Canaan*. Paris: Presses Universitaires de France, 1987.

———. *Dark Side of the Light: Slavery and the French Enlightenment*. Minneapolis: University of Minnesota Press, 2006.

Schmitt, Carl. *Constitutional Theory*. Durham, NC: Duke University Press, 2008.

———. *The Nomos of the Earth in the International Law of the Jus Publicum Europaeum*. New York: Telos, 2003.

Schoelcher, Victor. *Vie de Toussaint Louverture*. Paris: Paul Ollendorf, 1889.

Scott, David. *Conscripts of Modernity: The Tragedy of Colonial Enlightenment*. Durham, NC: Duke University Press, 2004.

———. *Omens of Adversity: Tragedy, Time, Memory, Justice*. Durham, NC: Duke University Press, 2014.

———. "The Paradox of Freedom: An Interview with Orlando Patterson." *Small Axe* 40, no. 1 (2013): 96–242.

Scott, James C. *The Art of Not Being Governed: An Anarchist History of Upland Southeast Asia*. New Haven, CT: Yale University Press, 2009.

———. *Domination and the Arts of Resistance: Hidden Transcripts*. New Haven, CT: Yale University Press, 1990.

———. *Seeing Like a State: How Certain Schemes to Improve the Human Condition Have Failed*. New Haven, CT: Yale University Press, 1998.

———. *Two Cheers for Anarchism: Six Easy Pieces on Autonomy, Dignity, and Meaningful Work and Play*. Princeton, NJ: Princeton University Press, 2012.

Scott, Rebecca. *Degrees of Freedom: Louisiana and Cuba after Slavery*. Cambridge, MA: Harvard University Press, 2005.

Scully, Pamela, and Diana Paton, eds. *Gender and Slave Emancipation in the Atlantic World*. Durham, NC: Duke University Press, 2005.

Sekora, John. "'Mr. Editor, If You Please': Frederick Douglass, *My Bondage and My Freedom*, and the End of the Abolitionist Imprint." *Callaloo* 17, no. 2 (1994): 608–26.

Selassie, Haile. *The Third Testament Ilect Verses: The Selected Speeches of Emperor Haile Selassie I, 1918–1967*. Chicago, IL: Frontline Distribution, 2010.

Sen, Amartya. *Development as Freedom*. New York: Anchor Books, 1999.

Sepinwall, Alyssa, ed. *Haitian History: New Perspectives*. New York: Routledge, 2013.

Shapiro, Ian, Rogers Smith, and Tarek Masoud, eds. *Problems and Methods in the Study of Politics*. Cambridge: Cambridge University Press, 2004.

Shelby, Tommie. *We Who Are Dark: The Philosophical Foundations of Black Solidarity*. Cambridge, MA: Harvard University Press, 2005.

Sheller, Mimi. *Democracy after Slavery: Black Publics and Peasant Radicalism in Haiti and Jamaica*. Gainesville: University Press of Florida, 2000.

Shepherd, Verene, ed. *Engendering Caribbean History: Cross-Cultural Perspectives*. Kingston: Ian Randle, 2011.

Shklar, Judith. *American Citizenship: The Quest for Inclusion*. Cambridge, MA: Harvard University Press, 1991.

———. *Redeeming American Political Thought*. Chicago: University of Chicago Press, 1998.

Shulman, George. "Acknowledgment and Disavowal as an Idiom for Theorizing Politics." *Theory & Event* 14, no. 1 (2011). Online at: http://muse.jhu.edu/journals/theory_and _event/v014/14.1.shulman.html.

———. *American Prophecy: Race and Redemption in American Political Culture*. Minneapolis: University of Minnesota Press, 2008.

Singham, Archie. *The Hero and the Crowd in a Colonial Polity*. New Haven, CT: Yale University Press, 1968.

Singham, Shanti. "Betwixt Cattle and Men: Jews, Blacks, and Women, and the Declaration of the Rights of Man." In Kley, *The French Idea of Freedom*, 114–53.

Skinner, Quentin. *Hobbes and Republican Liberty*. Cambridge: Cambridge University Press, 2008.

———. *Liberty before Liberalism*. Cambridge: Cambridge University Press, 1998.

Smallwood, Stephanie. *Saltwater Slavery: A Middle Passage from Africa to American Diaspora*. Cambridge, MA: Harvard University Press, 2007.

Smith, Matthew. *Red and Black in Haiti: Radicalism, Conflict, and Political Change, 1934– 1957*. Chapel Hill: University of North Carolina Press, 2009.

Smith, Valerie. *Self-Discovery and Authority in Afro-American Narrative*. Cambridge, MA: Harvard University Press, 1991.

Stauffer, John. *Giants: The Parallel Lives of Frederick Douglass and Abraham Lincoln*. New York: Twelve, 2008.

Suk, Jeannie. *Postcolonial Paradoxes in French Caribbean Writing: Césaire, Glissant, Condé*. Oxford: Oxford University Press, 2001.

Sundquist, Eric, ed. *Frederick Douglass: New Literary and Historical Essays*. Cambridge: Cambridge University Press, 1990.

Taylor, Charles. *Modern Social Imaginaries*. Durham, NC: Duke University Press, 2004.

Thomas, Deborah. *Exceptional Violence: Embodied Citizenship in Transnational Jamaica*. Durham, NC: Duke University Press, 2011.

Thomas, Deborah, and John Jackson Jr., directors. *Bad Friday: Rastafari after Coral Gardens*. New York: Third World Newsreel.

Thomas, Helen. *Romanticism and Slave Narratives: Transatlantic Testimonies*. Cambridge: Cambridge University Press, 2000.

Thompson, Alvin O. *Flight to Freedom: African Runaways and Maroons in the Americas*. Kingston: University of the West Indies Press, 2006.

Thornton, John K. "African Soldiers in the Haitian Revolution." *Journal of Caribbean History* 25, nos. 1–2 (1991): 58–80.

———. "'I am the Subject of the King of Kongo': African Ideology in the Haitian Revolution.'" *Journal of World History* 4, no. 2 (1993): 181–214.

Tocqueville, Alexis de. *The Old Regime and the Revolution*. Vol. 1. Chicago: University of Chicago Press, 1998.

———. *Writings on Empire and Slavery*. Baltimore, MD: Johns Hopkins University Press, 2001.

Todorov, Tzvetan. *The Conquest of America: The Question of the Other*. Norman: University of Oklahoma Press, 1999.

Trouillot, Michel-Rolph. *Haiti: State Against Nation. The Origins and Legacy of Duvalierism.* New York: Monthly Review, 1990.

———. *Silencing the Past: Power and the Production of History.* Boston: Beacon Press, 1995.

———. *Ti difé boulé sou Istoua Ayiti.* New York: Koléksion Lakansièl, 1977.

Tsao, Roy. "Arendt's Augustine." In Benhabib, *Politics in Dark Times,* 39–57.

Turner, Jack. *Awakening to Race: Individualism and Social Consciousness in America.* Chicago: University of Chicago Press, 2012.

Tyson, George, Jr., ed. *Toussaint L'Ouverture.* Englewood Cliffs, NJ: Prentice-Hall, 1973.

Vacano, Diego von. *The Color of Citizenship: Race, Modernity, and Latin American/ Hispanic Political Thought.* Oxford: Oxford University Press, 2012.

Vergès, Françoise. *Mémoire enchaînée: questions sur l'esclavage.* Paris: Albin Michel, 2006.

Villa, Dana. "Beyond Good and Evil: Arendt, Nietzsche and the Aestheticization of Political Action." *Political Theory* 20, no. 2 (1992): 274–308.

———. *Socratic Citizenship.* Princeton, NJ: Princeton University Press, 2001.

Viroli, Maurizio. *Republicanism.* New York: Hill and Wang, 2002.

Walcott, Derek. *Selected Poems.* New York: Farrar, Straus and Giroux, 2007.

Walsh, John. *Free and French in the Caribbean: Toussaint Louverture, Aimé Césaire, and Narratives of Loyal Opposition.* Indianapolis: Indiana University Press, 2013.

Ware, Malcolm. "Coleridge's 'Spectre Bark': A Slave Ship?" *Philological Quarterly* 40, no. 4 (1961): 589–93.

Washington, Booker T. *Frederick Douglass.* Honolulu: University Press of the Pacific, 2003.

White, Ashli. *Encountering Revolution: Haiti and the Making of the Early Republic.* Baltimore, MD: Johns Hopkins University Press, 2010.

Willett, Cynthia. *Maternal Ethics and Other Slave Moralities.* New York: Routledge, 1995.

Williams, Eric. *Capitalism and Slavery.* Chapel Hill: University of North Carolina Press, 1994.

Williams, Melissa, and Stephen Macedo, eds. *Nomos XLVI: Political Exclusion and Domination.* New York: New York University Press, 2005.

Wirszubski, C. *Libertas as a Political Idea at Rome during the Late Republic and Early Principate.* Cambridge: Cambridge University Press, 1960.

Wittgenstein, Ludwig. *Philosophical Investigations.* Oxford: Blackwell, 2001.

Wolin, Sheldon. "Fugitive Democracy." In *Democracy and Difference: Contesting the Boundaries of the Political,* edited by Seyla Benhabib, 31–45. Princeton, NJ: Princeton University Press, 1996.

———. "Political Theory as a Vocation." *American Political Science Review* 63, no. 4 (1969): 1062–82.

Wood, Gordon. *Empire of Liberty: A History of the Early Republic, 1789–1815.* Oxford: Oxford University Press, 2009.

Wynter, Sylvia. *Black Metamorphosis: New Natives in a New World.* Unpublished MS.

———. "The Ceremony Must Be Found: After Humanism." *boundary 2* 12, no. 3 (1984): 19–70.

———. "Unsettling the Coloniality of Being/Power/Truth/Freedom." *CR: The New Centennial Review* 3, no. 3 (2003): 257–337.

———. "1492: A New World View." In *Race, Discourse, and the Origin of the Americas,* edited by V. Hyatt and R. Nettleford, 5–57. Washington: Smithsonian Institution Press, 1995.

———. "Beyond the Word of Man: Glissant and the New Discourse of the Antilles." *World Literature Today* 63, no. 3 (1989): 637–47.

Young-Bruehl, Elisabeth. *Hannah Arendt: For Love of the World.* New Haven, CT: Yale University Press, 2004.

Young, Iris Marion. *Justice and the Politics of Difference*. Princeton, NJ: Princeton University Press, 1990.

———. *Responsibility for Justice*. Oxford: Oxford University Press, 2011.

Zamir, Shamoon. *Dark Voices: W. E. B. Du Bois and American Thought, 1883–1903*. Chicago: University of Chicago Press, 1995.

Zips, Werner. *Nanny's Asafo Warriors: The Jamaican Maroons' African Experience*. Kingston: Ian Randle, 2012.

———, ed. *Rastafari: A Universal Philosophy in the Third Millennium*. Kingston: Ian Randle, 2006.

Dessalines, Jean-Jacques: assassination of, 122; Césaire on, 5–6; as emperor, 131; in final battle of Haitian Revolution, 6; Haitian Declaration of Independence and, 122–25; as illiterate, 208n25; Jefferson and, 114–15; massacre of whites ordered by, 134, 210–11n51; postrevolutionary Haiti and, 108; refusal of slavery and, 113; vodou and, 208n34

diaspora: scholarship on, 184n21; unidirectional flight and, 11

Diawara, Manthia, 167

Diderot, Denis, 105, 204n31

Diouf, Sylviane, 184n19

disavowal: acknowledgment and denial and, 29, 35; Arendt's, 189–90n52, 189n48; *avow* and *disavow* as terms and, 28; Freud on, 29; object of, 187n8; political language and, 42; political-social divide and, 36; poverty in new American republic and, 35; republicanism and, 28; vs. silence, 28, 29, 49; of slave agency, 23–24, 43–44, 189–90n52, 191n69; social question and, 34, 35–36; trauma and, 29, 43; as untenable, 88; of US black slavery, 35; in vocabulary of slavery, 41–42

domination and non-domination: etymology of, 40, 190n67; freedom and, 29, 39–40, 191n73, 199n94; general strikes and, 46–47; neo-Roman republicanism and, 40, 41, 191n69; taxation and, 42; unfreedom and, 41–42, 191n77

Douglas, Stephen, 77–78

Douglass, Frederick: abolitionist philosophies and, 47, 58, 59–61; admiration for, 55; anti-lynching advocacy of, 87; assertion and, 78–80; assimilationism and, 59–61, 87; black political solidarity and, 57; black vs. white women and, 83–84, 200n117–18; Brown's raid and, 82–83, 85; on Caroline (slave woman), 198–99n93; Coleridge and, 67–71, 196n46, 197n62; on comparative freedom, 71–80, 84–85, 87, 120; conceptual breakthrough on freedom and, 198–99n93; on convict lease system, 201n127; Davis on, 53, 55–58, 71, 75, 200n127; definition of slavery by, 68–69; equivocations of, 86; escape contemplated by, 79; Firmin and, 86–

87; flux in reflections of, 195n24; on Fourth of July, 72–73; as fugitive chain theorist, 71; "The Fugitive's Song" and, 61, 196n35; fugitivity and, 55, 59, 192n96; on future, present, and past, 80; Garrisonians and, 58, 59, 60, 79, 195–96nn34–35; Haiti and, 85, 86–87, 88; Hegel and, 198n84; on holidays for slaves, 80; interpretations of works of, 55–56; life story of, 58–59, 60, 62; Lincoln and, 199n95; literacy of, 69; marronage of, 58; masculinism and, 83–84; on movement, 194n15; movement as inevitable for, 56; Mr. Covey and, 53, 63, 70–72, 74–77, 80–82, 84, 198–99nn93–94; name of, 69, 72; on paradox of slavery amid freedom, 56; philosophy of slavery and, 69; photograph of, 61; political language of, 72, 87–88; as political leader, 193n5; on poverty vs. slavery, 66; power as subsidiary concept for, 85; prefaces to works of, 61; as race man, 84; radicalism of flight of, 85, 87; on republicanism vs. republican governance, 73–74; on resistance vs. revolutionary violence, 80–83; role of the fugitive and, 193n7; Romanticism and, 58, 61–63, 66–68, 75, 80, 83–87, 195n23, 196n46; as schoolteacher, 78–79; on slavery and freedom in form vs. fact, 76–78, 199nn94–95; slaves as humans and property and, 69–71, 84–85; spiritual autobiography and, 85; structural devices of, 195–96n34; theorists who are slaves and, 15; theory of freedom of, 57; Transcendentalism and, 195n23; value of experience and, 24; on voting, 79–80; women's suffrage and, 83–84, 200n117; writings of, 57–58, 61–62, 81

Drake, St. Clair, 184n21

dread, 178

Dred Scott v. Sandford, 37, 62

Dreyfus Affair, 54

Dube, Lucky, 176

Dubois, Laurent, 12, 108, 113

Du Bois, Shirley Graham, 54

Du Bois, W. E. B.: on abolition-democracy, 48, 192n96, 193n5; alternative conception of freedom and, 43; on American assumptions about wealth creation,

www.ingramcontent.com/pod-product-compliance
Lightning Source LLC
Chambersburg PA
CBHW072103040426
42334CB00042B/2284